# LATELY I'VE BEEN THINKING III

# LATELY I'VE BEEN THINKING III

### Powerful ¶ Posts
### for an Awesome Life

## By SONDRA RAY

**IMMORTAL RAY**
BOOKS

# OTHER BOOKS BY SONDRA RAY

Books By Markus Ray

IMMORTAL RAY PRODUCTIONS
301 TINGEY STREET, SE #302
WASHINGTON DC, 20003

**IMMORTAL RAY**
BOOKS

WASHINGTON DC

Library Of Congress Cataloging in Publication Data

Ray, Sondra; Lately I've Been Thinking III

I. Relationships. 2. Self-Mastery. 3. Life Wisdom


Cover Design: Markus Ray
Cover Image: Judy Totton Photography of London
Back Cover Image: Judy Totton Photography of London.


ISBN 13: Paperback:  978-1-950684-23-6
ISBN 13: E-Book:  978-1-950684-24-3
ISBN 13: Hardcover:  978-1-950684-25-0

# DEDICATION

I dedicate this book to my wonderful husband Markus who always supports my writing and whose determination brings our books into manifestation. Without him, all the books I have written in the past couple decades would have been impossible. I love you more than words can express. You are my very best partner, the one who travels with me and helps me all the time. You always encourage me to pursue my spiritual experiences, all the while keeping me grounded. We make a great team.

I also dedicate this book to our three Masters of the *Dream Team* Who guide us always: Babaji, Jesus of ACIM, and The Divine Mother. I am deeply thankful to You for all your support which is beyond words.

And thirdly, I dedicate this book to all those Breathworkers out there throughout the world who are doing their best to make a difference. I acknowledge you and hope you will find inspiration here, within these pages of *Lately I've Been Thinking III*.

"All things are echoes of the
Voice for God."

—*Jesus of A Course in Miracles*—

# Table of Contents

# FOREWORD

I am happy to say this is the third installment of *Lately I've Been Thinking* by Sondra Ray. She writes every day on her Facebook some tidbit of wisdom. This volume covers 2019 and 2020. *Lately I've Been Thinking III* was started before we knew a "worldwide pandemic" was just around the corner. And in the middle of this book, it happened. What did we do about it? What did we think about it? How did we cope with it at the time? This book covers that important period in our life.

It starts out chronicling our "life on the road," and then it weaves its attention to experiences inside of us when, all of a sudden, we were forced to slow down and introspect in one place. Many of us had to change our trajectory—overnight.

Sondra Ray is always introspecting, trying to nail down the causative thought factors that precede our experiences. Although this third volume shows a slowing down in the physical movements of our life, perhaps it plots a speeding up in our inner sensitivity—given the nature of our physical stasis. We all went through this. Sondra and I went through it. And these entries show a shift in focus that flowed with the needs of the times.

I was stalled a bit in getting these entries ready for publishing. We are still coming into balance with a new way of working. ZOOM became a paramount tool of our trade during the pandemic. It fed our creativity and kept us alive—more than alive—as it helped us to actually thrive. One never would have thought a total "shut down" could initiate such a grand opening. We shifted our gears, as many did, to being online.

"Necessity is the mother of invention," is that common aphorism that rang true to our *great sequestered* days. It certainly got us to "see things differently" during the pandemic, and see the core of our work is in Relationships. We always knew this, but these Relationships were enhanced, not strained, by the unusual times. They were strengthened online, more than ever. It was inspiring to flow into the new intensity of this "invention."

One cannot avoid the massive presence of the internet in our daily lives. Think of it as a world wide web that makes communication more possible on a global scale than ever before. Nothing too new about that. But what the pandemic did was to rewire our brains to think along the lines of electronic connections and millisecond transmissions.

And, we would come to realize a new kind of exposure. More exposed, what did we have to share that was new and provocative to our age? To our situation? To our Relationships? To our challenges in this time of a modern-day plague? As much as the pandemic was a possible hazard to our bodies, it was an even bigger possible hazard to our mental and emotional lives. It had an impact on our souls.

As you dive into *Lately I've Been Thinking III*, you will most likely find some balm for your soul. It can be a treat, of course, but it can also be a necessary medicine, newly invented. Sondra Ray's usual pearls of wisdom are presented in the vernacular style of just plain talk that she is so good at. We feel relaxed in her presence. I know I do, and I spend 24 / 7 / 365 with her. I have a good idea that what she writes and the way she writes it is the same as the way she lives what she writes. She walks her talk, in other words, and describes that walk in the moment of these entries exactly just what is going on with her, which is common to what is going on with everyone. Her finger is on our pulse of feelings.

This book will make you laugh, and sometimes cry. It will insist you expand your possibilities and stretch your comfort zone to invent a new world for yourself, based on the necessity at hand. A better guide you will not find than in Sondra Ray, through the things she has "lately been thinking about." We are all fortunate that she writes down these impressions on such a regular basis on her Facebook, daily, that we may ponder them here in this consolidated volume.

It is a labor of love to crunch them all together. Barbara Milbourn, our literary advisor, copy editor, and transcriber, and I put these *LIBTs,* as we call them, in alignment. We have our individual talents in this. THANK YOU, Barbara, for doing the bulk of the transcription. I do the layout and the fine tuning. This leaves Sondra Ray "hands free," shouting her "Powerful ¶ Posts for an Awesome Life," her clarion calls for liberation, from the rooftops.

It brings me great joy to see these will be ongoing. *Lately I've Been Thinking IV* has already been written in 2021 through 2023. But for now, *LIBT III* is at hand. Onward and upward! Thank you for your ongoing readership.

*Markus Ray*

Washington DC
February 22, 2024

# PREFACE

I can't believe this is my third book about my daily Facebook posts. I never dreamed I would be doing it every day like this. It has been such a good feeling for me to start my day with high thoughts. To me, the purpose has always been to spread enlightenment, and it is fun for me to receive people's comments back. The other day when Markus was working on the table of contents for this book, he was reading out loud the titles of my topics. I happened to be lying down breathing in the next room. As I heard him read the titles of my posts, I was kind of shocked how just hearing the titles was healing to me. I could not believe that I had come up with all those topics.

Somehow it made me feel good just to hear those topics repeated. "Well," I thought, "that was brilliant...and I don't even remember writing THAT!" So, the very fact that I was there pretending I was a reader and liking what I heard made me feel good. Then I thought, "Well, if the mere titles made me feel good, then maybe people will really feel good reading those subjects." It was the first time I felt like my own student of myself, and I got something out of it!

Following this experience of just hearing the titles of the posts, I know you will get something special out of reading this book. The great thing is that you can open it anywhere and read a post whenever you feel like it. Or you can run your finger down the Table of Contents and find the subject that you need—one that appeals to you in the moment. You don't have to start at the beginning and read it like a regular book. You can open it anywhere and get the message for the day.

It is kind of a fun book to give as a gift to friends also. I love giving books away as gifts. Try it yourself. It will make you feel good. You can give away all three volumes—*Lately I've Been Thinking I, II, and III*—like a trilogy.

I love contributing to the beauty of the planet and the enlightenment of the people. Make it your habit that every day you are getting better and better and giving more and more to people. This I want to give to you AND I want to be your friend. You can write to me here:

Sonda@SondraRay.com

and I promise to respond.

LOVE,

*Sondra Ray*

# LATELY I'VE BEEN THINKING III

*January 1, 2019*

## ❡ LIBERATION BREATHING MISSION STATEMENT

❡ Our mission is liberation from all limitations, even from death, in all departments of our daily life. Through Liberation Breathing, a powerful and guided use of the breath, we invite you to join us in breathing in more life force and living with greater vitality. Join us in healing our minds and bodies and our relationships. Join us in creating conflict-free relationships everywhere. Join us in bringing joy to our work and job environment. Ultimately, join us in our mission to integrate spirit-mind-body and bring about a more peaceful world by serving the Greater Good and Humanity. May we all achieve a deeper level of peace within ourselves as we dedicate our Life's Highest Purpose to TRUTH, SIMPLICITY, LOVE, AND SERVICE.

**Love, Sondra**


*January 2, 2019*

## ❡ A DIFFERENT KIND OF FAST

❡ Since we spent a lot of time in India, Indonesia, and Thailand this year, I thought it was time for us to have a parasite cleanse. The really good one is when you take no food and you just fast on milk for eight days. The milk draws the parasites out of the crannies and then you zap them with strong herbs every two hours. We are committed to this; but I cannot say I like it.

**Love, Sondra**

*January 3, 2019*

## ℘ A SHIFT IS COMING

℘ Joel Osteen said, "If you take this as in *a shift is coming* it may not look natural, but we serve the supernatural—God. He will breathe in your direction in a new way. The shift is acceleration. The shift will take you where you could not have gone on your own. Your new attitude should be: "God, I am ready. I am taking the limits off You. I am enlarging my vision. I may not see the way, but I know you have a way. I declare I am coming into a shift." When God breathes in your direction, people change their mind. Closed doors suddenly open. *Not now* turns into *It is your time*. Now YOU need to get ready."

**Love, Sondra**

*January 4, 2019*

## ℘ MORE ON A SHIFT IS COMING

℘ Joel Osteen continues: "Stay in faith. God has a shift coming. God will not allow any person to keep you from your destiny. God knows how to shift things around and get you to where you are supposed to be. God knows how to move the wrong people out of your life and bring the right people in. God will get you where you are supposed to be. You are one shift from seeing a dream come to pass. This is the year that God will shift things into your favor. He is lining it all up. What you could not make happen on your own, God will cause you to accomplish. It will be bigger than you thought. It will happen quicker than you imagined, and it will be more rewarding than you ever dreamed possible. Whatever level you are at now, God is about to cross his hands and put you in a position you never could have reached on your own. Why don't you start expecting unprecedented favor believing for God to do something new in your life? A flood is coming!"

**Love, Sondra**

*January 5, 2019*

## ♪ HALFWAY THROUGH

♪ We are halfway through this fast. I am still convinced it is the most effective for getting ALL parasites. It is very interesting to do a strict fast with your mate. Very intimate and enlightening.

♪ So far Markus has done better than I have but we shall see if anything comes up for him the last half. What manifested for me was a strange dry cough. I thought it had to do with a publishing issue, so I kept processing that. However, nothing changed. So, I started doing a deep prayer. That worked.

♪ I had a dream where a very complex childhood pattern came up. After I got clear on it, I kept explaining it to people in the dream so I would not forget it. I am very grateful for this knowledge. I will share the prayer tomorrow.

**Love, Sondra**

*January 6, 2019*

## ♪ THE PRAYER

♪ Here is the prayer I used on myself:

𝕵 "I take responsibility for creating this condition caused by negative thoughts of mine such as...................I lay this at your feet. I allow you, the Holy Spirit, to undo all my wrong thinking that caused this condition and those thoughts that keep me from giving it up.

𝕵 I now choose to think that I can create peace instead of this. I place it all in your hands. I ask you to help release me from this and raise it from me.

𝕵 I ask to be taught the right perception of the body.

𝕵 I pray for release of the fear of the miracle healing. I pray for help in the cause of that fear which is my addiction to the thought of separation from God. I do not want to keep this error. I now ask for the part of the body affected to cooperate and let go. I cooperate with you and follow you (the mind of Jesus). I believe that you know what to do and will guide me. I choose union with you. I am willing to receive the solution."

**Love, Sondra**

*January 7, 2019*

𝕵 **7TH DAY OF FASTING**

𝕵 I am proud to say I have not cheated. Fasting is a willpower workout! It is supposed to give you the following:

* Superhuman confidence and self-control
* Superhuman brain functioning
* Increased longevity
* Enhancing learning
* Superhuman clarity and direction
* Awareness of incongruences (I can vouch for that!)
* Superhuman health
* Rebooted immune system

* Superhuman motor skills
* Superhuman emotions
* Weight loss
* Superhuman appearance
* Etc.

❡ I can say this is all true, but you have to go through your "stuff." Right now, my cranium is a bit stuck, and I may need acupuncture.

❡ I am really going to celebrate on Wednesday.

**Love, Sondra**


*January 9, 2019*

**❡ COMPLETED THE FAST**

❡ Yeah! During that time, I sent a manuscript to the publisher and Markus finished his wonderful book THE MASTER IS BEAUTIFUL. When he paints or writes, I get the pleasure of that energy that he puts out.5

❡ Usually there is a "gift" after fasting and I had one. I went to an acupuncturist at a healing center I have never been to. It was the best acupuncture session I have ever had in my life. Not only that, but the owner of the center is a very sophisticated, elevated, exciting woman and I really found a new friend. I really loved her right off the bat and the feeling is mutual.

**Love, Sondra**

*January 10, 2019*

## ꙅ THE DANGER OF ANGER

ꙅ Dalai Lama: "We lose control of our mind through hatred and anger. If our minds are dominated by anger, we will lose the best part of human intelligence—wisdom. Anger is one of the most serious problems facing the world today."

ꙅ Guru Mai: "It is said that if you are a true ascetic, you are completely devoid of anger. If there is any trace of anger in you, you are called a scoundrel, not an ascetic. A great being will go to any extent to remove the fire of anger. The greatness of a Saddhu Monk is that he can drop something once he realizes he has it."

**Love, Sondra**

*January 11, 2019*

## ꙅ MORE ABOUT ANGER

ꙅ Mata Ammachi: "Anger and impatience will always cause problems. Suppose you have a weakness of always getting angry easily. Once you become normal again, go and sit in the family shrine room or in solitude and regret and repent your anger. Sincerely pray to your beloved deity or Mother Nature, seeking help to get rid of it. TRY TO MAKE YOUR OWN MIND AWARE OF THE BAD OUTCOME OF ANGER. When you are angry at someone, you lose all your mental balance. Your discriminative power completely stops functioning. You say whatever comes into your mind and act accordingly. You may even utter crude words. You lose a lot of good energy. Become aware that these negative feelings will only pave the way for your own destruction! Anger makes you weak in every cell of your body."

**Love, Sondra**

*January 12, 2019*

### ♫ A COURSE IN MIRACLES ON ANGER

♫ This is ACIM Lesson 348 about the "highest thought" about anger.
♫ "I have no cause for anger or for fear,
For You surround me. And in every need
That I perceive, Your grace suffices me."

**Love, Sondra**

*January 13, 2019*

### ♫ AN UNCONSCIOUS ADDICTION TO SUFFERING

♫ Many people cannot heal all their symptoms completely because they unconsciously have an addiction to suffering. Religious upbringing is affecting them more than they realize. They get one thing in their body cleared up and then they get another ailment. They may have been told it is actually "holy" to suffer. They may have been told "If you suffer now, you get all the good later in Heaven." (What a brainwashing for torture!)
♫ On top of that they were probably told it is not right to be perfect. That is blasphemy. That was my case. For some reason I was really brainwashed on that dogma. So I unconsciously made sure I was not perfect by keeping some low-grade condition in my body.

❦ Then when I started working on my enlightenment and became happier and happier; that was wrong too as you are not supposed to be TOO happy according to the church. I really, really had to work out my church dogma which took me quite a long time.

❦ The final part I had to work out was to let go of the guilt that I was NOT suffering because others were.

❦ On top of all this, when I had a father who died and a sister who died, I somehow unconsciously felt I should be like them and have something wrong with me so I could still be close to them. CRAZY! So I had to work all of the above out and I hope you can too.

**Love, Sondra**


*January 14, 2019*

❦ **FEAR IS SELF-CONTROLLED**

❦ Fear may seem beyond our control at times but it is not. Fear is self-controlled. We are responsible for what we think, and fear comes from thoughts. ACIM says that when we have fear it is a sure sign we have allowed our minds to mis-create. When we have fear, we have chosen wrongly. The correction of fear then is our responsibility. When we ask God to take away our fear, we imply that it is not our responsibility.

❦ We must ask instead for help in the conditions that brought about the fear. Those conditions are a desire to remain separate from God. Our fear prevents us from letting the Holy Spirit be in charge. If we let the Holy Spirit be in charge, no fear will exist.

❦ ACIM says the only way to overcome fear is to master love.

**Love, Sondra**

*January 17. 2019*

## ℘ SOMETHING ABOUT GERMANY

℘ It so happens I am 50 percent Swedish and 50 percent German. My German side used to get really activated when I came to Germany. Stuff would come up in my body, etc., so I was concerned coming back here that it might happen again.

℘ Well, what I manifested this time was the following: The day I arrived, my email was hacked! This has never happened to me before and Markus is having a hard time figuring this one out. The other thing that happened is that my crown fell out in Thailand, and I had to go to a dentist there to put it back. Now it is painful and feels loose and somewhat painful. Always something in Germany for me.

℘ Anyway, went out with the team here last night and had a blast. So I am enjoying myself despite of the other issues. Our translator Ursina is also lovely as is our assistant Dirk.

**Love, Sondra**

We had a great dinner tonight with Dina Wolter, Dirk Voss, and Ursina Minck in Cologne. Loving Germany!

*January 18, 2019*

## ℐ BEING STRONG AND COMMITTED OR NOT

ℐ We're having a lot of fun with the team here in Germany. It is very strong, and they are very committed. It is fun to go out with Rebirthers, as they are always upbeat with high thoughts and working on themselves.

ℐ Lately we have seen some documentaries and films about famous people who tragically ended up with huge messes in their lives—catastrophes, terrible illnesses, etc. Why? They did not work on themselves throughout their lives. They did not clear their subconscious to be exact. Then it finally all comes up sooner or later. It is inevitable. Who wants to end up like that? Nobody. But how many are willing to devote their lives to clearing themselves?

**Love, Sondra**

*January 19, 2019*

## ℐ NEW TO BREATHWORK

ℐ We have quite a few people who are totally new to breathwork. It is so exciting to see them have their "initiation." Some were saying it was an experience of a lifetime! Now you know why I travel around the world spreading the good news that this work is available.

ℐ But imagine this: Some people have ancestors who were Nazis. They really have to deal with the family guilt.

ℐ I feel privileged that we can help them with this.

**Love, Sondra**

*January 21, 2019*

**♪ AMAZING TRAINING**

♪ The thing that stood out was this: When I asked who had not forgiven themselves at 10 (100%) to stand up, practically the whole room stood up. They have a lot of guilt, so we had to help them with that. So glad to be of service.
♪ The team was absolutely fantastic. All equals and people we love to hang out with.
♪ Markus sold his painting "Christ of Cologne." It is so beautiful.

**Love, Sondra**


*January 22, 2019*

**♪ THE CATHEDRAL OF COLOGNE**

♪ Yesterday we visited the great cathedral of Cologne which is renowned for its gothic architecture. Twenty thousand people visit it per day. It has the tallest twin spirals. Its construction began in 1248. Work was halted in 1473 and not restarted until l840. It is the largest cathedral in northern Europe. It has the largest facade of any church in the world and is considered a masterpiece. Apparently, it took 14 hits during the bombing when the city was flattened.
♪ We did not stay too long as it was just as cold inside as outside.

**Love, Sondra**

The Cathedral of Cologne

*January 24, 2019*

## ♫ GOING TO THE KARMA

♫ Had a client who was wonderful inside and out. She is successful and in a good relationship. She is nice looking, well dressed, and great to be with. You would never imagine that she had so much self-hatred. It was really heavy. The only thing we could come up with was her past lives. She had lost two children due to carelessness. That was the thing she needed help with.

♪ Sometimes you just have to go there to the karma.

**Love, Sondra**

*January 25, 2019*

## ♪ THE PERVASIVENESS OF ABUSE

♪ We have had quite a lot of clients who were physically and/or emotionally abused as children. They feel like victims. However, they have to look at how they created that in this incarnation.

♪ When I process them on what thought they had that attracted abusive parents in this incarnation, it is often the thought "I am bad." They then attracted this as a punishment. They so often create a mate who abuses them also.

**Love, Sondra**

*January 26, 2019*

## ♪ SUGGESTIONS FOR GREATER RELATIONSHIP

♪ Along with your partner, dedicate your relationship to something greater than both of you.

♪ Always pursue a holy relationship, committing to holiness above all else.

ℐ Do spiritual purification techniques together with your mate regularly.

ℐ Make it your purpose to become a "superbeing." Transform your relationship into a sacred space where that can happen.

ℐ Become part of a spiritual family that helps you progress. Join with others.

ℐ Balance work on yourself with efforts to serve humanity and the planet.

**Love, Sondra**

*January 27, 2019*

**ℐ SIGNS OF BEING STUCK**

ℐ Some people do not realize they are really stuck, and they need help to get out of it. Here are seven signs:

- You feel unhappy and isolated.
- You feel anxious or moody, rarely experiencing joy.
- You feel helpless, can't move forward or accomplish activities.
- You are sick, in pain, or your vital energy is blocked.
- You feel a nagging urge to attack someone verbally or physically.
- You can't get your personal relationship to clear.
- Your financial situation is shaky or faltering.

ℐ If any of these are true for you, you need spiritual purification techniques such as Liberation Breathing. We give sessions via ZOOM often. You can also study A Course in Miracles and do some chanting of a mantra.

**Love, Sondra**

*January 29, 2019*

**❡ WILLING TO FORGIVE**

❡ If you find you are stuck and cannot forgive someone even though you have tried, look to see if you are willing to change the thought, *I cannot forgive him*. It is not that you can't, it is that you won't. So you have to pray for the release of your stubborn refusal to do it. The prayer for that is: "I pray to God, a power greater than myself, for the willingness to change." Write that 108 times in a row. Usually, you will shift. ❡ Or maybe you actually have a fear of forgiving. So write out "My fear of forgiving this person is.........." The answer you get might be surprising. It might come out as, "Well then I would be really happy!" Some people have a fear of happiness. Then you go on to process what their fear of happiness is.

**Love, Sondra**

*January 30, 2019*

**❡ KEEP THE VITALITY IN YOUR RELATIONSHIP**

❡ Take note if you are killing off the vitality of your relationship by these ways:

- Not being in present time
- Not being spiritually awake or nourished
- Buying into prophesies of doom
- Failing to express your creativity
- Expressing constant put-downs and disapproval
- Failing to forgive
- The silent treatment

- Stuffing your feelings
- Addictions
- Stuffing food, getting fat
- Control and dependency
- Giving your power away

**Love, Sondra**

*January 31, 2019*

## ₰ EXTERNAL INFLUENCES AND YOUR HAPPINESS

₰ We have had several clients who are "drained" and feel "put under the bus" by family members. Not by their partners but grown siblings and families of the siblings for the most part. Or it could be exes, etc. Often there is money involved such as inheritances and so on.

₰ One client was so depressed over this that she did not feel like living anymore. We needed to lift them up and direct them to the following thoughts:

- *I disconnect from the family mind.*
- *I no longer give them so much power.*
- *I rise above the need for approval or disapproval from them.*
- *It is okay to put them in a kind of quarantine for some time.*
- *My happiness is more important than that drama.*

₰ It helps to take a vow of happiness wherein you firmly decide that you are not going to let anything in the external ruin your happiness.

**Love, Sondra**

*February 2, 2019*

**❡ COUPLES IN STRESS**

❡ Today we will give a ZOOM session to a couple in stress and tomorrow to another couple in stress.

❡ We always work first with each person separately and then we have them come together for our comments. It does not work to have a stressed-out couple speak together at first. Too hard! We tried that only once and they got in a big fight in our presence.

❡ Once I made the mistake of counseling a couple in a restaurant. She stormed out and left her food. He ran after her. We were on one of the Caribbean islands and did not even know how to get back to the place we were staying. So we just had to sit there and wait and wait, hoping one would come back for us. Finally, he did. What a disaster. Won't make that mistake again.

**Love, Sondra**

*February 3, 2019*

**❡ ABOUT WORKING WITH COUPLES**

❡ The first couple we worked with did very well. The husband had asked the wife if she wanted to go into couple's therapy, but then they chose to work with us instead. I am glad because most marriage counseling has no idea about what a personal lie is, and you have to know how to process someone's subconscious to get that. And that was the issue.

❡ I am always in awe of this work we do, and it is very rewarding to be involved with it. I love my career and I wish

I could talk more people into becoming Breathworkers. Especially men. We need more male breath workers.

**Love, Sondra**

*February 4, 2019*

## ♫ THE TOUGHEST COUPLES

♫ The toughest couples to give sessions to are those who were both physically and emotionally abused. You would think they would NEVER want to be in a relationship as adults where they are abused. But the mind seeks what is familiar and so they attract partners who abuse them. They both provoke it also. They set it up to make sure their partners will abuse them and then they complain how hurtful the relationship is. They usually have victim mentality. But we take them back pre-conception to look at the thought they had about themself that attracted an abusive parent in this lifetime.

♫ It is often a thought like "I am bad" and so they come in thinking they deserve this abuse. So then end up in what ACIM calls a "special hate relationship." They need to give up their addiction to pain and drama. It is very hard work to make progress with them, but nevertheless we try to do our best.

**Love, Sondra**

*February 5, 2019*

**♪ REPAYING DEBT**

♪ We had some clients who owed people a lot of money for a very long time...even 10 years! They say they don't have the money to pay them back. But the reason they don't have the money to pay them back is that they did not chip away at the debt by paying on a payment plan. Then their guilt really came up which keeps them from having the money to pay them back. So it's a catch-22. If they would only start paying this debt, they would be getting out of debt.

**Love, Sondra**

*February 7, 2019*

**♪ LEAVING A RELATIONSHIP**

♪ Have lately had several people who want to leave their relationship. Of course, they are not obligated to stay with someone while they continue to behave in a toxic manner. If the partner is not working on himself or herself or there is no visible change, it is a red flag.

♪ If you feel you got the lessons you were supposed to get, then it is not a failure to end the relationship. It is a success because you got the lessons.

**Love, Sondra**

*February 9, 2019*

## ♪ CONFLICTS OVER MONEY

♪ Conflicts over money rank as one of the most frequent causes of divorce. This is no surprise as money is easy to fight about. In any case, money conflicts differ in essence very little from any other kind of conflict. The ego loves a conflict. When we give up the addiction to conflict, we stop fighting about everything, including money. The best book on money I have ever read is *The Path to Wealth* by May McCarthy.

**Love, Sondra**

*February 10, 2019*

## ♪ MONEY REJECTION COMPLEX

♪ Some people have what we call a "money rejection complex." It could stem from the belief that money is sinful or bad and so they block the receiving of it. Or it could come from the thought in one's subconscious "I am a failure" so then they will always block money so they can prove they are a failure.

♪ Money is innocent. It is just paper and energy. Any negative thought you have about it, you made up. Your own energy determines whether money flows to you or not. The higher your energy, the more money you can attract and handle. As you develop higher spiritual qualities you can change your vibration.

♪ Only you can deprive yourself of anything. One teacher told me, "You can go to the ocean with a teaspoon or a bucket; the ocean does not care."

**Love, Sondra**

*February 12, 2019*

## ♪ DON'T JUST SETTLE

♪ God is not in the business of giving you lackluster relationships or giving you mediocrity. That happens when you settle for less than you deserve. Settling affects your emotional, mental, physical, and spiritual health. When you are with someone who you are not happy with, you will always feel a void. That is no way to live. That situation must change because it does not glorify God. God always has your best interests in mind.

♪ Some people say, "Oh we get along," but you want something deeper than that. God wants you to be with your counterpart and have a deep connection. Your mate has to love God.

**Love, Sondra**

*February 15, 2019*

## ♪ OUTSTANDING ORGANIZER AND TRANSLATOR

♪ Our organizer Adailton is a miracle worker here in Brazil. He told me yesterday that the training is SOLD OUT. He wanted 60 people to fill that room and he created exactly that. This is exciting. He is very clear that his thoughts will produce his results. We are very blessed. He even had tee shirts made with our logo on them.

♪ I also love the translator he chose. Her name is Simone, and she has worked on herself a lot and is very clear. She can be a real girlfriend for me also.

**Love, Sondra**

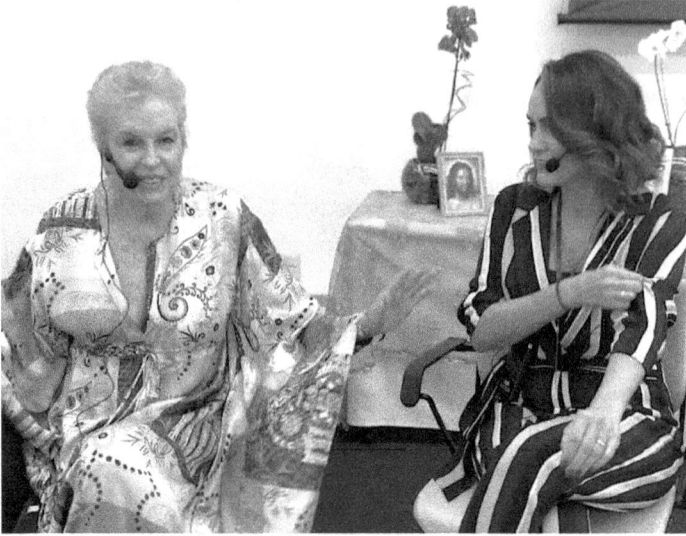

With our great translator, Simone

*February 17, 2019*

## ♪ A GREAT SATURDAY IN BRAZIL

♪ On Saturday we did Ho'oponopono long form first. Then we chanted Om Namaha Shivaya. Then I talked about Babaji and went over His teachings, and we showed a video of Him. After that I taught spiritual healing, and everyone worked on a symptom they wanted to get rid of and we processed it. After that was the breathwork. Great day!

♪ In the evening we went out with Simone, the translator, and her husband. It is amazing to meet such an outstanding woman. I am really fascinated by her. She is really advanced. She bought Markus' painting of Jesus. He also got commissions to do more paintings!

**Love, Sondra**

Teaching in Brazil – wonderful people in this training.

*February 18, 2019*

### ♫ SUNDAY'S TEACHING IN BRAZIL

♫ On Sunday I talked about the Divine Mother and the miracles I have seen her perform. I went over the teachings of Amma, The Hugging Saint, and I went over physical immortality. We had a lot of beautiful meditations on spiritual music with devotees of Babaji chanting devotional songs to the Divine Mother also.

♫ Then the breathing and closing with a Divine Mother puja with rose petals. The Brazilians were so very grateful. Some even said it was the most beautiful experience in their whole life! It was all really GRAND.

**Love, Sondra**

A successful training completed at the San Francisco Hotel. Thanks to Adailton Soares, an angel.

*February 19, 2019*

### ♫ WORST POSSIBLE BIRTH TRAUMA

♫ On rare occasions we have a client whose mother died at their birth. Can you imagine? This is the worst possible birth trauma of all. The consequences of the soul coming in are major to say the least. One client lost hearing when she was told this. Another had migraines for FORTY years! The guilt they have is horrendous. They really suffer. This really stirs my compassion.

**Love, Sondra**

*February 20, 2019*

## ♫ STILL LEARNING

♫ After 40+ years I am still learning so much about rebirthing/Liberation Breathing. It is still absolutely fascinating to me, and I love to be a facilitator with Markus.

♫ Often we have clients with the personal lie "I am not wanted" which is their conception trauma. The problem they have in relationships is they attract people who don't want them. Then if someone wants them, they don't want that person.

♫ It takes quite a long time to unravel this problem. They also feel like victims. So one has to take them back to pre-conception and get them to take responsibility for choosing those parents. Why did they incarnate with parents or a parent who did not want them?

**Love, Sondra**

*February 22, 2019*

## ♫ A NEW TECHNIQUE

♫ Lately I have been trying a new thing in sessions. After the whole interview when the client is lying down, I ask them what the biggest fear is that they have in their whole life. Then I ask them if they are guilty about anything. These questions put them immediately into a cycle and it is like opening a can of worms. Things start moving really fast then. So it is important that they are lying down when responding to these questions.

**Love, Sondra**

*February 23, 2019*

## ♪ REBIRTHING IN BRAZIL

♪ We have 33 participants in Curitiba thanks to Tom Cau, a great Rebirther and organizer. People write down the miracle they want from this training and then on a card they write "I am so happy and grateful I now have........." and they write the miracle they want as if they already have it. Then they stand up and introduce themselves and read the card and place it on the altar. We take these cards home with us, place them on our Divine Mother altar, and leave them there until we return to Brazil.

**Love, Sondra**

Participants in Curitiba, Brazil

*February 24, 2019*

## ♪ FEELINGS OF SADNESS

❡ I was feeling sad most of the day while teaching and I thought that was odd. But then during the breathe, so many people were crying that I understood I was channeling their sadness. I asked Markus later why he thought they were all so sad. He immediately said "infidelity." It is true that there is a lot of that going on in South America. Once we saw 17 clients and 16 out of the 17 had fathers or husbands that were disloyal. It is almost an epidemic. So, it is a macho thing, I guess. I am glad they are letting go.

**Love, Sondra**

With my sweet translator, Samantha, in Curitiba, Brazil.

*February 26, 2019*

## ℐ THE ERRORS PEOPLE WANT TO KEEP

ℐ Sometimes we get a client who is in such a toxic marriage that they are very ill as a result. We ask them if they had considered leaving and they say, "Many times." We say, "Well, you have to choose if you want to leave and get well or stay and be sick." They say they want to be well but when we ask them when they are going to bring up leaving, they say they don't have the courage. Usually, they have pity on the partner even if he is an alcoholic, or they are afraid to be alone.

ℐ One woman broke a leg. After she healed it, she broke the other one. She was afraid to take the necessary step.

ℐ These sessions are really hard and sometimes I feel slightly ill afterwards.

ℐ The point is: "Truth cannot deal with errors people want to keep." What do you do about their unwillingness? They pay for a session but then they are unwilling to do what it takes. Unwillingness is a big problem in the world.

**Love, Sondra**

*March 1, 2019*

## ℐ LAST DAY IN BRAZIL

ℐ Our last day in Brazil was VERY interesting. First Tom took us to meet a spiritual master who can heal any disease. That is a relief because John of God, who everyone went to see, is in jail for sexual abuse. Five hundred women came forth to accuse him!

ʃ After that we went to see the woman who is the head of Family Constellations. She is amazing in that she has a kind of ashram for kids, and she has adopted seven children, some of them deformed. She is super powerful. She had over 40 people to hear us talk!

ʃ Tom is busy enrolling already for August when we go back. We usually don't go to a country twice in a year, but they want that, and they can handle that. We gave the talk on the way to the airport, so we were busy right up to the last minute.

**Love, Sondra**

*March 2, 2019*

### ʃ REJECTING FEEDBACK

ʃ We have clients complain that they cannot give ANY feedback to their mates. On the plane I was reading a book that talked about how it looks when you reject feedback.

- You get angry at the person giving it even if he or she says it in a kind way.
- You make excuses for the mistake or fault that was pointed out.
- You brush it off even though you would give the same feedback if the roles were reversed.
- You deny the feedback is even accurate.
- You avoid the person in the future because you don't want to address the issue.
- You point out the flaws of the person giving the feedback.
- You gather up evidence of others who do not agree with the assessment (even if you assess it was valid).
- You try to put the feedback out of your mind.

(From the book *Successful Women Speak Differently* by Valorie Burton)

**Love, Sondra**

*March 3, 2019*

### Ꝯ THE LIE "I AM UNWANTED"

Ꝯ I must confess I feel sorry for people who have the personal lie "I am unwanted." Naturally, they have a difficult time in relationships. They are unconsciously attracted to people who don't want them so they can feel unwanted. The people that want them, they are not interested in. They will push them away. It is a no-win situation. It takes quite a long time to get over one's personal lie because it is an addiction. These people really struggle in no-win relationships over and over. They feel like victims from their conception trauma.

Ꝯ The only way out is to see that they chose those parents. I ask them what the reason was they did not want to be wanted in this incarnation. It is usually a past life where they did something bad or wrong and then they think they don't deserve to be wanted. That is step one. Step two is that they really have to become willing to be wanted and re-program and have a lot of Liberation Breathing sessions.

**Love, Sondra**

*March 4, 2019*

### Ꝯ SHOW GENUINE PROGRESS

Ꝯ I read a lot of books on relationships to see if I have missed anything as it is my field. I also read them to see if they are something I could recommend to students. Recently I read *The Man God Has for You* by Stephan Labossiere.

⚶ There is a chapter called "There has to be Genuine progress." The partner has to be willing to acknowledge the issue and own it, and they have to show genuine progress trying to do things better. They need to understand the issue.

⚶ We all slip up, but if they don't care about how their mistakes affects you, then look out. You are not obligated to remain with someone while they continue to behave in a toxic manner. They need to be actively trying to correct it. There has to be a visible change.

**Love, Sondra**

*March 5, 2019*

### ⚶ OVERCOMING BETRAYAL

⚶ We often see couples where there has been betrayal of trust or infidelity. They want to know if this can be overcome, and they are really struggling. Of course, both partners have to have a really strong desire to heal. In the best-case scenario this crisis could lead to a deepening in the relationship. But what we usually see is that there is a punishment factor. This does not help. The one feeling betrayed might not be speaking to the "guilty" one or may refuse to sleep in the same bed, etc. This is unhelpful. Withdrawing from the relationship as a punishment can take many forms. Punishment is intended to inflict pain, but it just creates more pain. Then this affects the children also.

⚶ The one feeling betrayed would have to look at their part in creating the betrayal. When I have seen that done, then they have the possibility of staying together and moving on.

**Love, Sondra**

*March 6, 2019*

## ℘ RECORDS OF WRONGDOING

℘ I went to a metaphysical church in Los Angeles where a female Black minister said, "LET US NOT KEEP ANY RECORDS OF WRONGDOING." Wow! What a great lesson for relationships.

℘ So often couples are hanging on to something their partner did long ago. This statement calls for complete forgiveness and forgetting the whole thing. Really a statement to live by.

**Love, Sondra**

*March 7, 2019*

## ℘ WHEN YOU FEEL MISTREATED

℘ Make a list of those you feel have mistreated you and hurt you. Then try this prayer:

℘ "I (your name) am making room to forgive all those who inflicted pain and suffering on me in the past. I choose to forgive them so that their actions of the past can no longer affect my present. My wish is to see them through the eyes of unconditional love. I also forgive myself for anything related to these events. I was doing my best at the time. I pray that these people and myself can experience love and peace going forward."

(From the book *The Seven Secrets to Healthy, Happy Relationships* by Don Miguel Ruiz, Jr. and Heather Ash Amara)

**Love, Sondra**

*March 9, 2019*

## ꝶ MAKE EVERY ACTION AN OFFERING

ꝶ From Ammachi: Try not to create suffering or difficulties for others. You may wonder how this can be done. The easy way is to make every action an offering to the Supreme Being. Think of every action as a form of worship. Then our actions will make both us and others happy and will benefit us and others as well.

ꝶ From now on, try to imagine that everyone who comes to you has been sent to you by God. If you can do this, then surely you will change.

**Love, Sondra**

*March 12, 2019*

## ꝶ PEACE IS INEVITABLE

ꝶ People think we have to live a certain kind of life to be happy or we need to have certain possessions to be happy. And yet it is the happiness that will bring these good things to you. People have it backwards. People also want abundance, health, peace, and harmony. These things come to you as a RESULT of your happiness.

ꝶ Be happy FIRST. Live in the moment. That is the key.

**Love, Sondra**

*March 13, 2019*

## ꝶ THE "I AM" MEDITATION

❡ I AM is the first name of God. When you want to think of God, think of I AM with your respiration. Inhale and say "I", exhale and say "AM." Doesn't that make you feel good?

❡ Just by saying I AM to yourself lifts you up. So the thing to do is this: Whenever you have a problem, forget about yourself and think about God instead. Forget about the problem and do the I AM meditation above and keep doing it. If your mind wanders, bring it back again to the I AM meditation.

(From *Silence of the Heart* by Robert Adams)

**Love, Sondra**

*March 14, 2019*

## ❡ UNFOLDING SPIRITUALLY

❡ I read through the book *Silence of the Heart* by Robert Adams. I found it too complex in places, but I kept reading on the plane. Got to the last chapter and I really was glad to say that what he said was totally clear.

❡ He stated that the very fastest way to unfold spiritually and get enlightened is to be of service to the guru. He stated that when you really love the Master, you will see very fast changes in your life. You should give your ego to the master and become empty and free. If you surrender to the master, the master will always be with you and never leave you. You will never be alone again. You will stop worrying about anything and everything. The master is pure awareness, absolute reality, all pervading, everywhere present. And, the master will kill your ego so you can be liberated. There is nothing more powerful than being with the master.

❡ Now you know why I am always trying to get everyone to come to Babaji, Ammachi, and Jesus with us.

**Love Sondra**

*March 15, 2019*

**℘ WHAT IS GOD ?**

℘ A devotee of Ramana Maharishi had a son who died, and he was totally grief stricken. So, he begged to have an audience with Ramana. When he entered the hall, Ramana was reclining on a couch with his eyes closed. The devotee started to cry and tell him all his troubles and how much he loved his son. And then he asked Ramana, "What is God?" Ramana didn't answer and kept still for 15 minutes. Then he opened his eyes and he said very softly "What IS, is God."

℘ I liked his answer.

**Love, Sondra**

*March 17, 2019*

**℘ I AM AN ASSET**

℘ Once we had clients who were failing in business and getting a lot of disapproval from their bosses. In one case the client was outright fired. In checking their subconscious thoughts, we found out that they had the personal lie "I am a screw-up." At first, I wondered what the right affirmation was to dilute that. We came up with "I am an asset."

℘ A personal lie can ruin everything. You have to know what your personal lie is, and it has to be breathed out. Changing it to the opposite is not enough. It has to come out of the cells.

**Love, Sondra**

*March 19, 2019*

## ℐ BLESSING INSTEAD OF JUDGING

ℐ The kahunas of Hawaii teach that even mentally criticizing others affects your body. They teach that criticism of the self or of others causes stress and inhibits awareness, memory, and energy flow, making you weaker and more susceptible to illness.

ℐ When someone displays a behavior that is intolerable, we usually don't feel like praising them for it. To break the habit of judging that person, try blessing the situation instead. Support the person moving through the offensive pattern, bless them, and see them healed of it. Then honor and respect their God Self. This is easier to do if the relationship is already placed in the context of conscious blessing.

**Love, Sondra**

*March 22, 2019*

## ℐ AS SO OFTEN HAPPENS

ℐ We are doing a training in Michigan. I needed an ironing board, so Barbara called her next-door neighbor to see if he had one. He did not. However, later, there was a new ironing board outside our door. He must have gone out and bought us one. So, I told Barbara I would like to meet him. He is a bachelor who has a very beautiful home as he is in the tile business. I invited him to the training, and he said yes and asked if he could bring his best friend. I was happy about this as he is in a new relationship. However, later, all his fear came up so I don't know if he will make it. This so often happens.

**Love, Sondra**

*March 23, 2019*

## ℘ THE WRONG PERSONAL LIE

℘ We have a sweet group. What is interesting to me is this: Most have had rebirthing before, BUT they have the wrong personal lies. So they were obviously not processed correctly before. So glad I can straighten this out as it is absolutely KEY that you know EXACTLY what the correct personal lie is. It affects your whole life. The group is very happy to be corrected on this.

**Love, Sondra**

*March 24, 2019*

## ℘ THE PERSONAL LIE AFFECTS EVERYTHING

℘ Today when I taught the spiritual healing class I had them all select one symptom in their bodies they wanted to process. Then they shared this with me, and we did the process to find out the cause of the condition. What was amazing was how often the condition was occurring in their bodies because their personal lie was stuck in that area of their body. Once again, I am stunned how much the personal lie affects everything.

**Love, Sondra**

*March 27, 2019*

## ℐ CONSCIOUS UNCOUPLING

ℐ In Michigan there was a couple splitting up and they were doing the program of "conscious uncoupling," and it seemed to be helping so I thought I had better buy the book and check it out to see if I could recommend it. It is written by Katherine Woodward Thomas who also wrote *Calling in "The One."* I think this book is very good for people who are splitting up. It helps you accelerate your own awakening and helps you get a sane, new beautiful life. It helps you get good will, generosity, and respect while doing minimal damage. I have not finished it yet, but I would recommend it.

**Love, Sondra**

*March 28, 2019*

## ℐ A LIFE-ALTERING OPPORTUNITY

ℐ "Conscious uncoupling is a breakup or divorce that is characterized by a tremendous amount of goodwill, generosity, and respect where those separating strive to do minimal damage to themselves, to each other, and to their children, as well as intentionally seeking to create new agreements and structures designed to set everyone up to win, flourish, and thrive moving forward in life."

ℐ Awaken to this breakup as a life-altering opportunity to transform your disappointing and destructive patterns in love at the deepest level.

(From *Conscious Uncoupling* by Katherine Woodward Thomas)

**Love, Sondra**

*March 29, 2019*

## ℐ TREATING DYSFUNCTION IN A RELATIONSHIP

ℐ It is a good idea to treat dysfunction in a relationship like a physical illness you would treat right away. If you don't deal with the problem right away, your upset becomes suppressed, tension builds, and your relationship becomes unhealthy. By the time you get help, it may be too late. Processing the issue does not have to be hard. Working on it can even be fun. Clearing the relationship moment to moment is the answer. At least clean it up before going to sleep. You can share without attack using compassionate communication. Say:

1. What I notice in our relationship is . . .
2. The way I feel about this is . . .
3. What I need and recommend is . . .

ℐ I am happy to announce *The New Loving Relationships Book*.

**Love, Sondra**

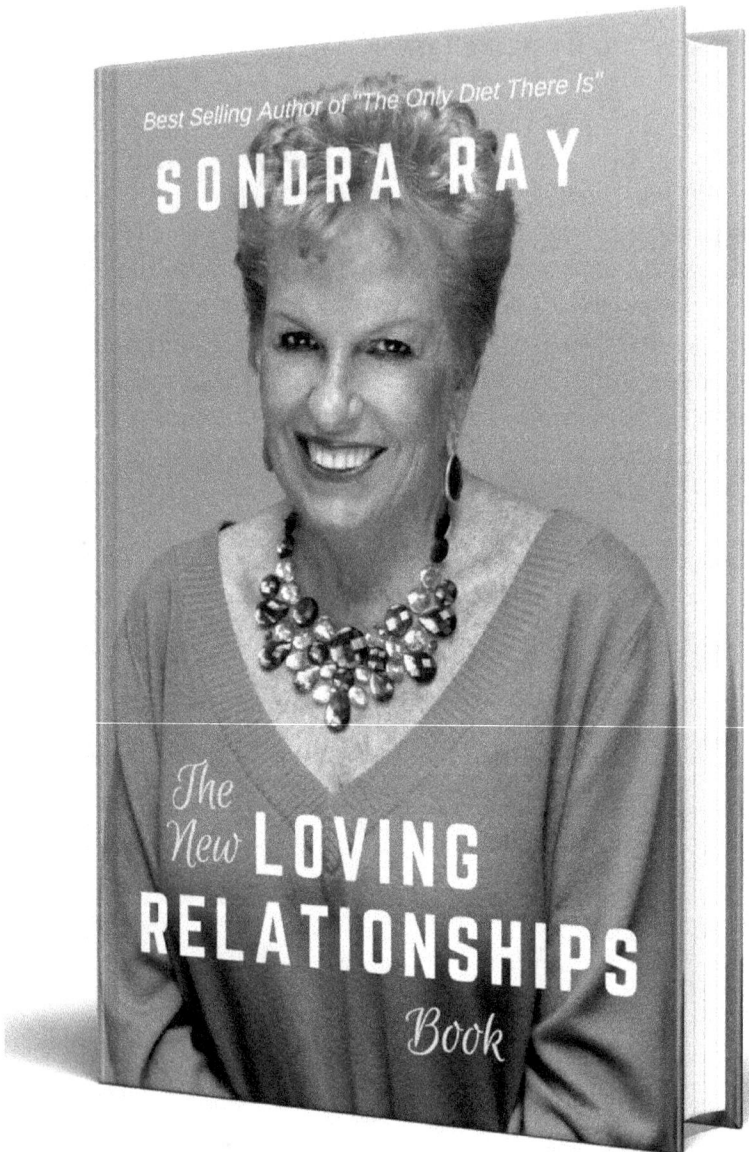

Best Selling Author of "The Only Diet There Is"

# SONDRA RAY

*The New* **LOVING RELATIONSHIPS** *Book*

Sometimes I paint these and then come back a couple years later and wonder how I did it. This Jesus I painted in Melbourne in 2017. . . Markus Ray

*April 1, 2019*

## ℘ PROVIDING A SAFE EXPERIENCE

℘ Since I have come to India over 40 times, I can provide a really safe experience for everyone. For one thing, we start out in the La Lit Hotel in Delhi. I call it Babaji's hotel as he found it for me. It is very beautiful and has altars and sacred art and statues all around. The best part is the staff really knows us and they always say "Welcome back" to us. There is a beautiful spa which is a great place to get treatments after 14 hours on an airplane. The group arrives today and tonight we will have a group meal.

**Love, Sondra**

*April 2, 2019*

## ♫ TAKING THE GROUP THROUGH STAGES

♫ We take the group through stages, starting out in a 4-star hotel where they can recover from the trip, and then slowly taking them to lesser hotel. (Most people go directly to the ashram from the airport on a train and I think it is too abrupt for new people.)

♫ Last night we had a group dinner that lasted several hours and everyone pretty much surrendered to each other. Today we will do a briefing and put them in groups with an assistant leading each group and they will have their first breathwork session.

♫ In our group they have breathwork every day and that is why they stay healthy. At the ashram people go through everything and other people always want to be in our group because they see how much fun we have and how everyone stays in good shape.

**Love, Sondra**

*April 3, 2019*

## ♫ OPENING THE INDIA QUEST

♫ We open the India Quest at the La Lit Hotel with a breathwork session.

Our India Questers after a good breathe

♫ We're leaving New Delhi today to begin the journey to Herakhan ashram.

**Love, Sondra**

*April 4, 2019*

**♫ WHILE IN HALDWANI**

♫ Stayed in Haldwani last night. To ashram today.

♫ Yesterday was our tenth wedding anniversary. The group wanted to hear our whole love story which was fun to relive with them.

♫ We both did a breathwork session with them, and the assistants led the session. It has been a glorious ten years.

**Love, Sondra**

*April 6, 2019*

Our friend Uday Chatterjee making offerings at the Havan (holy fire).

*April 15, 2019*

## ♪ ONE BIG MIRACLE

♪ Just came out of Herakhan ashram (where we were off the grid). The group did fantastic, and they loved it. One half of the group did mundun (head shaving) and they got so much out of that. We always get really clear on things by going to this Navaratri (nine-day festival to the Divine Mother). We always see the truth of what must be done. It is all one big miracle.

♪ Leaving for Dehradun today to visit Uday and Retu, our wonderful guides.

**Love, Sondra**

India Questers at Babaji's quarters

*April 19, 2019*

### ₰ LIVING OUT THE PRINCIPLE OF KARMA

₰ For Indian people, karma has a very vivid and practical meaning in their everyday lives. They live out the principle of karma and this the basis of their ethics. They understand it to be a natural and just process. Karma inspires in them a sense of personal responsibility.

₰ Buddha said, "What you are now is what you have been, and what you will be is what you do now." In other words, whatever is happening to us now mirrors our past karma. If we know that, whenever suffering and difficulties befall us, we do not view them as a failure. We see the suffering as a completion of past karma. Tibetans say that suffering is a "broom that sweeps away negative karma." It is an opportunity to evolve. Good fortune is a fruit of good karma.

♫ It is through our actions, words, and thoughts that we have a choice.

**Love, Sondra**

*April 20, 2019*

## ♫ HAPPY EASTER

♫ Today we celebrate the release of God's Son. Easter is the sign of peace. The risen Christ becomes the symbol of the Son of God's forgiveness on himself: the sign he looks upon himself as healed and whole. The white lilies are the sign the Son of God (you) is innocent. We celebrate life now and we honor the perfect purity of God's Son. Jesus says this: "This Easter I would have the gift of your forgiveness offered by you to me and returned by me to you. The time of Easter is the time of joy. Look on your risen Friend and celebrate his holiness along with me. For Easter is the time of your salvation, along with mine."

**Love, Sondra**

*April 21, 2019*

## ♫ WHEN ANXIETY IS LOWER

♫ Why is it that relationships between friends follow a smoother course than relationships between lovers? Somebody asked Ammachi that once and her answer was this: Expectations and criticism. We don't tend to be critical of friends.

⨌ Another possible explanation might be that in a friendship a sense of play is preserved affording relaxation and lowering the emotional intensity and subsequent anxiety. When anxiety is lower, each person can maintain equality and openness.

**Love, Sondra**

*April 26, 2019*

### ⨌ FEELING VULNERABLE

⨌ I am feeling vulnerable after India. But that does not mean I feel weak. One can stay in one's power and be vulnerable. It is good to feel vulnerable really because it implies openness, sensitivity, and lack of defense. It also makes one know that one has to care for oneself. It is also good in a relationship as it makes me feel more intimate and sensitive to interactions.

**Love, Sondra**

*April 28, 2019*

### ⨌ A WAY TO MEASURE SELF-ESTEEM AND VITALITY

⨌ It's great to be living in an impeccable apartment. Did you know that your home and the various spaces and objects that comprise it offer a clear, tangible way to measure your level of self-esteem and vitality? Have you ever considered the idea that grime, dirt, filth, and things falling apart represent your death urge? Notice the difference in your vitality and the vitality of your relationship when your space is pretty and clean. Careful maintenance of your property and belongings creates a cycle of positive energy.

**Love, Sondra**

*April 29, 2019*

### ♫ BEING READY OR BEING AFRAID

♫ Women: Are you ready to be in a relationship with an exact equal? Or

1. Are you afraid of your own power and standing out?
2. Are you afraid you will be lost without someone controlling you?
3. Are you afraid to stand up to a man and be yourself?
4. Are you afraid of your REAL SELF?
5. Are you afraid of being different than your mother?
6. Are you afraid you are not as good as a man?
7. Are you afraid people will criticize you if you are different?
8. Are you afraid you won't be able to keep the peace unless you give in?
9. Are you afraid of the energy, the excitement, the aliveness of being with an equal?

♫ To be with your true equal you will need to handle the upsurge of energy and you will need good methods of clearing. It is so worth it.

**Love, Sondra**

*May 1, 2019*

## ♫ THE WORD "PROBLEM"

♫ Instead of using the word *problem*, use *situation* or *challenge* or even *opportunity*. Situation is a more neutral word. Then look for something good in what initially appears to be a setback.

♫ One manager said the following when his staff would come and tell them there was a big problem. He would say, "GOOD!"

♫ Great souls learn great lessons from even small problems.

**Love, Sondra**

*May 3, 2019*

## ♫ ASK FOR WHAT YOU WANT

♫ When we first got here to the UK, we were tired as we could not sleep on the plane. We ended up with a terrible hotel room that was kind of in the basement near the housekeeping rooms. It was very dark. It was depressing. My computer got stuck and would not connect with the hotel internet. An expert worked on it for an hour and gave up.

♫ The next day we asked to change rooms. We manifested a beautiful room with large windows looking out on the trees. There is a lot of light. Markus tried my computer again and it was unstuck! Sometimes you just have to ask for what you want.

**Love, Sondra**

*May 6, 2019*

## ℘ TOTALLY DIFFERENT VIBRATIONS

℘ Wonderful training with so many young people this time. They loved it. I maintained good energy throughout and so we all had fun. One of our Rebirthers was so impressed with the last training that he treated his three children AND their partners to the training as a gift. Two of the male partners left after Friday night as it was too much for them. That was a shame for their girlfriends who remained and changed a lot in the weekend.

℘ Now those partners are also in totally different vibrations. Let's see if they can make it work anyway.

**Love, Sondra**

Wonderful LRT in Leamington Spa, UK.

*May 7, 2019*

## ℘ THE FULLY FUNCTIONING PERSON

ℐ The Fully Functioning Person (FFP) is one who enjoys high levels of self-esteem and personal contentment, and who is completely relaxed with himself and the world. The most identifiable characteristic is that he is completely non-defensive. He does not feel the need to justify or explain himself to anyone for anything. He lives his life completely in accordance with his own thoughts, feelings, values, and ideals. He is warm, gracious, happy, and charming and is called a fully mature, fully integrated personality. To reach this level is one of our most important goals.
(From the book *Believe It to Achieve It* by Brian Tracy)

**Love, Sondra**

*May 9, 2019*

**ℐ A DAY IN VALENCIA**

ℐ We had a wonderful time with Bela our organizer and our translator Dipika visiting the old palace gardens at Jardin de Monforte.
ℐ After that Bela gave me a fantastic treatment for clearing my aura. Then we all went out to celebrate and have tapas with some assistants. Really happy to be in Spain, especially since I can understand Spanish!
ℐ Following is a prayer from Isis. I was a priestess in Her temple in Egypt and Bela gave me this prayer which is fantastic. It expresses my teaching role in this lifetime perfectly.

**Love, Sondra**

"The only thing I ask of you is that you enter my house with respect. To serve you I don't need your devotion or your sincerity. I don't need your beliefs, just your thirst for knowledge. Enter with your vices, with your fears, with all the things you hate, from the biggest to the smallest. I can help you to dissolve them. You can look at and love me as a female, as a mother, as a daughter, as a sister, as a friend, but never look at me as an authority that is above you. If the devotion for any god is greater than that which you have towards the god INSIDE of you, you offend both of them and you offend the ONE."

*May 10, 2019*

♫ FUN, FUN, FUN!

❡ The Spanish know how to have fun, fun! Went out with Bela and her assistants last night. They wanted to hear Babaji stories from me and since that group is so advanced, I told some of the more outrageous stories. Bela started channeling Babaji, and we all got very much in bliss. The room is going to be full tonight as we have around 40 people!

❡ P.S. Markus tried a scooter for the first time (in his suit jacket) on the beach.

**Love, Sondra**

Markus on Marta's scooter in Valencia

*May 13, 2019*

## ∮ A MIRACLE AT THE END OF THE TRAINING

∮ At the end of the training we had a miracle after the puja to the Divine Mother. A couple who had had a rough marriage renewed their vows in front of everyone and vowed to re-conceive their marriage in the new paradigm we covered on Sunday. It was very beautiful.

∮ Markus sold his painting of the Virgin Mary. It was also the day in Valencia when they celebrate the Virgin Mary and throw loads of rose petals from balconies onto the Virgin. Happened the same time we were offering rose petals to the Divine Mother!

**Love, Sondra**

Our great team here in Valencia. Headed up with Bela and her wonderful assistant Dipika.

*May 16, 2019*

## ♪ LEARN HOW TO RELATE

♪ On the plane I read the following:

♪ "Forget relationships and learn how to relate. Relating means you are always starting; you are continuously trying to become acquainted. Again and again, you are introducing yourselves to each other. That is the joy of love: the exploration of consciousness. You are always finding new ways of loving each other, new ways of being with each other. The other becomes mysterious . . . then love is a constant adventure."
(From Osho)

**Love, Sondra**

*May 18, 2019*

## ♪ TREMENDOUS SUPPORT IN BARCELONA

♪ Started the training. We have 27 great people. One half had never had a breathwork session. It is so rewarding to see them happily responding to the process.

♪ I also had a situation with someone that needed healing. I wanted it handled before I started the training, so I wrote to Babaji and told him it was urgent, and I needed help with the tricky situation. He never lets me down. After lunch I came back, and it was all cleared up! Love having this tremendous support.

**Love, Sondra**

Babaji in Barcelona by Markus Ray

*May 21, 2019*

### ꙮ DOVETAILING PERSONAL LIES

ꙮ I am always amazed at how a couple will have their personal lies dovetailing. For example, if he has a thought, *I am not enough* she is always criticizing him for not doing enough or being enough and then she gets angry. When she gets angry, he wants to avoid her and not be affectionate.

Then she feels unwanted which is her personal lie. This goes back and forth all the time!

**Love, Sondra**

*May 24, 2019*

### ♪ OSHO'S THOUGHTS ON LOVE

♪ "Love cannot be pretended, and love cannot be managed. There is no way to manage love. It is bigger than you. Only those people who are capable of being alone are capable of love because they can go to the deepest core of the other without possessing, without becoming dependent."
(From Osho)

**Love, Sondra**

*May 25, 2019*

### ♪ MIRACLES AS EXPRESSIONS OF LOVE

♪ Miracles occur naturally as expressions of love. Miracles bring more love both to the giver and the receiver. Miracles are natural, but purification is necessary first. Prayer is the medium of miracles. Through prayer love is received and through miracles love is expressed. Miracles are a sign of love between equals.
♪ THE GREATEST MIRACLE IS WHEN WE AWAKEN FROM THE DREAM OF SEPARATION.
♪ We are to become miracle workers . . . working for the spiritual underground!

**Love, Sondra**

*May 26, 2019*

## ꙋ GUILT

ꙋ When you are attracted to guilt, you are deciding against happiness. Guilt feelings induce fear and retaliation. When we choose to exchange guilt for joy, God offers us eternity. When we lay guilt upon a brother, we will feel guilty, and we can never understand what love is. Love and guilt cannot co-exist. Guilt hides Christ from our sight. If we did not feel guilty, we could not attack. If we attack, we are judging another as unworthy of love and deserving punishment.

**Love, Sondra**

*May 27, 2019*

## ꙋ PERFECT LOVE

ꙋ We have built an insane belief system (ego) because we think we would be helpless in God's presence, and we want to save ourselves from His love. We think it would crush us into nothingness. We are more afraid of God than the ego. Love cannot enter where it is not welcome.
ꙋ We do not realize how much we have denied ourselves by staying in the ego. God however will never cease to love us. We somehow have chosen not to love, or fear could not have risen. Fear comes from lack of love. The only remedy is perfect love. Perfect love is the Atonement.
(From A Course in Miracles)

**Love, Sondra**

*May 28, 2019*

## ♪ CHOOSING TO BE LED

♪ The ego sets us on a journey which leads to futility and depression. But under the guidance of the Holy Spirit, we are led to joy. The Holy Spirit's love is our strength. We cannot learn love with a split mind.

♪ We need to say to the Holy Spirit "decide for me" and it is done. We must learn of His wisdom and love. We must unlearn isolation through His loving guidance. If we want to be conflict free, we have to learn only from the Holy Spirit.

♪ Think how great our release will be when we are willing to receive correction from the Holy Spirit for all our problems.

**Love, Sondra**


*May 31, 2019*

## ♪ LOVE EVERYTHING GOD CREATED

♪ We must love everything God created, or we cannot learn of His peace and accept His gifts. We cannot have salvation when we disengage from the Sonship. God will come to us only as we will give Him to our brothers. If we do not give the love of God to everything we see and touch, we are denying Heaven to ourselves. We are our brother's savior, and he is ours.

(From A Course in Miracles)

Love, Sondra

*June 1, 2019*

**ℐ THOUGHT PRECEDES EXPERIENCE**

ℐ We often have clients who have the thought *I don't want to be here*. They don't want to be here because they don't like the way their life goes. We have to constantly remind them that thought precedes experience. Their life is not working, in fact, because they don't want to be here. They did not want to be here since birth. Maybe they had a rough birth trauma or maybe it is due to past lives.

ℐ The correct affirmation for them is this: "The more I choose to be here, the better everything gets. The better everything gets, the more I want to be here."

ℐ Often they don't even realize they have that thought in their subconscious. That is why they really need a session.

**Love, Sondra**

*June 2, 2019*

**ℐ LOVE CANNOT JUDGE OR CHANGE**

ℐ "Love cannot judge. Love is not found in darkness and death. There is no love but God's. Probably you think that different kinds of love are possible. You think there is a kind of love for this, and a kind of love for that. A way of loving one, another way of loving another. Love is ONE. It has no separate parts, no degrees. It never alters with a person or circumstance.

ℐ "Love's meaning is obscure to a person who thinks that love can change. People think that they can love at times and hate at other times.

ℐ "Love is freedom. Love increases as it is given."

(From A Course in Miracles)

Love, Sondra

*June 3, 2019*

### ❡ AFFIRMING LOVE AS OUR PRIORITY

❡ "I will not be afraid of love today. When we want only love, we will see nothing else. If we offer love, it will come back to us. Love is within us. It cannot be destroyed but can only be hidden. When we choose love, life is peaceful. When we turn away from love, then pain sets in. By affirming that love is our priority in any situation, we actualize the power of God."
(From A Course in Miracles, Lesson 282)

**Love, Sondra**

*June 4, 2019*

### ❡ TEACH LOVE INSTEAD OF FEAR

❡ "When we love, we are placing ourselves in a context that leads to events at the highest level of good for everyone involved. God's plan calls for God's teachers to heal the world through the power of love. Every situation we find ourselves in is an opportunity planned by the Holy Spirit to teach love instead of fear. Every problem, inside and out, is due to separation from love."
(From A Course in Miracles)

**Love, Sondra**

In Estonia, one of our favorite European countries

*June 7, 2019*

### ♫ AN EVENING IN ESTONIA

♫ We went for dinner at our favorite Russian restaurant on the square. The atmosphere is heavy Russian decor, and the beet soup is divine. After that we did an evening with rebirthing. Two new guys went through A LOT, and I was worried they would not like it, but they came up later at the end and said that nothing else they had done had ever worked except for this! Real converts. Starting the training tonight.

Love, Sondra

*June 7, 2019*

**⚐ THE FOUR ELEMENTS OF TRUE LOVE**

⚐ *Loving Kindness* is being able to offer happiness.
⚐ *Compassion* is the capacity to understand the suffering in oneself and in the other person.
⚐ *Joy*. When you know how to generate joy, it nourishes you and the other person.
⚐ *Equanimity*. No boundary between you and the other person What happens to you, happens to your loved one.

**Love, Sondra**

*June 10, 2019*

**⚐ HAPPY TO REPORT**

⚐ I am happy to report that the training turned into a miracle. First, it cooled off which helped. Second, Markus got to an emergency dentist on Sunday and was treated for a start on his root canal. The procedure with X-rays only cost $40 euros. This would have cost about $600 in USA. Third, a brilliant scientist in the training had a mystical experience with Ammachi and Babaji whom she had never heard of before this training. That turned her whole life around for a big miracle. The LRT ALWAYS works no matter what I go through.

**Love, Sondra**

*June 13, 2019*

**ꢢ ARRIVED IN LATVIA**

ꢢ. We arrived in Riga yesterday. Staying near embassy row and it is beautiful. Our organizer Jānis is an amazing man and so fascinating to talk to. I love it when communication flows and everyone is having a good time.

ꢢ This morning we had coffee with Jānis and his partner Inta. Lovely!

**Love, Sondra**

Sondra with Jānis and Inta

*June 15, 2019*

### ℐ A WELL-BALANCED TRAINING

ℐ Jānis has produced around 35 wonderful people for the training. It is well balanced with a lot of men! This is unusual as usually there are more women. The men are doing great.

ℐ Everyone is going for it. One gal is vomiting but we encourage her to stay in the room and be in the energy. Hopefully she is better today. I really like Latvia, especially the Italian restaurant we have one block away. I want to come back next year and see all these people again!

**Love, Sondra**

Jānis Bruns and Sondra sharing intensely in one of the provocative sections of The LRT in Riga, Latvia

*June 17, 2019*

## ♪ LOVING COMMUNICATION

♪ "Please tell me your difficulties, your suffering, and your deepest wishes." (To know how to love someone we have to understand them.)

♪ "If a relationship cannot provide joy, then it's not true love. Offer only things that can make the other person happy. Ask, "What would make you happy?" "What can I do for you that would make you happy?"

**Love, Sondra**

*June 18, 2019*

### ℘ A LITTLE MIRACLE

℘ Sitting in a random restaurant last night and a woman approached our table. Turns out she is a strong Babaji devotee from here and not only that, she stayed in India three whole years to look after Muniraj who was the guru after Babaji. Such devotion! We will give her a session tomorrow before leaving. Love these little miracles!

**Love, Sondra**

*June 21, 2019*

### ℘ OUR HOLY TEMPLE HOME

℘ We are back in our Holy Temple Home after seven weeks in Europe and four weeks in India before that. We are ready for a good rest in Washington. A lot to take in. We give thanks at our Divine Mother altar. All the people we met on the tours we keep in touch with on WhatsApp. What a great tool for communicating!

℘ Love to all of you who attended our events around the world and who help make them possible. Our Holy Relationship with you is truly the best part of our work. It is the real altar upon our marvelous Earth. We are truly blessed by You and our meetings in Divine Service.

**Love, Sondra**

*June 22, 2019*

## ♪ A LOVING RELATIONSHIP

♪ What is a loving relationship? The loving part is already handled. You are love and your partner is love. All you have to do is remove the blocks to the awareness of love's existence. The relating part is where the "game" comes in. It is a game you negotiate: Shall we date and see each other twice a week? Shall we move in together? Try out the game plan and if it does not work, renegotiate. It is important not to impose the exact form or pacing from a previous partnership on your new one. Each new person has a unique history, unique patterns, fears, and desires.

**Love, Sondra**

*June 23, 2019*

## ♪ AFFIRMATIONS I MADE FROM ACIM

- I cannot be hurt unless I give something power to hurt me. Therefore, all blame is off the track.
- I see my brother as sinless. I am committed to see him differently than I have. I constantly appreciate the value he or she provides for me to see myself.
- I am now clear that death is a result of a thought called the ego, and therefore all death is suicide.
- Now I give my body new orders. Since I was the thinker that thought death is inevitable, I am also the thinker that can now think Life is inevitable and I am safe and immortal.
- When anything seems to cause me fear, I pray this: Teach me how not to make of this an obstacle to peace. I let You use it for me.

**Love, Sondra**

*June 24, 2019*

## ℑ MORE AFFIRMATIONS FROM ACIM

ℑ I pray for forgiveness regarding the distortions I have made that kept Spirit out. I choose not to maintain these distortions that cause separation. I do not want these errors any longer. "I am one with Spirit, one with joy, one with life, and one with abundance and all that God is."

ℑ "Since God's will for me is only perfect happiness, I am no longer afraid of God's will. (When bad things happened, that was not God's will for me; it was the creation of my own impure subconscious mind.) God's will brings me everything I want. God's will and my will are one now."

**Love, Sondra**

*June 25, 2019*

## ℑ LOVE AND OUR IMMUNE SYSTEM

ℑ Research studies prove that love boosts our immune system. When we stay alone our energy is unbalanced. If you are single, it is recommended you find a partner! Don't stay alone. When the energy of a man and woman connect, there is a meeting of yin and yang energy. This synergy forms a powerful mix to improve your health. Studies worldwide have unequivocally proven that people in relationships are healthier. Holding hands is a merger of yin and yang energy.

ℑ When we share and receive love, many chemicals in the brain are activated allowing our overall energy to grow stronger.

**Love, Sondra**

*June 27, 2019*

### ♫ INVISIBLE DIVORCE

♫ I read in a book by Dr. Harville Hendrix about the concept of an "invisible divorce." It happens with couples usually in a power struggle or with people afraid of intimacy. In other words, what does your spouse (or mate) do to avoid you? The list they got is very long: reading romance novels, disappearing into the garage, Facebooking, tweeting, or snapchatting, camping out on the phone, worshiping the car, spending too much time with the kids, being wedded to the computer, volunteering for every committee at church, spending too much time with the boat, having an affair, avoiding eye contact, spending hours reading the *New York Times* , falling asleep on the couch, being a sports junkie, coming home late for dinner, fantasizing during sex, being sick and tired all the time, not wanting to be touched, four scotches a night, living on the tennis court, etc. The list goes on and on.

**Love, Sondra**

*June 28, 2019*

### ♫ BECOMING A COUPLE

♫ Some experts say that it takes from nine to fourteen years for a couple to truly "create and form a being." Which means when we first get married our brains are stuck in "singleness" grooves. We don't think of ourselves as part of a couple, but as one individual trying to relate to another. In other words, they say that the journey from "me" to "we" is about a decade. All this apparently means that when couples break up after just six or seven years, they have not begun to experience what being married is really like. It is like climbing halfway up the mountain; they never get to see the sights. (From Gary Thomas, evangelical minister.)

ℐ I wonder: Wouldn't it be different if one was enlightened?

**Love, Sondra**

*June 29, 2019*

**ℐ HO'OPONOPONO**

ℐ I recommend that everyone learn the true Ho'oponopono process (not the 4-step short form). Ho'oponopono is a simple yet profound method of resolving problems and removing stress in a non-stressful way. It does not deal with the coping, controlling, and management of stress; it releases stress. The essence of it is KNOWING WHO YOU ARE. This knowledge is the key. With the key of self-identity, man is able to be one with himself and the Source of Creation. This is how you free yourself.

ℐ To take the course, contact IZI LLC on Google. Markus has written a beautiful chapter on my Kahuna teacher, Morrnah Simeona, in his new book *The Master is Beautiful*. I highly recommend this book!

**Love, Sondra**

*June 30, 2019*

**ℐ AMMACHI IN WASHINGTON**

❧ Today we are checking into the hotel where Ammachi will be giving Darshan. We are very thrilled to say the least. She is the real Divine Mother. She is also called the Hugging Saint. She has been known to hug 20,000 people in one sitting which seems theoretically impossible. I have been with her before in Dallas, Santa Fe, California, New York, and India, but it has been several years since I have been able to get my schedule clear to see her here in Washington, D.C. So this is wonderful.

**Love, Sondra**

*July 1, 2019*

## ❧ AMMACHI CONNECTED TO PARASHAKTI

❧ Amma is connected to Parashakti, the all-pervasive, pure consciousness, power, and primal substance of all that exists. She has this supreme energy of the Divine Mother. She is in a state of Divine Joy all the time. It is normal for her to feel ecstatic. She is covering the world with love. We are getting up early to get in line for our token. We are in the Marriott in Crystal City. Going now to get in line.

**Love, Sondra**

*July 2, 2019*

## ❧ WONDERFUL HUGS FROM AMMA

❧ Amma was wonderful to say the least. Markus offered her his books *Odes to the Divine Mother* and *The Master is*

*Beautiful*. She took a real interest in those and gave him a special hug. Then she hugged us both together. Come to find out she has done more to give aid than some countries. ॐ Came back to our room and WWII was on with Auschwitz. It was like seeing the very best humanitarian and the worst evil in the world all in one swoop. Just shows what we are capable of. Hoping to get another hug tonight.

**Love, Sondra**

*July 3, 2019*

## ॐ ANOTHER HUG FROM AMMA

ॐ For our second hug we had to wait seven hours from the time we got the token. That was not a problem as we have a hotel room. Anyway, I will never forget that hug. First, she hugged us each individually and then she put us together for another hug. This time she looked us right in the eyes and smiled while putting rose petals over us. Her look was one of recognition as if she knew everything about us, which she does of course. It was extremely uplifting to be so close to her.

**Love, Sondra**

*July 6, 2019*

## ॐ DOCTORS, PATIENTS, AND MASTERS

ॐ Someone asked Amma if she was like a doctor and if she considered her devotees like patients. She said, "It is more important that THEY realize they are patients." Then she was asked what percentage of success she had with these patients. She answered this: "Son, successful operations are very rare." The questioner then asked, "Why?" Amma answered, "Because the ego doesn't permit most people to cooperate with the doctor. It doesn't let the doctor do a good job."

♪ She added, "When a True Master works on you—on your ego—he or she prefers to do it while you are conscious. The Divine Master's surgery removes the disciple's cancerous ego. The whole process is much easier if the disciple can remain open and conscious."

**Love, Sondra**

*July 7, 2019*

♪ **AMMA ABOUT GRACE**

♪ The questioner asked Amma about Grace. "What is it? And even if you dedicate yourself to your work would the result depend on Grace?"

♪ Amma: "Grace is the factor that brings the right result at the right time in the right proportions to your actions. Dedication is the most essential part. The more dedicated you are, the more open you remain. The more open you are, the more love you experience. The more love you have, the more grace you experience. Grace is openness. It is the spiritual strength and the intuitive vision that you can experience while performing an action. By remaining open to a particular situation, you are letting go of your ego and narrow-minded views. This transforms your mind into a better channel through which divine energy can flow. That flow of shakti and its expression through our actions is grace."

**Love, Sondra**

*July 8, 2019*

**ꗊ AMMA ABOUT TRUE LOVE**

ꗊ Someone asked Amma: "What is true love?"
Amma said: "True love is the state of complete fearlessness. Fear and genuine love cannot go together. As the depth of love increases, the intensity of fear decreases. The more love you have, the more divinity is expressed within you. The less love you have, the more fear you have and the more you move away from the center of life."
(From the book *From Amma's Heart* by Swami Amritaswarupananda Puri)

**Love, Sondra**

*July 9, 2019*

**ꗊ HAVING A DIRECT LINE**

ꗊ A devotee of Amma said with concern, "Amma, so many thousands of people pray to You. It seems that almost all the lines will be busy when I call for help. Do you have a suggestion for me?"
ꗊ Hearing the question, Amma laughed and replied: "Don't worry son. You have a direct line. However, the quality of the line depends on the fervor of your prayer."

₰ One thing that people cannot understand is how the guru can help thousands at the same moment. How does She know everything about everyone and all their needs? This is the great mystery. She is tapped into cosmic consciousness and can hear your prayer. This I experience with Babaji, Jesus, and Ammachi.

**Love, Sondra**

*July 10, 2019*

**₰ WORK IS WORSHIP**

₰ Someone asked Ammachi if she ever wanted to stop the work she was doing. Here is her reply: "What Amma does is not work. It is worship. There is only pure love in worship. Therefore, it is not work. Work is tiring and dissipates your energy, whereas love can never be tiring or boring. On the contrary, it keeps filling your heart with more and more energy. Pure love makes you feel as light as a flower. You won't feel any heaviness or burden. Boredom occurs only when there is no love. Nothing gets old when there is love. Everything remains eternally new and fresh."

₰ That applies to everyone not just Amma. That is what Babaji always said to us. He used to shout: WORK IS WORSHIP. IDLENESS IS DEATH! So, no matter what your job is, turn it into a form of worship. Know you are serving humanity by whatever you are doing. You are among the ministers of God, and your ministry is everyone who comes to you during the day. Lift them up!

**Love, Sondra**

*July 11, 2019*

## ♫ LOVE OR ATTACHMENT

♫ Often people come to Amma complaining how sad they are after a divorce or break-up. She usually talks to them like this: "Am I really in love or am I too attached? Ask yourself this question as deeply as you can. Contemplate on it. And soon you will realize that the love we know is really attachment. Most people are craving attachment, not real love. So Amma would say that this is an illusion. In a way, we are betraying ourselves. We mistake attachment for love. Love is the center and attachment is the periphery. Be in the center and detach yourself from the periphery. Then the pain will go away."
(From the book *From Amma's Heart* by Swami Amritaswarupananda Puri)

**Love, Sondra**

*July 12, 2019*

## ♫ KNOW NO SORROW

♫ People complain to Amma that they are never free from sorrow. All Amma will say to such people is that they have not really called upon God at all because their minds were filled with other things. Those who really love God know no sorrow. There is only bliss in the lives of those who are fully immersed in their love for God. Everywhere and in everything they see only their beloved deity. If we pray to God, it should be only for the sake of loving God and not to gain material things. We should forget ourselves in the presence of God.

♫ Say this prayer: "Make me love You and let me forget everything else!" This is the lasting wealth of life, the wellspring of bliss. If we develop such devotion, we have succeeded in life.
(From Amma's book *Lead Us to Purity*)

**Love, Sondra**

*July 13, 2019*

## ♫ THE FRUITS OF OUR ACTIONS - KARMA

♫ Amma talks about one's karma. She says that if life at present is a struggle for some and easy for others, it is the result of fruits of their previous actions. Our success today is the fruit of the good actions performed yesterday. And if this success is to continue in the future, we have to do good deeds today, otherwise, we will have to experience suffering tomorrow. If we are compassionate towards those who struggle today, we can avoid suffering tomorrow. By helping those who have fallen into a ditch to climb out, we can avoid our own fall tomorrow.

♫ The suffering that arises from one's past actions is, in a sense, a divine blessing because it helps us remember God. By turning to the spiritual path, one experiences a lot of relief from karma.

**Love, Sondra**

*July 14, 2019*

## ♫ THE WAY TO FACE EXPERIENCES

♪ Amma talks about the way to face experiences. She says we confront the experiences in life in three different ways.

1. We try to run away from the situations.
2. We try to change the circumstances, believing that such a change will solve all our problems.
3. We curse our circumstances and proceed somehow.

♪ These don't really work. But there is a fourth way. There is a way to overcome difficult situations, and that is to change our state of mind. This is the only way to find joy.

♪ It is impossible to change the external environment completely to suit our needs. So we need to change our state of mind to suit the environment. This is possible only through spirituality. If we transform our minds, we can face any situation with a smile. Pray for the ability to change your present mental attitude.

(From Amma's book *Lead Us to Purity*)

**Love, Sondra**

*July 15, 2019*

**♪ FORGIVENESS AND WRONG THINKING**

♪ You cannot cancel out your past errors alone. They will not disappear without the Atonement. (The Atonement is total forgiveness and allowing the Holy Spirit to undo all your wrong thinking.)

♪ "Joining in the Atonement is the way out of fear. Therefore, I invite in the Holy Spirit and ask Jesus to bring Him down to me. I can ask for immeasurable gifts. The gift I ask for is healing. The Holy Spirit lives with me. I renounce the role of guardian of my thought system and give it to Him. I unite my

will with the Creator. I bring my mind completely under the Holy Spirit's guidance. I join in His resurrection. Until I do, my life will be wasted."
(From A Course in Miracles)

**Love, Sondra**

*July 18, 2019*

**♪ CALIFORNIA LIFE**

♪ Ahh . . . the California life! We are staying at Jane and Ernie's in Glendale. The house is really expansive and there is a wonderful terrace and pool, so we sit outside and relax. The place is impeccable and in such fabulous taste. This really gets one high.
♪ Going out on the town tonight to celebrate.

**Love, Sondra**

*July 19, 2019*

**♪ TWIN FLAME LOVE**

♪ We're out on the town with our "twin flames." The twin flame love carries an intensity that can be translated into productive work and service to others. You have a great love to share as well as power and creative energy to elevate humanity. We four waited a long time to manifest these mates! We definitely did not find that in our first marriages, and we had to go through karmic relationships before we got this blessing!

**Love, Sondra**

*July 20, 2019*

### ❡ YOUR DIVINE COUNTERPART

❡ The twin flame is your divine counterpart. "The twin flame is at the highest level of the white fire body of your God Presence, and this is the other half of the spiritual being that you were in the beginning.

❡ "Soul mates are loves of close kindred souls and they tend to be complimentary . . . soul development is often at the same level. They can work well together. But they may be more like brother and sister and are not as profound as twin flames.

❡ "If the other person is more advanced than you are, you have a great opportunity. But if you are the one more advanced, you may be carrying a heavy burden and be pulled down."

(From *Finding a Higher Love* by Elizabeth Clare Prophet)

**Love, Sondra**

*July 21, 2019*

### ❡ CELEBRATING IN PASADENA

❡ We went out to celebrate how well this Southern California training is going. We went to the Langham Hotel in Pasadena which is very posh. I love to go into fine hotels and absorb the atmosphere. Even when I did not have any money, I did this, and it helped me to increase my prosperity consciousness. I used to go to the finest hotel in San Francisco with red silk walls. Back then when I was a beginning Rebirther I did not have money to order from that menu so I would just sit at the bar and order artichoke soup and that is all I would eat. It made me feel rich.

¶ The training is somehow easier than most partly because Jane has already rebirthed these people a lot before the training. Makes such a difference!

**Love, Sondra**

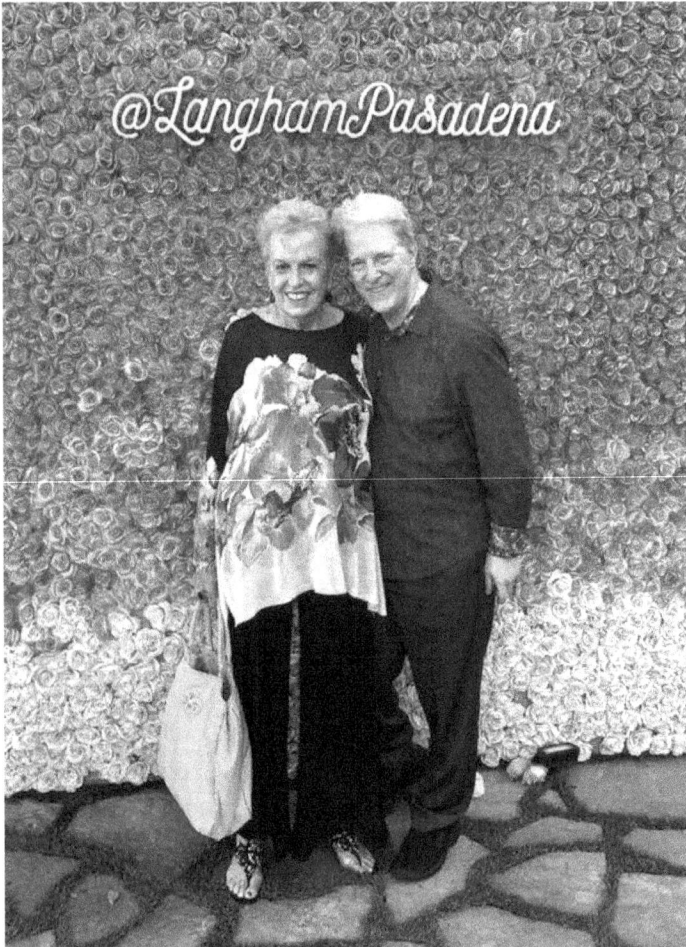

Enjoying one of the nicest hotels in Pasadena

*July 23, 2019*

**❡ KNOTTY RELATIONSHIPS**

❡ The question was this: "How do I handle a relationship when the person is frequently angry and that causes me to get upset also?"

❡ When dealing with anger: "At the point of releasing anger there is a split second when you can decide not to vent it, not to let the anger be expressed to hurt others. I realized that I had the CHOICE. If I didn't exercise that choice, I would be making tremendous karma. We can control anger by buttoning up our lips. We can decide not to say something we will regret that will hurt the other. We must prefer a higher love to our problems." (This is from Elizabeth Clare Prophet.)

❡ Well, I like that, but I don't think we should stuff our anger either because that hurts our bodies. You don't dump it and you don't stuff it. Babaji gave me an even higher teaching, I think. He said you locate the thought that causes the anger, confess that, and breathe out the charge.

❡ What we do is this: We say calmly, "I am feeling activated." (That way you are not stuffing it like one might do when buttoning lips.) You are not dumping it either as you are taking responsibility for your thought. Say to your mate, "The thought I am having that makes me feel activated is . . ." Then you breathe out the bad energy and do not dump it on your mate. I agree that if you vent it, you are creating tremendous karma.

**Love, Sondra**

*July 25, 2019*

## ♪ KARMA AND FORGIVENESS

♪ People often get a very low score on forgiving their parents on a scale of 0 to 10 (10 being total forgiveness). I am always trying to get them to go to ten. For one thing, forgiveness is the key to happiness. Also, what you don't forgive you attract.

♪ Someone said to Elizabeth Clare Prophet that he was having trouble forgiving his mother because he did not respect her. The teacher said first he had to forgive himself and God for giving him that mother. Then she said it was his own karma that gave him that mother in this life. That it was by his karma and his actions that he had to have this mother. Then she told him he had to forgive himself for his actions and karma . . . and that when he would do that, he was forgiving God who set it in motion. She said God's law of karma had worked irrevocably in his life because his own soul demanded it. Then she reminded him that he should pray for forgiveness for projecting upon others the traits he found in his mother. After all this, he could, she said, send forgiveness to his mother. She also said he would also see his past misuse of the mother energies! She said he would eventually love God for the opportunity to see this.

♪ Then one can say, "I made a mistake. The mistake was not good, but I am good because God created me."

**Love, Sondra**

*July 27, 2019*

## ♪ JUDGING

♪ Judge not, that ye be not judged. It means that if you judge the reality of others, you will be unable to avoid judging your own. The choice to judge rather than to know is the cause of loss of peace. Judgement always involves REJECTION.

♪ You have no idea of the tremendous release and deep peace that comes from meeting yourself and your brothers totally without judgement. The strain of constant judgement is virtually intolerable. Only those who give over all the desire to reject, can know that their own rejection is impossible.
(From A Course in Miracles)

**Love, Sondra**


*July 28, 2019*


**♪ SEE THE GLORIOUS CREATIONS**


♪ "Whenever you are not joyous, then know this need not be. In every case, you have thought wrongly about some brother that God created. Look at yourself and your brother and see in both the glorious creations of a glorious father. You and your brother will yet come together in my name and your sanity will be restored. Whenever you act egotistically toward another, you are throwing away the graciousness of your indebtedness and the holy perception it would produce."
(From A Course in Miracles)

**Love, Sondra**


*July 30, 2019*

**♪ A HOLY ENCOUNTER**

꽃 "When you meet anyone, remember it is a Holy Encounter. As you see him, you will see yourself. As you treat him, you will treat yourself. As you think of him, you will think of yourself. Whenever two sons meet, they are given another chance at Salvation. Do not leave anyone without giving Salvation to him and receiving it yourself.

꽃 "Whenever you are with anyone, you have another opportunity to find him. The Holy Spirit teaches you that if you look only at yourself, you cannot find yourself because that is not what you are. Whenever you are with a brother, you are learning what you are because you are teaching what you are. He will be imprisoned or released according to your decision and so will you. The Kingdom cannot be found alone.

꽃 "Communication ends separation, and attack promotes separation. Would God have created a voice for you alone?" (From A Course in Miracles)

**Love, Sondra**

*July 31, 2019*

## 꽃 OVERCOMING THE CROSS

꽃 Sometimes we waste time helping people who do not want to be helped. ACIM says, "Truth cannot deal with errors people want to keep." It also says, "Jesus can erase all misconceptions from your mind if you will bring it under His guidance." Further, "You are free to join my resurrection, until you do so, your life is indeed wasted. You are free to crucify yourself as often as you choose. The only message of the crucifixion is that you can overcome the cross. Your ego self and your GOD SELF are in opposition."

❡ He adds, "If you are willing to renounce the role of guardian of your thought system and open it up to me, I will correct it very gently and lead you back to God."
(From A Course in Miracles)

**Love, Sondra**

*August 2, 2019*

### ❡ OUR SOUL IS WORTHY

❡ Had some clients recently that were putting themselves down because of overweight, etc. I want to share what I read on the plane: "We should never condemn ourselves for our shortcomings and mistakes, but we can resolve to do better next time. If we condemn ourselves even a little, it's like poking a hole in a water bottle. The water slowly but surely leaks out. No matter how much water we put in the bottle, it will not stay full. ❡ That is what happens to our energy when we allow anything or anyone, including ourselves, to condemn us so that we feel we are not worthy of God's love. Our soul is worthy. So have profound mercy on yourself and forgive yourself."
(From *Finding a Higher Love* by Elizabeth Clare Prophet)

**Love, Sondra**

*August 3, 2019*

### ❡ ADVERTISING FOR A MATE

❡ I saw on the internet that a lady in New York City was advertising in taxi cabs for a mate for herself. She had to pay

$5,000 and the video ad was in 7,000 taxi cabs. I wonder how long the ad stays in place. Anyway, she is daring.

꿈 A safer and more sure way to attract a mate is to use the "Cosmic Dating Service" where you ask God or your guru to line you up with the perfect mate for you and your mission. Then you say, "If I am not ready, make me ready." I know two LRT grads that did that, and they did not even have to go out of the house. Their perfect mate came to their door! It beats going to a bar or using a dating service. God knows more single available people than you do! I asked Babaji for this and he gave me Markus.

**Love, Sondra**

*August 8, 2019*

꿈 **FATAL DISTRACTION**

꿈 A client of ours has a young baby. Her babysitter went to the store and left the baby in the car in hot weather! The police were called. Our client was beside herself and really needed our help. The baby is okay, thank God. This problem is becoming very serious in our country. Recently a man left his twins in the car in the heat, and they died.

꿈 One of our students is actually doing a documentary on this. She already did one about a man who had a adopted a baby in Russia and all he and his wife went through to get that baby. The baby was left in the car by him in the heat and the baby died. So the Russians banned adoptions from the USA after that.

꿈 Now she is doing another documentary on the general problem and calling it *Fatal Distraction*. That is certainly the right name. Maybe we have too much ADD (attention deficit disorder).

**Love, Sondra**

*August 10, 2019*

**¶ WHERE NEED ENDS TRUE LOVE BEGINS**

¶ Had some clients recently that were too needy. I always say that where need ends true love begins. Too much dependency on a person can kill love. Relationships based on emotional insecurity and need can become self-destructive. They don't work. Too much need drives people away and smothers love. It scares people away and it attracts the wrong kind of people. You also end up resenting the person because you have given away your personal power and rights. Also, if you are desperate and looking for someone you may end up in a very bad situation that would not be good for you.

¶ Before I met Markus, I asked myself if I could be happy all by myself for the rest of my life (even being an immortal) and the answer was a sincere YES. Then I knew I was really ready for a relationship.

**Love, Sondra**

*August 11, 2019*

**¶ BOTH AGREE TO BE CONFLICT FREE**

¶ A client questioned: "Isn't it good and just normal that couples have fights and conflicts in the course of their relationship?" I answered: "It cannot be all good if it is that way. Both partners have to agree to have a conflict-free relationship. To do that one has to have overcome anger and one has to know how to be at peace. This requires enlightenment. If only one partner is angry the other needs to look at why he or she is attracting that also. You are the one you live with."

ℱ The cure is to take the Loving Relationships Training that we teach and to read the following books:
*Loving Relationships* by Sondra Ray & Markus Ray
*Spiritual Intimacy* by Sondra Ray & Markus Ray

**Love, Sondra**

*August 12, 2019*

## ℱ LEARNING SO MUCH MORE

ℱ I learned so much more about Liberation Breathing yesterday. We had a client in a foreign country who is a new organizer. It was his first session. He got so much out of it, and he changed so much in 1-1/2 hours that I could not believe that we had not done him sooner. I was about to beat myself up for that mistake but then I suddenly understood why.

ℱ His birth was very rough. His mother should have had a C-section, but the doctor was switched at the last minute and the new doctor did not even know how to do a Cesarian! The mother was in huge stress with severe bleeding and was taken away to the ICU immediately. The father went with her. When he came out, they were not there for him. So he ended up with two strong negative thoughts: "I hurt women" and "I am alone."

ℱ This was his first time to realize this, and it totally explained his relationships with women. It also explained to me why we did not connect with him earlier. We got set up as parents who were not there! We could not even contact him sooner as he was not connected with us. He was not connected with people either which is why the enrollments were low. I think they will change now . . . but it is all the last minute.

**Love, Sondra**

*August 13, 2019*

## ♪ TWO REQUIREMENTS

♪ Elizabeth Clare Prophet said that when people want to know whether they should get married or not, she asks them two questions.

♪ First: "Have you considered if your individual service to life would be enhanced, enriched, and greater in marriage than it would be separately?"

♪ Second: "Are you deeply in love? Do you have a fire burning deep in your heart; the fire that can commemorate your love for God?" If you are hesitant, she suggests that you wait.

♪ Therefore, marriage has two requirements: a greater service to God that is greater than you can render alone and intense, fiery love.

**Love, Sondra**

*August 15, 2019*

## ♪ BONDING OVER FOOD

♪ Our new Brazilian "family" took us out to a very long lunch (like they do in Spain). I think we were there for more than two hours. It was very socially intense and wonderful with our translator (who is pregnant) working overtime.

♪ They ordered for us the national drink of Brazil called caipirinha made from sugar cane liquor and lime. They told us that people drink this together while cooking and "hanging out." We had a four-course fresh seafood meal. When you order something, they bring enough of the same for the whole table, so we are all eating the same thing.

Everyone is so loving. Really bonding over the food! We really did get grounded in Brazil.

**Love, Sondra**

A wonderful start to our month here in Brazil with our LRT team in Rio

*August 15, 2019*

## ℥ LAUGHING AT OUR MISTAKES

℥ Since we wrote the book on personal lies, I have had a new one come up: "I am careless." It is like my old one, "I am not perfect" and yet slightly different. I thought I packed perfectly, but today I realize I did not pack any purses or shopping bags which we need for carrying books, paints, etc. So I told Markus and he said, "We always need that. Didn't you have that on your list?" I said, "Yes, but I obviously did not read my list carefully because I was careless." Then in the elevator he made kind of a joke saying, "Well, most of the time when you are careless, it is no big deal but other times like this it is just plain stupid." I did not take this as a criticism because he said it in a very light funny way. We both cracked up laughing in the elevator. You have to laugh at your case.

ℐ Later we had to go out and try to find his painting supplies. It was very intense out there in Rio and we were not even downtown. It was like NYC or worse. Parking is impossible. We could not find the canvas he needed that was the right size anywhere. So I was teasing him about making the mistake of not asking the organizer to do it ahead of time like he usually does. The whole scenario became very complicated and now the team has to take the subway to go downtown in Rio and find the right size. Anyway, we really had the experience of trying to shop in Rio and look for shopping bags and canvases. It turned out to be really funny. I hope people in the USA appreciate our country. So much easier! I finally recovered from my temporary culture shock.

**Love, Sondra**

*August 15, 2019*

**ℐ OUT AND ABOUT IN RIO**

ℐ The city sidewalks are made with marble mosaics, just like in Lisbon, Portugal. Very BEAUTIFUL, but labor intensive, to say the least. Markus and I are by the sea, and there is a man repairing the sidewalks here.

Markus & I by the sea admiring the mosaic sidewalks.

§ Rio has such fantastic energy. It's almost magical. It is by the sea and there is a very famous stature of the Christ on a hill overlooking the bay. One wonders if this "blessing" keeps the city in another dimension.

§ The Portuguese colonized Brazil, so it has a much different vibe that the rest of South America, which was colonized by Spain. We love Portugal and we can appreciate the cultural transference that is carried over in things like the mosaic sidewalks!

**Love, Sondra**

Man making sidewalk repairs

*August 16, 2019*

### ❡ THE NEED TO LET GO

❡ We had yet another South American drama to deal with. Our Liberation Breathing client came to our hotel for a session (after flying in from another city). The desk forbade her from coming to our room saying they have a rule that no outside people can be visiting the rooms. So, I thought this must be a misunderstanding as that never ever has happened to us in any other hotel in the world in my whole career.

§ I went downstairs to greet her, and the desk personnel stopped me and made it very clear this was not allowed. We asked to speak to the manager, but that person did not come. So now we have to move to the place where we are doing the training. This woman, being Brazilian handled it fairly well, but I was nearly in a spontaneous rebirthing in the lobby.

§, We are checking out of this hotel and going to stay at the venue where the training is. I am trying to remain cool, but this is a bit much! Fortunately, Babaji trained me to handle sudden shifts or else I think I would be freaked out.

§ It is back to the lesson: "Today I will judge nothing that occurs." (ACIM Lesson 243)

§ Apparently the hotel does not want prostitution coming in and out of their hotel, so they have made this rule of no outside visitors. Go figure!

**Love, Sondra**

The Divine Mother is blessing us now

*August 19, 2019*

### ꝶ A VERY TOUGH TRAINING

ꝶ Everyone loved the training. They always do. It always works. For me, it was the first time in my life I tried to introduce A Course in Miracles to an all-Catholic group in a Catholic center. When they realized that it made the church obsolete, which it does, they had tremendous resistance. Some went into spontaneous rebirthings. I nearly fainted the energy was so heavy. After that when Markus spoke about ACIM however, he was able to completely win them over.

¶ And again later, when I presented the new paradigm, they became very shocked at how off they had been in relationships. They became extremely restless, and some got up out of their chairs. It was so intense I nearly fainted again. This has never ever happened to me before.

¶ Because they were "newbies" and had never had rebirthing before, and because of all that went down with that which I just shared, it was one of the hardest trainings in my life,

**Love, Sondra**

*August 24, 2019*

¶ **YOU ARE SPIRIT**

¶ We have a lot of new people in the training here in Belo Horizonte, Brazil who had their first session of rebirthing last night. They went through a lot, but they were very grateful for it. Always a good sign. Mostly women; only two men in the training. These women are all hoping for a partner who is willing to work on himself like they are.

¶ Today is my birthday and I am so happy that I have the knowledge of physical immortality. If you do not, please read our book *Physical Immortality: How to Overcome Death*. It will change your life just as it has mine. Imagine if I was thinking *oh, I don't have a lot of years left*. I would then be getting sick. The body grows old and dies because the mind is sick.

ℐ Jesus said that the power of life and death are in the tongue. So, what you say is what you get with your body. Remember this:

- Spirit is that which cannot be destroyed.
- Mind is condensed Spirit.
- Body is condensed Mind.
- Therefore, body is utmost Spirit.
- You are Spirit.

**Love, Sondra**


*August 25, 2019*

### ℐ SUCCESS IN SOUTH AMERICA

ℐ Our Loving Relationships Training helped a lot of souls rise up here in Belo Horizonte, Brazil. Adailton Soares and his great team were determined to bring success to our travels and work in South America. Bole Baba Ki Jai! Praise to the Brazilians and the Divine Mother.

**Love, Sondra & Markus**

The Brazilians in The Loving Relationships Training

*August 26, 2019*

## ♪ HAPPINESS – AN ATTRIBUTE OF LOVE

♪ I am feeling really happy that this training went off perfectly.

♪ "God being love is also happiness. Happiness is an attribute of Love. It cannot be apart from love. Nor can it be experienced where love is not. Love has no limits being everywhere. Therefore, joy is everywhere as well. But the mind can deny this, believing there are gaps in love where pain and sin can enter. This belief would redefine love as limited and introduce opposition to what has no limits. Fear then is associated with love. To fear God is to be afraid of joy. God being Love is also happiness and it is happiness I seek today. I cannot fail because I seek the truth."
(From A Course in Miracles)

**Love, Sondra**

*August 27, 2019*

## ℐ BLAMING THE PAST

ℐ Had some clients really stuck in the past and using the past to blame all their present problems. Here is the prayer Jesus would recommend.

ℐ LET US GIVE THANKS TODAY THAT WE ARE SPARED A FUTURE LIKE THE PAST. TODAY WE LEAVE THE PAST BEHIND US.

ℐ There is one thing we have to remember about the past. It is not here. You have to get over it. Forgiveness is the master eraser. So that is how you get over it.

**Love, Sondra**

*August 28, 2019*

## ℐ CONSCIOUSLY INVITE THE HOLY SPIRIT

ℐ As we demonstrate love towards others, we learn that we are lovable, and we learn how to love more deeply. If we choose to bless another person, we will always feel more blessed. If we project guilt onto another, we will always end up feeling more guilty. Each person will be our crucifier or our savior, depending on what we choose to be to them. Focusing on their innocence sets us free. The ego is the great fault finder.

ℐ Consciously invite the Holy Spirit into every relationship to deliver us from the temptation to judge and the tendency to condemn. Say, "Dear God, I surrender this relationship to You." People who make us angry are our greatest teachers.

(From A Course in Miracles)

**Love, Sondra**

Awaiting our arrival in Curitiba Tom Cau and Selda Chuilki at Madalosso

*August 30, 2019*

### ♫ FORGIVENESS IS UNDOING

♫ Recently a client received a Liberation Breathing session from us, and we sent her some notes about her session. We also sent some affirmations to study with instructions to memorize and recite them frequently, and to "breathe them in" a few times a day.

♫ She asked if there was anything else she "needed to do" to which I answered there is "nothing to do."

♫ It is true, there is nothing to do.

♫ But there is a lot to "undo."

♫ We call this process Forgiveness in Liberation Breathing. And the true kind of "undoing" is self-forgiveness and taking 100 percent responsibility for all aspects of our life.

❦ We teach that thought forms always precede manifestations. Even death. The cause of our problems is always within us, just as the solutions are within us as well.

❦ This being said, all we can do when we see a negative aspect, condition, or event in our life taking shape, is to be the Sherlock Holmes of our own mind, and discover the culprits (thought forms) that "made up" this problem. Then we forgive those thought forms (memories) that are replaying as the "problem." One of the biggest is our personal lie.

❦ Forgiveness is undoing. Without any self-judgment, or judgment of others, we LOOK AT OURSELVES. All we need to do is just look. You would think that is "easy." But people generally do not want to LOOK. They want to avoid and deny. This "makes it hard." People are generally unwilling to take 100 percent responsibility. Part of their mind would like to remain a victim of "circumstances beyond their control."

❦ In this looking we are "taking responsibility" to forgive anything we see inside of ourselves. This "neutralizes" the thoughts and memories responsible for the problem. We do not even need to "know" all the thoughts which made up the problem. We only need to take responsibility and ask DIVINITY to transmute them to light. TO FORGIVE THEM. In this way, Jesus is absolutely right in A Course in Miracles when He says, "Forgiveness is the key to happiness." So we are learning to be "Masters of forgiveness," like Him.

❦ LIBERATION BREATHING is simply this FORGIVENESS PROCESS in action—not only at the "mind level," but also at the subconscious "body level." This is why the breathing is so important. It helps to release the negative thoughts and memories that are actually "held in the cells." So the continuum of the causation is dealt with over the "complete spectrum" of the "problem." SPIRIT renders help to the MIND—BODY to rebalance us and return our WHOLE SELF to its DIVINE CONNECTION of PURE JOY.

❦ This is why traditional "therapy" does not really work or takes too long. It does not address the "cellular memory" with attention to a physical process like the breathing to release the "cellular memories." This is why the allopathic approaches do not fully work to heal "disease" because they do not deal with the mental causation of "thought forms" which made up the disease in the first place.

ℐ People are in the "right place" for optimum healing in their personal life, family life, and public life, when they are practicing Liberation Breathing. Each step taken in this practice moves a person closer to PURE JOY (LIBERATION). We send our clients many blessings daily who stick with their process. Liberation Breathing is really for the "rest of your life," which could be as long as you want it to be.

**Hugs, Markus & Sondra**

*August 30, 2019*

## ℐ WORK ON YOURSELF REGULARLY

ℐ We gave a session via Skype to an elderly woman at the request of her wonderful adult children who are our students. This woman has had headaches for twenty years and now she has M.S. This is how people end up who do not know to work on themselves regularly. The end is always suffering if you don't work on yourself throughout your life. It was so sad.

ℐ Amma says it is inevitable that your shadows will come out. She talked about the fact that you have to handle three shadows if you want to be enlightened. The personal shadow is your "case," your birth trauma, your death urge, your negative thoughts. The family shadow is the negative family mind that you took on. The religious shadow is all the false religious theology you learned. All this will inevitably come out. Most people suppress all that and then they suffer in old age.

ᵍ Yesterday we had a mother and both of her teenage daughters who she inspired to come. Now that is the right idea.

**Love, Sondra**

*August 31, 2019*

### ᵍ PRAYING FOR AND REMEMBERING LEONARD ORR

ᵍ I am praying for Leonard however it comes to be. I thank him profoundly for giving me this wonderful career. I am so honored that I could be at his side at the beginning of Rebirthing and help spread it around the world. Those two years I had with him are still some of the best of my life. I feel so happy that he was in his prime then and I could support his mission and take Rebirthing around the world which I continue to do. His brilliance was always stunning to me. Since I was not afraid of him like some were, I could download what he said so people could understand it. This was a joy for me to be able to do.

ᵍ I was with Leonard on our first trip to meet Babaji. That was a mind blower, of course. What a time we had!

**Love, Sondra**

Elvi Orr, Sondra Ray, Leonard Orr, Markus Ray

*September 1, 2019*

### ℐ KNOWING YOUR PERSONAL LIE

ℐ I am always shocked when we get a client who has been rebirthed for years but does not know what a personal lie is and have no idea what theirs is. The Rebirther they had was not trained well. I always try to get it in the very first session. ℐ Sometimes the client does not want to look at it. I keep asking questions until I get it. But it is not always easy. Lately I had to ask one client this: "What don't you want to reveal to me about yourself?" Then it finally came out. Her personal lie was "I am dirty." She did not want to reveal that to me, but it explained everything that was happening in her life. Well, that is why I finally wrote a book on this subject. It is called *Liberation.*

**Love, Sondra**

*September 2, 2019*

## ♪ PURIFICATION TECHNIQUES FOR COUPLES

♪ We had a wonderful training. It always works. Had a very enlightened female doctor in the training with her mother. It was thrilling to meet them.

♪ In the training we talked about spiritual purification techniques that a couple could do together.

- Liberation Breathing
- A Course in Miracles
- Chanting mantras
- Writing affirmations
- Fasting
- Conscious silence
- Praying
- Fire purification
- Sweat lodges
- Listening to spiritual music
- Networking
- Doing a peace project
- Going to the ashram
- Visiting holy places
- Mundun (head shaving)

♪ All these things bring the wonder of spiritual intimacy.

**Love, Sondra**

The LRT in Curitiba

*September 3, 2019*

## ♪ BEING CAPABLE

♪ We have had several clients with the personal lie "I am not capable." They say they are not capable of doing a good job at the workplace, or not capable of receiving love, or not capable of healing themselves, or whatever. If I ask them what their fear is of giving up that thought, they often say that if they were capable, they would be too powerful. One said she could not be capable as then she would lose the love of her father because he is not capable. She thought she had to be like him to get his love! In this case we had to give her the affirmation that it was okay to be different than her father. What finally worked was this: "I disconnect from my father's mind."

**Love, Sondra**

*September 4, 2019*

## ♪ DO YOU ACCEPT GOD'S LOVE?

♪ We must not only understand God's love for us, but we must choose to open up and receive it. Choosing to receive God's love means getting close to Him or Her (Divine Mother). This means spending time letting in The Presence. It means becoming more like that Presence.

♪ Then how do we choose to express our love to God? How do we show our love for God? If we do that, it will transform our life.

♪ After that we must choose to love others. If we do these three things our good will be magnified.

♪ The greatest force in the world is God's love.

**Love, Sondra**

*September 5, 2019*

## ♪ AFFIRMATIONS FROM CHAPTER 16 IN ACIM

1. I no longer use special relationships to deny my need for God.
2. There is nothing lacking in me. I do not need a special person to complete me.
3. I do not limit my love to just one special person, nor expect him to stop loving others because of me.
4. I let go of the past and the illusion and insanity of one special relationship.
5. I pray to be forgiven now for putting other gods before Him and decreasing my magnitude.

6. I am a whole individual. I attract another whole individual. I love myself, therefore I don't need another self to replace me.
7. I no longer make form more important than love. I remember that love is always more important than form.
8. I turn over my relationship to the Holy Spirit to be used for His purpose and enter with Him into the Holy Instant.
9. I am willing to expose all my relationships to the light.

**Love, Sondra**


*September 6, 2019*

### ♪ HONORING THE LEGACY OF LEONARD ORR

♪ Leonard passed while I was teaching a Rebirthing school. I know he would be glad I was doing that. After we took a few minutes of silence I told the group that he would want me to carry on.

♪ I will certainly carry on with more drive than ever to honor his legacy. I am very very grateful to him for all he taught me and especially for giving me such an absolutely wonderful career. I am honored that I was there right at the beginning alongside him to help him develop and spread our mission. These were some of the best years of my life and I have continued daily since then to move Rebirthing forward. I am happy he is with Babaji now.

**Love, Sondra**

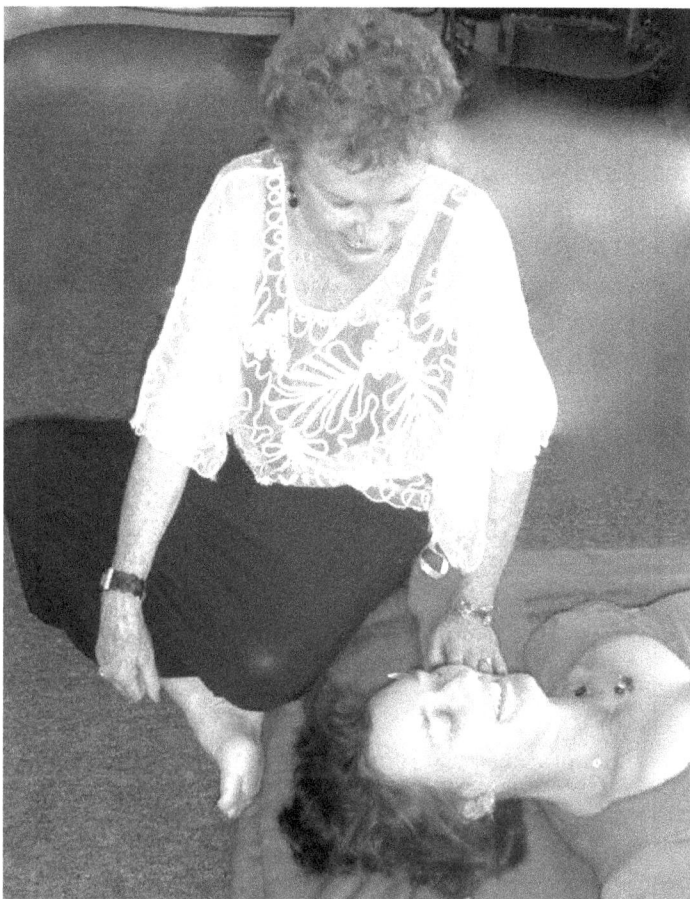

The rebirthing experience

*September 7, 2019*

## ꧁ MEDITATING ON ONE'S DEITY

꧁ We ALWAYS have an altar in every room of our home and in the training room. Markus is painting Ammachi right now and I love to stare at his painting. I like the lure of Divine Love from Her. It brings bliss and rapture. Her love is beyond

111

anything. The motherly way is a pure and sweet path. We children are precious to her. You can always go to her.

𝕵 One should focus on one's beloved deity as a meditation. You can choose any representation of the Mother that appeals to you. You should gaze at the picture and then shut your eyes and focus on the memory. Imagine her standing in front of you.

𝕵 The Mother is the primal feminine force. Her love will bring you light. The light is a state of consciousness—God expressing itself in form.

𝕵 Whatever you ask for in faith will be given to you. Believe that as you ask.

**Love, Sondra**

Ammachi by Markus Ray

*September 8, 2019*

### ℻ MAKE ROOM FOR MIRACLES

℻ Forgiveness is the choice to see someone as they are NOW. What people said or did is not who they are. Relationships are reborn as we let go of our brother's past. By bringing the past into the present, we create a future just like the past. By letting the past go, we make room for miracles.

❡ Only love is real. If a person behaves unlovingly, their behavior was derived from fear. They have forgotten who they are. Whenever we are contemplating attacking someone, it is as though we are holding a sword above their head. But the sword falls on us. To condemn another is to condemn ourselves.

❡ Every loving thought is true, everything else is an appeal for help. Even if they mistreat us, it is an appeal for help.
(From A Course in Miracles)

**Love, Sondra**

*September 9, 2019*

**❡ TODAY THINK OF GRATITUDE**

❡ The Liberation Breathing Training went extremely well, and I was honored to teach them how to give sessions to others. Everyone had so much gratitude.

❡ "Our gratitude will pave the way to Him and shorten our learning time by more than you could ever dream of. Gratitude goes hand in hand with love and where one is the other must be found. Your gratitude toward your brother is the only gift I want. To know your brother is to know God. If you are grateful to your brother, you are grateful to God. Today think of gratitude in place of anger, malice, and revenge."
(From A Course in Miracles)

**Love, Sondra**

*September 10, 2019*

## ♌ OVERCOMING THE CROSS CONTINUED

♌ "You are free to crucify yourself as often as you choose. The only message of the crucifixion is that you can overcome the cross. You are free to join my resurrection, and until you do so, your life is indeed wasted. I can erase all misconceptions from your mind if you will bring them under my guidance. But truth cannot deal with errors you want to keep. Your self and your God Self are in opposition. If you are willing to renounce the role of guardian of your thought system and open it to me, I will correct it very gently and lead you back to God. The abilities you possess are only shadows of your real strength."
(From A Course in Miracles)

**Love, Sondra**

*September 13, 2019*

## ♌ STUCK IN PARENT'S MIND

♌ Lately we have had quite a few clients totally stuck in their parent's mind. During the interview of one, I did not know if he was talking about himself or his father. He kept going in and out of his father's mind. His father was depressed, and he was depressed. He also had his father's mind on money.
♌ During the session I gave him the affirmation "I disconnect from my father's mind." This thought changed him completely. He began to channel very high spiritual thoughts. It was very beautiful. He went from his father's mind to the mind of the Divine. That was real liberation. Liberation Breathing really worked for him.

**Love, Sondra**

*September 14, 2019*

## ♫ AFFIRMATIONS FROM CHAPTER 26 IN ACIM

1. I am willing to receive correction for all my problems. There is not one for which I cannot get a solution if I give it to the Holy Spirit.
2. I do not imagine that one illusion is true. None of them are true.
3. I do not impose sin on my sisters and brothers, nor limit them to a body. I am careful not to sacrifice my oneness by seeing my brother or sister in another body apart from mine.
4. My wishes are the same as the will of God. God wills that I have everything. This is natural since he created me as everything.
5. It is natural for me to use the power God has given me.
6. I accept salvation and happiness now. There is no reason to delay.
7. I cannot be unfairly treated. People treat me the way I treat myself. The way I treat a brother is my opinion of myself. God is in my brother. I always regard him gently.
8. I am willing to have all my relationships totally cleaned up. I do not allow any ancient hatred to come between me and any other person.
9. I welcome the angels and do not interfere with their help.

**Love, Sondra**

*September 15, 2019*

## ♫ THE MOTHERLY ASPECT OF GOD

♫ Mother Teresa said that the only thing that should make us sad is if we don't become saints! Meditate on that statement for some time and it will change you. She is saying that it is our duty to become a saint. After all, the Bible says, "Be ye perfect even as your Father which is in heaven in perfect." That was also an order! Mother Teresa wanted us all to become like Jesus. That was the life she wanted to live and the love she wanted to reflect and express, and she did that.

❡ I was in India at the time of her passing. If you watched her funeral on TV, you might remember that she was laid out on a plank and was totally visible from all sides because she was not in a casket. The cameras were on her body 24 hours a day. They made you just look at her and look at her and look at her. It was very deep.

❡ We need to connect with the Divine Mother like that. Focusing on the Divine Mother will soften our hearts. It will make us more affectionate to the children of the world. It will make us have more kindness, tenderness, cooperation, and love in our relationships. We need to develop the motherly aspect of God.

**Love, Sondra**

*September 16, 2019*

**❡ GETTING YOURSELF UNSTUCK**

❡ The first step is to recognize you are stuck.

- Do you feel unhappy and isolated?
- Do you feel anxious or moody, rarely experiencing joy?
- Do you feel helpless, and that you can't move forward or accomplish ordinary projects and activities?

117

- Do you feel sick, in pain, or is your vital energy blocked?
- Do you feel an urge to attack someone verbally?
- Do you feel you can't get your relationship to clear?
- Do you find your financial situation is shaky?

ℐ If so, give yourself some attention by doing spiritual purification. You can ask for a Liberation Breathing session. You can do some chanting, you can do some mantras or read A Course in Miracles.

ℐ A humble person recognizes his errors, admits them, and does something about them!

**Love, Sondra**

*September 17, 2019*

**ℐ LIBERATION BREATHING IS THIS AND MORE**

- A baptism of the Holy Spirit with power
- A physical experience of Infinite Being
- A technique of spiritual healing
- A removal of tension and blocks to full awareness and health
- A renewal of divine nature in human form
- A regeneration of human perfection
- A release of mortal bondage
- A breathing mantra
- A practical mystical experience
- An inflow of divine energy
- A growth experience focused on releasing trauma
- An energy release
- A cure for sub-ventilation
- A learning to relax at the cosmic level

- A cleansing of the mind and body of negative. mental mass
- A production of a perpetual state of health and bliss
- A dynamic energy
- A "youthing" process
- An experience of God loving you at the cellular level

❡ HAVE YOU TRIED IT?

**Love, Sondra**

*September 18, 2019*

❡ **HARMFUL TENDENCIES IN A RELATIONSHIP**

❡ Beware of these harmful tendencies in a relationship.

1. Making the relationship top priority over everything else and neglecting the other parts of life.
2. Making your mate more important than God, yourself, and everyone else. Idolizing or worshiping this person to the detriment of your self-esteem.
3. Assigning the relationship over to a priority other than spirituality.
4. Being afraid to communicate your own ideas.
5. Being afraid to confront your mate on weak areas and stuffing your resentment about them.
6. Giving your personal power away to your mate.
7. Sinking into old family patterns.
8. Lacking self-esteem.
9. 9.Being addicted to bickering.

❡ A negative unholy relationship feels depleting, like a depressing burden. A holy relationship is a totally different game. It nourishes each mate's individuality, strength, power, creativity, and productivity in the world.

**Love, Sondra**

*September 19, 2019*

## ♫ THE EGO IS AN ADDICTION

♫ The ego says this: "Seek love and never find it" and "If you find it, get rid of it." It wants you to always be in frustration of the search. It does not want satisfaction. Even if you find love and are still stuck in the ego, your subconscious could sabotage the relationship and get rid of the love. People are often not aware of this trap.

♫ Clearing this aspect of the ego takes spiritual work on oneself. ACIM explains this point. Reading it will help get your mind clear and so will Liberation Breathing.

**Love, Sondra**

*September 20, 2019*

## ♫ LEARNING AND ENJOYING BREATHWORK

♫ Imagine installing a hot tub or jacuzzi in your bedroom or outside. As a daily routine, a couple soaks together and rebirths each other instead of arguing. During the Breathwork session they let go of the tension, pain, and disease producing stress They channel new ideas for their business and future. They get clear on potential relationship problems. Does the scenario sound far-fetched? It is not.

There are loads of Rebirthers already living like this now. Some just use their bathtubs. I always say it is Heaven to be living with a Breathworker.

℘ But you say you are not a Breathworker. Well, we can teach you! I love teaching this because I have all my knowledge built up since 1974!

**Love, Sondra**

*September 21, 2019*

℘ **HEALING**

℘ "Your body shows where you are in alignment with the flow of well-being and where you have stepped out of alignment. Illness is an indication that there is a blockage in the current life force. Your body is at the effect of your mind. Illness is a wakeup call to recognize where the flow has been obstructed. No adverse physical condition need be permanent. Many people have been healed of every disease.

℘ Jesus was able to achieve healing because his vision of his patient's wholeness was more powerful than their belief in the disease.

℘ Healing is a result of shift in consciousness from separation to wholeness, a return to your true Self."
(From *A Course in Miracles Made Easy* by Alan Cohen)

℘ So we can help you find the thought that is causing the blockage and you can breathe it out in Liberation Breathing.

**Love, Sondra**

September 22, 2019

## ꞓ THE EGO IS THREATENED BY CHANGE

ꞓ The ego takes refuge in familiarity and is threatened by change. It defines the known as preferable to the unknown, even if the known sucks. This is one reason why so many people stay in abusive or bad relationships. The relationship, although painful, is at least predictable. The ego equates predictability with safety, even if the predictable is disaster. To the Holy Spirit, this thought system is insane."
(From *A Course in Miracles Made Easy* by Cohen)

**Love, Sondra**

September 23, 2019

## ꞓ PRAYER FORMULA #1

ꞓ I learned this in Sunday school when I was a kid. It's very effective!

1. Opening: Read one or two pages from a holy book like A Course in Miracles text.
2. Forgiveness:
3. State to the Divine Mother what you want to be forgiven for. State to the Divine Mother who you want to be forgiven by. State to the Divine Mother who you want to forgive.
4. Gratitude: State to the Divine Mother all the things you are grateful for.
5. Petition: State the problem you face.
6. Closing: Read from a holy book again. Try A Course in Miracles lesson for the day.

**Love, Sondra**

*September 24, 2019*

## ♩ PRAYER FORMULA #2

♩ Remember **FACTS**.

**F** aith: (Babaji said "Faith is everything.")
**A** doration: (Only after the Divine Mother has rightly been honored do petitions assume their proper place. Offer flowers, fruits, and genuine love.)
**C** onfession: (If we don't admit our mistakes, this will cause a break in our communion.)
**T** hanksgiving: (We must be overflowing with gratitude.)
**S** upplication: (Pray to become God-like. Pray to become all that you really are. Pray to conform to the higher purposes.)

**Love, Sondra**

*September 25, 2019*

## ♩ EXCEPTIONAL EXPERIENCES

♩ Yesterday we visited the newly opened Washington Monument (now with an elevator to go to the top), and the Museum for African American History. Both were exceptional experiences.

**Love, Sondra**

The Washington Monument in Washington D. C.

*September 25, 2019*

## ℐ ALL YOU NEED WITHOUT STRUGGLE

ℐ "A Course in Miracles is the ultimate prosperity manual. The Course is uncompromising in its affirmation of your right

to all the riches and wellness in the universe. It does not however, tell you how to get stuff. It teaches you how to get peace and happiness. When you are established in soul serenity you are in the perfect position to attract all you need, supplied by grace. When you dwell in a wealth mentality, you will have all you need without struggle."
(From *A Course in Miracles Made Easy* by Alan Cohen)

**Love, Sondra**


*September 26, 2019*

**♪ A TEASPOON OF PURIFIED ENERGY**

♪ The mantra is a sacred word or sacred set of words through the repetition of which one attains perfection. Babaji said the most important mantra (and the highest thought) is Om Namaha Shivaya. This mantra means Infinite Spirit, Infinite Being, and Infinite Manifestation. Babaji said it removes all obstacles and miseries and bestows eternal bliss and immortality. He who does repetition of this mantra is freed from births and deaths.
♪ "Namaha" represents the individual soul. "Shiva" represents the universal soul. "Aya" denotes the identity between the individual and the universal soul. The mantra also means "I surrender to Shiva, or the part of God that destroys my ignorance." It also means "I surrender to the God within" or "Thy will be done."
♪ Chanting the mantra is like taking a teaspoon of purified energy. It is like plugging yourself into the God socket and at the same time wiping out your negativity.

**Love, Sondra**

*September 27, 2019*

## ♌ A PRAYER TO THE GREAT COSMIC MOTHER

♌ When 9/11 happened I wrote to all my colleagues in different lineages and asked them what we should do. The best answer was from Tom Kenyon who told me the only hope now was the Divine Mother. Then he sent me a prayer. Based on what is going on in our government right now, I think it is time to review this prayer. I am glad I could find it.

♌ A PRAYER TO THE GREAT COSMIC MOTHER
O GREAT COSMIC MOTHER
COME TO US WE PRAY
COME TO US IN THIS DARKEST HOUR OF THE WORLD
DIVINE BIRTHER OF THE COSMOS, WE CALL UPON THY NAMES
ARISE WITHIN US, AND GIVE US STRENGTH
MAKE THY FIERY PRESENCE KNOWN
IGNITE US WITH YOUR ALL-PERVADING LIGHT
FROM WITHIN THE HEART OF EVERY WOMAN
FROM WITHIN THE HEART OF EVERY MAN
REVEAL YOURSELF
O MOTHER OF ALL WORLDS
UNVEIL YOURSELF IN THE MIDST OF US
IGNITE US WITH YOUR ALL-PERVADING LIGHT
GIVE US STRENGTH TO KNOW YOU
GIVE US THE PURITY TO HEAR YOU
GIVE US INSIGHT TO SEE PAST THE LIES THAT HAVE OBSCURED YOU
OH, FIERY MOTHER OF THE COSMOS, GIVE US COURAGE IN THE DARKEST HOUR OF THE WORLD.

**Love, Sondra**

*September 28, 2019*

## ♌ PRAYER TO THE GREAT COSMIC MOTHER CONTINUED

♌ FOR YOUR SAKE AND THE SAKE OF THE EARTH,
SHAKE US FROM OUR UNCONSCIOUS STUPOR,
FOR THE SAKE OF ALL LIFE, WE PRAY TO YOU.
LIFE IS IN DANGER.
TRUTH IS BEING WITHHELD.
GRANT US THE SPIRITUAL POWERS AND INSIGHT TO SEE EVIL IN ALL FORMS,
THE WOLVES PRETENDING TO BE LAMBS,
THE PERPETRATORS DISGUISED AS VICTIMS,
GRANT US THE SPIRITUAL VISION TO SEE CLEARLY AND GRANT US THE BLESSING OF THY DIVINE WILL.
(By Tom Kenyon)

♌ I think that the planet has to get "rebirthed" by the Great Cosmic Mother. For me the solution to have a smooth birth is surrender to the Divine Mother. It is said that worship to the Divine Mother is the highest thing possible. It can be said that everything you possess is a gift from the Mother. She is the original spark of creation. Everything is possible with the Divine Mother.

**Love, Sondra**

*September 29, 2019*

## ♌ BABAJI PROCESSES ME DURING THE NIGHT

♌ I had a dream that I was in Herakhan, Babaji's ashram. But every time I would go to my room a white, very ugly dog would jump on me and hang on me and I could not get him off. This went on every time I came out of my room and every time I went into my room. I was very disturbed about this and wanted someone to get rid of this dog. I went to speak to the yogis as to what they could do with the dog. One yogi only said to me, "It is ALL Babaji." Why was Babaji appearing to me as dog hassling me?

❧ Then I was sitting at some bleachers and two very interesting characters were there. I was very attracted to one who was dressed very unusually, and he could speak many languages. I kept asking him where he was from, but he did not answer that. Suddenly he pulled out a long sword with jewels on it. (Later I was very sure that was Babaji himself.) I was still upset about the dog, so I decided to go to a ceremony. I ran into those two guys again and then the one said, "Choose another animal." So I chose a swan. Then everything changed and I woke up.

❧ I immediately understood the dream. I was in a battle in my subconscious mind over something and I had not realized it. I was guilty about that, and the mad dog was the fight in my mind. Babaji did not disapprove of me at all. In fact, he was completely loving and just said, "Choose again." I was so glad he showed me this fight in my mind. Babaji never misses a beat!

❧ I looked up the symbolism of the swan. It read: "To see a swan is a very important moment. It is like a message from the angels. It is a symbol of purity, beauty, and grace with spiritual evolution. It indicates a good period for you. Angels will protect you and you don't have to worry. Leave all the past behind and start a new phase."

❧ BHOLE BABA KI JAI!

**Love, Sondra**

*September 30, 2019*

**♪ FEAR OF BEING TOTALLY ALIVE AND HAPPY**

♪ The reason you might not want to be healed is you would be 100 percent alive and then it would seem like you had no escape valve called death in case it got bad! But if you hang on to that escape valve, you will be creating a gap between you and God so that itself creates misery.

♪ Besides if you are 100% percent God, it is too exciting for most people. People often don't feel safe with happiness and excitement. They think *If I am THAT happy, the shoe will drop afterwards.* Or they might think they are not worthy of so much happiness. Therefore, some people make an unconscious underlying commitment not to be happy as it is too dangerous.

♪ The problem is one might not realize one has made that agreement because it is unconscious. They keep wondering why they cannot find happiness.

**Love, Sondra**

*October 1, 2019*

**♪ LEADING A LONG LIFE**

♪ The ability to lead a long life comes when the body is not forced to do what it does not want to do. You must clear out of yourself everything that holds you to a reality you do not like. Then the Holy Spirit can put you in your right place, which will not have anything you do not like because you will not have anything within you that attracts it.

♪ Pain and suffering is denying the magnetic energy its role of guiding you in your right place.

**Love, Sondra**

*October 2, 2019*

## ♌ EVERY INSTANT CAN BE REBORN

♌ The Holy Spirit offers you release from every problem that you think you have. He has no greater difficulty in resolving some than others. Every problem is the same to Him. One mistake is no more different to bring to truth than another. But He cannot use what you withhold, for He cannot take it from you without your willingness.

♌ Every problem is an error. He does not judge whether the hurt be large or little. He takes the thorns and nails away.

♌ You have the right to all the universe, to perfect peace, complete deliverance from all effects of sin and to life eternal, joyous, and complete in every way.
(From A Course in Miracles)

**Love, Sondra**

*October 3, 2019*

## ♌ SUPPRESSED BIRTH TRAUMA

♌ Your misery is often caused by birth trauma that is suppressed in the body. The trouble is you tend to heal your birth trauma the same way you had it. If your birth was slow, you will be slow to heal your birth trauma. Mine was all about waiting for my father to come back in the room so I spent a lot of time waiting to get healed rather than being healed. One piece of your birth trauma could be stuck for years.

♌ Also, how can you receive God's help if you have the thought "help hurts"? Many people felt hurt by the delivery team that was trying to help them. So maybe you have God set up as your delivery team and you have to change that.

♫ I realize by writing this I am assuming you are looking at your birth trauma. If you are not having breathwork sessions, you may not even consider that. Suppressed birth trauma causes pain in the body. I hope you will be looking at it and getting sessions.

**Love Sondra**


*October 4, 2019*

### ♫ PAST LIVES AND SICKNESS

♫ Here is what Dr. Roger Woolger says in his book *Other Lives, Other Selves:*

♫ "The body and its various aches, pains, and dysfunctions is a living psychic history when read correctly. Even though the physical ailment may have very specific origins in a person's current life, I have found more and more that there are certain layers to every major syndrome of physical illness, accident, or weakness. The existence of a past life level of physical problems has been confirmed over and over again in the cases I have seen."

♫ During Liberation Breathing we can access past lives. I agree that sometimes you have to locate one to really create the necessary healing.

**Love, Sondra**


*October 5, 2019*

### ♫ A WAY TO SEE YOUR SUBCONSCIOUS THOUGHTS

꽃 Perhaps you feel you cannot trust God because you were let down before. But probably you did not realize that only you can deprive yourself of anything. God did not let you down. You could not receive what you asked for.

꽃 God always says yes to your thoughts. So, you likely had a negative thought that blocked your ability to receive. You need a way to see your subconscious thoughts. That is why Liberation Breathing is so helpful.

**Love, Sondra**

*October 6, 2019*

꽃 **REGRET AND GUILT**

꽃 "Regret and guilt result from equating the present self that "is" with the former self that "was" but actually is no more. It is another form of egotism in which error is inflated instead of being relinquished to a higher power. Excessive guilt and remorse are a disguised form of egotism in which the self becomes blown up, exaggerated, and the hero of the tragedy. Wallowing in guilt is feeding the ego and is an indulgence.

꽃 By spiritual alignment, the past circumstances underlying the guilt are re-contextualized under the influence of spiritual energy. By invitation, the Holy Spirit transforms it by the presence of the healing power of grace. What the ego cannot lift with all its might, is like a feather to the Grace of God.

꽃 Undoing guilt: confession / forgiveness / penance / renewal of spiritual principles / good works / selfless service / humanitarian efforts."
(From the writings of Dr. David Hawkins)

**Love, Sondra**

*October 7, 2019*

## ℥ KARMA MEANS ACCOUNTABILITY

℥ Karma really means accountability. Every entity is accountable to the universe. To undo negative karma, you need to do good works / prayer / selfless service / benevolent acts / karma yoga (work dedicated to God). Negative karma is sometimes known as debt. As people evolve spiritually at each ascended level, corollary tests or temptations are there (wealth, power, prestige, pride).

℥ It is an error to ascribe the source of power to the ego (I instead of Divinity). What appears as misery or catastrophe may be the doorway to liberation for those who have negative karma to undo.

**Love, Sondra**

*October 8, 2019*

## ℥ A TRANSFER OF SPIRITUAL ENERGY

℥ A blessing is the natural expression of the fiery love of our inner Spirit. A blessing is an affirmation of our inner connectedness. Every time you create safety and reassurance where before there was fear, you are giving a blessing. A blessing has the power to empower, transform, and restore wholeness. A blessing is a force of love that passes between people . . . a transfer of spiritual energy.

℥ Who will you bless today?

**Love, Sondra**

A typical Tudor building in Guildford, United Kingdom

*October 9, 2019*

### ℌ HABITAT OPENED MY HEART

ℌ Before I left home, I was thinking about what charity I would support if I was rich. Then of course I realized I don't have to wait until then; I can start now giving small amounts. So, I chose Habitat (Habitat for Humanity), the one that Jimmy Carter supports. I also wrote him a letter. This opened my heart, and I more or less went into an altered state for several hours. I was in love with all people everywhere and everything.

꒾ Now I am having trouble with the time change and big issues to be handled over here so I have not been able to sleep for two days. This has never happened to me before a training. Yikes!

**Love, Sondra**

*October 12, 2019*

**꒾ HEALING SICKNESS**

꒾ The group is doing fantastic. Today we will cover healing and physical immortality.

꒾ All healing is essentially the release from fear. Sickness is not right-mindedness. Healing is accomplished the minute the sufferer no longer sees any value in pain. For sickness is an election, a decision conceived in madness for placing God's son on his Father's throne.

꒾ Healing must occur in the exact proportion to which the valuelessness of sickness is recognized. One need but say: "There is no gain at all to me in this" and he is healed. It is the mind, not the body, that makes the sickness.

꒾ The physician is the mind of the patient himself.
(From A Course in Miracles)

**Love, Sondra**

*October 13, 2019*

## ♫ ATONEMENT IS THE WORD OF GOD

♫ Healing and the Atonement are identical. Accept the Atonement and you are healed. The Atonement is the word of God, i.e., allowing the Holy Spirit to undo all your wrong thinking plus total forgiveness. To forgive is to heal.

♫ A sick person perceives himself as separate from God. One who has perfectly accepted the Atonement can heal the world. He has overcome death because he has accepted life. There is now no limit to his power.

♫ There is no problem the Holy Spirit cannot solve by offering you a miracle. Miracles arise from a mind that is ready for them. They cannot be performed in a spirit of doubt and fear. Say this: "I accept the Holy Spirit's purpose for my body. My body is for the word of God. Atonement is the word of God." (From A Course in Miracles)

**Love, Sondra**

*October 14, 2019*

## ♫ THE EGO'S USE OF GUILT

♫ Guilt demands punishment. Guilt is a symbol of attack on God. The guiltless mind cannot suffer. Being sane, the mind heals the body. The sane mind cannot conceive of illness because it cannot conceive of attacking anyone or anything. Give no reality to guilt if you want to be healed. The end of guilt will never come as long as you see a reason for it. You must learn that guilt is insane and has no reason because it is not in the mind of God.

℩ When the pain of guilt seems to attract you, remember that if you yield to it, you are deciding against your happiness. No penalty is ever asked of God's son except by himself and of himself. All salvation is the escape from guilt. Only in the exchange of guilt for innocence can one be free of pain. (From A Course in Miracles)

**Love, Sondra**

"Jesus of Guildford" by Markus Ray

*October 15, 2019*

**ꝯ PROCESSING PEOPLE CORRECTLY**

ꝯ The group did fantastic. One thing we teach them is how to process people correctly.

ꝯ Leslie Temple Thurston says, "Processing is a form of self-inquiry. To process means to examine deeply the nature of our conditioned ego patterning with the intention of finding the truth. We process our consciousness to become clear and find our wholeness. Letting go of baggage streamlines the system of mind, body, and emotions to make maximum use of time and energy.

ꝯ "A cleared consciousness is the most valuable asset in life! It allows us to cope with life's challenges and makes our awareness more flexible and free. It gives us enormously increased energy. It creates balance in mind, emotions, and body.

ꝯ "It means letting go of all the old reactivity and stored emotional memories. It is a very fast path to spiritual awakening."

**Love, Sondra**

*October 16, 2019*

**ꝯ THE BENEFITS OF PROCESSING**

- Fewer personality clashes with others
- Healing of physical, mental, and emotional traumas
- Ability to deal with anger
- Greater harmony and equanimity
- More energy for things that bring joy
- Feeling less drained

- Higher level of productivity
- More creativity
- Better communication skills
- Ability to resolve conflicts more easily
- Ability to let go of self-destructive behavior
- Greater tolerance, love, compassion, and appreciation
- More fulfilling work
- More fulfilling relationships
- Ability to let go of negativity and fear
- Increased flow of abundance
- Increased spirit of generosity
- Ability to love with an open heart
- Greater alignment with your highest path
- A more tangible connection to the soul
- More psychic ability
- Experience of peace
- Bliss states
- Greater levels of spiritual awakening

(Leslie Temple Thurston)

**Love Sondra**

*October 17, 2019*

### ♫ TWINS AND TRIPLETS

♫ We have had several students who were twins and even triplets, and their siblings died in utero. Some were passed, some were absorbed, and one had a twin that remained dead in the womb until delivery. Her womb was a tomb! Can you imagine the effect this has on the remaining soul? They could have a preverbal thought *someone has to die for me to live*. They feel abandoned and have a lot of abandonment issues in their lives. They feel betrayed. They could spend their whole life searching for someone. They could have survivor's guilt. One was punishing herself for that by having severe pain. One was projecting all this on her mate and was afraid he was going to die. She was always saying to him, "Start living!"

ℐ It is curious why people come in as twins or triplets in the first place. I want to do more research on this. If that is your case, please write to me and tell me why you think you created that.

**Love, Sondra**

*October 18, 2019*

**ℐ A DISCOVERED PRAYER**

ℐ We finally took a day off in London. First, we visited Taj in Ealing and went to a wonderful French restaurant and now we are staying in the Little Venice area doing sessions. I opened a book on the bedside table in our friend's bedroom and discovered this prayer:

ℐ. "Dear God,

You are always a thing of beauty in my eyes, a word of love in my ears, a sense of glory in my body, a thought of joy in my mind, and a wave of compassion in my heart. Please let me remember the sacred lineage of my being, as it is my soul's force. Please let me bring forth my light into the world, and not diminish my power. Please let me proclaim the truth of my spirit as though it were as sweet as an angel's song. Thank you, dear God. So let it be."

**Love, Sondra**

*October 20, 2019*

## ♪ ATTEMPTING TO SAVE A MARRIAGE

♪ We have a couple who are clients by Skype. We try never to see couples together because they get in a fight. So, we do a breathwork session on one and then on the other and then talk to them together. But in this case, we were in London where they live so we literally moved in with them to try to save their marriage. This is intense, especially in small places like in London. But you can know almost everything by living with them and seeing the kids and so on.

♪ How do you move a couple who is in a special hate relationship to a holy relationship? It took everything we knew and all our abilities and prayers. I think we did it. But of course, time will tell. Fortunately, they are sticking with us.

**Love, Sondra**

*October 21, 2019*

## ♪ RELATIONSHIPS ARE ASSIGNMENTS

♪ Relationships are a vast plan for our enlightenment. They are the Holy Spirit's laboratories in which He brings together those who have the maximum opportunities for mutual growth. Think of it as a giant computer.

♪ Consciously invite the Holy Spirit to enter every relationship and ask to be delivered from the temptation to judge and the tendency to condemn. Say, "Dear God, I surrender this relationship to you." (People who make us angry are our most important teachers.)

**Love, Sondra**

*October 22, 2019*

**ℐ ONLY LOVE IS REAL**

ℐ "If a person behaves unlovingly, their behavior was derived from fear. They have forgotten who they are. When we are contemplating attacking someone, it is as though we are holding a sword above their head. The sword does not fall on them, it falls on us."
(From A Course in Miracles)

**Love, Sondra**

*October 24, 2019*

**ℐ READ THIS LESSON AND FEEL GOOD**

ℐ "I feel the love of God within me now."
ℐ To feel the love of God within you is to see the world anew, shining in innocence, alive with hope, and blessed with perfect charity and love. Who could feel fear in such a world as this? It welcomes you, rejoices that you came, and sings your praises as it keeps you safe from every danger and pain. It offers you a warm and gentle home. It blesses you throughout the day and watches through the night as the silent guardian of your holy sleep. It sees salvation in you. It offers you its flowers. This is the world of love that God reveals.
ℐ The world of hatred is unseen and inconceivable to those who feel God's love in them. What is felt within is a sure reflection everywhere. You will look upon that which you feel within. If you feel the love of God within, you will see a world of mercy and love. We feel its all-embracing tenderness, its love which knows of us as perfect. Now lay aside all

concepts you have learned about the world and all images you hold about yourself. Empty your mind. Hold on to nothing. Do not bring with you one thought the past has taught nor one belief you ever learned.

℘ Come with holy hands unto your God. Ask and receive.
(From A Course in Miracles, Lesson 189)

**Love, Sondra**


*October 25, 2019*

**℘ HAVING TOTAL GRATITUDE**

℘ "When your forgiveness is complete, you will have total gratitude. You will see that everything has earned the right to love by being loving. Today think of gratitude in place of anger, malice, and revenge. Our gratitude will pave the way to Him and shorten our learning time by more than you could ever dream of. Gratitude goes hand in hand with love; and where one is, the other must be found. Your gratitude toward your brother is the only gift I want. To know your brother is to know God. If you are grateful to your brother, you are grateful to God.

℘ Gratitude can only be sincere if it is combined with love. We offer thanks that all things will find their freedom. Therefore, give thanks but in sincerity. We thank our Father that we are one with Him."
(From A Course in Miracles)

**Love, Sondra**

*October 26, 2019*

**♫ I AM SURROUNDED BY THE LOVE OF GOD**

♫ "Father, you stand before me, behind, beside me, and in the place I see myself and everywhere I go. You are in all things I look upon, the sounds I hear and every hand that reaches for my own. For what surrounds His son and keeps him safe is Love itself. There is no Source but this and nothing is that does not share its holiness or without the love which holds all things within itself. Father, your son is like yourself. We come to you in your own name today to be at peace within your everlasting love."
(From A Course in Miracles)

**Love, Sondra**


*October 28, 2019*

**♫ THE UNFORGIVING MIND**

- The unforgiving mind is full of fear and offers love no room to be itself.
- The unforgiving mind is sad without the hope of respite and release from pain.
- The unforgiving mind is torn with doubt, confused about itself and all it sees.
- The unforgiving mind is afraid to go ahead and afraid to stay.
- The unforgiving mind does not believe that giving and receiving are the same.

♫ Those who withhold forgiveness are binding themselves to illusions. Forgiveness is acquired. It is not inherent. Forgiveness must be learned. Forgiveness is the key to

144

happiness. You who want peace can find it only by complete forgiveness. All forgiveness is a gift to yourself. The holiest of all the spots on earth is where an ancient hatred has become a present love.
(From A Course in Miracles)

**Love, Sondra**


*October 31, 2019*

### ♫ A MORNING SPIRITUAL RITUAL

♫ Every morning we make the bed together, take our showers, and do these devotions"

- First, we read a few pages of the text of ACIM.
- Then we do forgiveness.
- Then we do gratitude.
- Then we do the petition.
- Then we read ACIM lesson.

♫ Yesterday we reviewed Lesson 152 "The Power of Decision is My Own." The first paragraph is very strong:
"No one can suffer loss unless it be his own decision. No one suffers pain except his choice elects this state for him. No one can grieve nor fear nor think him sick unless these are the outcomes he wants. And no one dies without his consent. Nothing occurs but represents your wish, and nothing is omitted that you chose. Here is your world complete in all details. Here is its whole reality for you. And it is only where salvation is."

**Love, Sondra**

*November 1, 2019*

**♪ PRAYER FOR MONEY**

♪ "I hereby ask and humbly pray with all my heart and soul and mind for Divine Abundance made manifest through personal fortune and success. I am willing to move beyond fear to fulfill God's Plan on Earth and Beyond. I personally pledge to open myself to financial wealth to fulfill my group and individual service commitments. In God's name, I accept my divine heritage right now and give thanks for the timely answer to this prayer. God's will be done. Amen."
♪ Repeat this aloud three times.

**Love, Sondra**

*November 2, 2019*

**♪ EVERYTHING WE KNOW IS WRONG**

♪ ACIM explains that everything we know is wrong so we must start over. Everything is wrong because we interpret everything through the ego. The ego is a false self we made up to compete with God. It is based on the erroneous thought *I am separate from God*. Once we believed that, we went into weakness, helplessness, fear, anxiety, suffering, anger, misery, sickness, aging, and death.
♪ In the ego's interpretation this separation is real and actually happened. Therefore, we are sinners and God is out to destroy us for this. So, we try to bargain with God saying, "You don't have to go to the trouble of punishing me, I will punish myself." The idea of sacrifice was then formed: "I will suffer and deprive myself to prove I am good, so you won't be angry, God." In the ego's thought system, we get the

insane notion that sacrifice is salvation . . . and that God's will for us is misery and we do not deserve to be happy. All of this is wrong thinking.

**Love, Sondra**

*November 3, 2019*

### ♪ RELATIONSHIP-RELATED AILMENTS

♪ Had a client who, on the surface, told us she was doing great. She also went on to praise her partner who is living in a different country. She does not see him often. But it turns out she has three ailments, and they are all related to that relationship. Her eyes feel pressure, her legs hurt, and her back hurts. When we processed her, it came out that she did not want to see the reality of her relationship. Her legs were heavy because of this heaviness she has to carry in the relationship. Her back hurts because she does not feel supported by the man. She has been involved with him for five years.

♪ She is making a lot more money than he and she says he is failing. She defended the relationship a lot at first. However, it is causing a real toll on her body, and she is not winning because he does not even live in the same country. I am always amazed at what people put up with. She said an astrologer said she would always make more money than a man because of her planets. We told her Babaji can change astrology readings. We will see what happens.

**Love, Sondra**

*November 4, 2019*

### ♂ A GUILT TRIP

♂ Yesterday I did something stupid, and I was judging myself and so I got stuck in guilt. This caused my cranium to get stuck. It was stuck most of the day and uncomfortable.

♂ Markus said that during the night in my sleep I said out loud,

"I can't give up this guilt because I am guilty." The pain was my punishment. So, I got up and did a lot of prayers like "I allow the Holy Spirit to undo my guilt," and then I got in a warm bath with my snorkel and did some breathwork until I broke through. Guilt always demands punishment. ACIM says that guilt is not only not of God, it is an attack on God.

♂ I feel sorry for people stuck in guilt for a long time. I could not stand 12 hours of it. The reason it lasted that long is I forgot to do the prayers and the breathing sooner. I couldn't even think straight, and we were busy. If you can't get off guilt, you really need a Liberation Breathing session.

**Love, Sondra**


*November 6, 2019*

### ♂ BABAJI IN WASHINGTON

♂ Markus just finished this Babaji in Washington before we left for Down Under.

**Love, Sondra**

Babaji in Washington, D.C.

*November 8, 2019*

### ꙮ FEAR OF GIVING UP CONTROL

ꙮ Had a client whose personal lie was "I am not perfect." I explained to her that the personal lie is an addiction and the way we process addictions is we have to know what the fear is of giving up the addiction. Her fear of giving up that thought was she would be out of control. So then I asked her what her fear was of giving up control. She said, "I would die!"

ᔍ So with that wiring, she was never going to give up her personal lie. This answer is not uncommon. I noticed she did not seem very happy even though everything in her life was more or less working. She also had the thought *I cannot be happy until I am perfect.* All this was a total set-up not to work at all.

ᔍ One has to explain to the clients that when one is actually out of control and letting God do the controlling, that is where the happiness is. Most people are in control with their ego and not letting the Divine be in charge. When one stays in control this stops the Divine energy. She was also exhausted because of all this. Her control pattern was stopping the Divine Energy. This has got to be explained clearly so they can really get it. She really needed this session and was so pleased she referred to us to new clients!

**Love, Sondra**


*November 9, 2019*


ᔍ **NEARLY DEAD IN MELBOURNE**

ᔍ We have a wonderful training here in Melbourne. There is one student who almost died at her birth and her mother almost died then also. She has a history of Chronic Fatigue and Epson Bar Syndrome. She had that for years. She thought her personal lie was "I am not good enough" but I told her I was sure her personal lie was really "I am nearly dead." This would explain quite clearly her sicknesses.

When she introduced herself, she put her boyfriend down in front of everyone and everyone was embarrassed. (One should never put down one's mate in public.) She complained he was not keeping up. She wanted him to be more with it—like more alive. I told her she has him set up as her mother who was nearly dead. Interesting case.

**Love, Sondra**

*November 10, 2019*

### MY TOUGHEST PATTERN

I have been a healer in many lifetimes. In those old days I used to take the patient's illness through my body and take it from them. I was good at it. At my birth in this lifetime, they let my grandfather out of the mental institution to see me and he was healed and never went back. The problem is in this life I want people to heal themselves in my presence and I don't want that old pattern. It slows me down. But frequently I go into the old habit and take on the client's case. This is too hard on my body. It is kind of an addiction.

Having been a nurse for 14 years, I apparently think I need to save people. This is a trick of my ego. Recently I had an alcoholic client who was suicidal. I took on her energy and it got stuck in my body. My cranium got stuck. This was painful and it is taking me too long to let it go. The "pattern" must go but I am having trouble changing it. Please pray for me. Obviously, I need to acknowledge that God is doing the healing.

**Love, Sondra**

*November 11, 2019*

## ❡ PAST LIVES AFFECT CURRENT PATTERNS OF THINKING

❡ I appreciate all your comments and prayers. The thing is I don't really need to learn more techniques to keep from taking on energies of clients. I know them. The thing is I keep them from working because my pattern of thinking that I have to save people myself is so strong. That is due to past lives and being a nurse. It is an ego trip, and I am trying to undo this habit, which is an addiction. Addictions are not so easy to deal with. I am better each day as I am doing a lot of prayers. And I had some cranial work.

❡ These are my prayers:

- Holy Spirit, I no longer deny you your ability to bestow your blessing of healing on me.
- I decree, I declare, I determine, I decide, and I order in the name of the I AM Presence to let go of this condition.
- I know you Holy Spirit can and will resolve this problem by offering me a miracle. I allow this. I allow healing to happen. I give up my addiction to thinking I have to do the healing.
- I let go of my power trip of not letting anyone heal me so I could be the king (ego).
- I give up my competition with God.
- I am united with Jesus, Babaji, and Divine Mother.

**Love, Sondra**

*November 12, 2019*

## ℘ GET LIFTED OUT OF QUICKSAND

℘ The only way we can be free is if help comes from outside the system, i.e., from the Holy Spirit. In other words, you cannot clear your ego with your ego. You will just be stuck. The Holy Spirit lifts us out of quicksand. We should take Jesus' hand. The Holy Spirit is the answer. He is not in this world. He acts in our minds.

℘ This is why we read the Divine Mother names at the end of the sessions. We turn it all over to a higher power and that is what works. The ego says the world is NOT the effect of the mind. We therefore think the problems are in the world. Problems therefore seem to be separate from the mind that created them. The ego switches it all around and says, "What is done to me is what causes my problem." This is denial. It is the projection that *You caused me; I did not cause you*. We have denied that we made up the world. We did make up this world with the thought of separation. A victim says, "I can't help the way I am because something was done to me."

℘ There is nothing outside of us that can hurt us except by our own thoughts. We are at cause of everything.

**Love, Sondra**

*November 13, 2019*

## ℘ THE FAST TRACK TO GOD

℘ Romantic relationships are the fast track to God. Anyone can maintain Christ consciousness by living in a cave.

♪ Each time you react with negative emotions to your partner's behavior, bless him/her for allowing you the opportunity to pass another spiritual test!

♪ When you are right with yourself and right with God, becoming right with your mate is a lot easier. The negative ego, if not checked, will contaminate and subtly poison your life including your romantic relationship.

**Love, Sondra**


*November 15, 2019*

## ♪ BEAUTIFUL KAMALAYA

♪ We have arrived at beautiful Kamalaya on Koh Samui, Thailand. It is a multi-award-winning wellness sanctuary and holistic spa retreat located among a tropical landscape on the south coast of Koh Samui. Words cannot describe the sheer beauty that puts you in bliss. It is such a special feeling. Every little detail is considered. We are here to rest and do private sessions with the guests. Our friend Karkhu has built this place. He was with Babaji and Muniraj in India for decades. He has created a temple here also and a room to honor Babaji. There is every kind of treatment and therapy imaginable. We are lucky to meet people from all over the world!

**Love, Sondra**

At beautiful Kamalaya, Koh Samui, Thailand

*November 16, 2019*

## ℐ THE BLESSINGS OF A TRUE MASTER

ℐ I am getting better. My master is healing me. A master (Babaji) emanates beneficial elements for his group. His sole care is to give you elements of a higher nature. You find nothing but blessings near a true master. The master

155

corrects your mistakes and encourages you. Under his guidance you can end up being a virtuoso. With a master, you cannot fall back into inertia; you feel continuously stimulated. He draws you along by his words and example. One should find a master who will give you the best ways to work so you can advance on the spiritual path. Babaji is the guru of gurus since he was not born of a woman. How can you get higher than that?

꽃 A master may have to be severe on his disciples by telling them certain truths for their progress and advancement. Most people are afraid to tell you the truth. A teacher tells the truth to his disciple to help them. The master will also give you love you never found even in your own family.

꽃 A master helps you become beautiful. What he wants is the best for you.

**Love, Sondra**


*November 17, 2019*


## 꽃 YOUR HELP TO REAL FREEDOM

꽃 The master is here to help you to real freedom so that you are strong, despite all difficulties. The master will warn you about what awaits you if you continue your present path. A master can open doors for you, but it is up to you to walk through them. Each time the master sees you are making progress it is likely he will give you a harder task to achieve.

꽃 You must tune yourself to the master's note. He has a tuning fork. You end up vibrating quite differently. Get yourself on the same wavelength and plug into the master's wavelength.

♪ The master is like a conductor. You must synchronize with him. You must always love and serve a higher being than yourself so that you can, thanks to him, perform miracles and do good. There is a sort of osmosis that goes on between you and the master and you benefit from his light. When you concentrate on him, you receive his emanations of purity and light.

♪ I must imagine that I enter his spirit, and I can think like him, feel like him, and act like him. I want to replace all my imperfections with the quality of my master.

**Love, Sondra**

*November 18, 2019*

## ♪ YOUR PARTNER'S LESSONS AND YOUR LESSONS

♪ It has been recommended that you don't take on any aspect of your partner's lessons or try to solve them. Your job is to provide a safe and loving atmosphere in which your partner can come to terms with the situation and learn what is needed and transcend it. Of course, if you are a Breathworker you can help him better to process it. I always say it is heaven to be a Breathworker and to have a Breathworker as a partner. You can really support each other! And you can get over stuff fast.

♪ If you yourself are going through a major lesson, try not to dump it on your partner and drain them. You need to know how to handle your own case or how to get the help you need if your mate is not a Breathworker. You can have a session with a Liberation Breathing practitioner. We can help you via Skype.

꒐ Crises are blessings in disguise that present the opportunity to accelerate your ascension process and realize God at a more expanded level.

**Love, Sondra**

*November 19, 2019*

## ꒐ A RELATIONSHIP IS A PROCESS

꒐ It is not a destination. It goes through many unending undulations that give it texture and character which shape and reshape the two people.

꒐ It is about movement and growth. It is a holy interpersonal environment for the evolution of the two souls. You should celebrate the change rather than not wanting to rock the boat.

꒐ We make the mistake of assuming that just because we love someone, he or she knows it and feels it and no special behavior is needed. Everyone needs more love. Nobody had a perfect childhood. Nobody got enough praise.

**Love, Sondra**

*November 20, 2019*

## ꒐ PATH OF ASCENSION AND RELATIONSHIPS

꒐ If both people in a relationship are on the path of ascension, then the one more centered at the time can serve as an anchoring point for Christ energy to be demonstrated. The transcendence of issues is why we are here in the first place. All of humanity is on the path of ascension but there is a big difference between those who are consciously on the path of ascension and those who are not. Those who are conscious are functioning at quite a different frequency. God realization becomes their very reason for being.

ᔕ If both of you are rather advanced on that path, the work that can be done is tremendous and of extreme value to humanity. If you make God the center of your work and life together, you will have a relationship of the highest order. Merging with a master, the couple invokes his divine presence to permeate their being, thus making those extremely high energies available to all of humanity.

**Love, Sondra**

*November 21, 2019*

### ᔕ COMMUNICATION

ᔕ I read these shocking statistics: most couples who are married communicate only 35 minutes in a whole week! And yet communication is the key to keeping a relationship committed. Communication is to a relationship what breathing is to living. When communication lines are not open, it is doomed to failure. But one should never communicate when one is caught up by negative ego or a lot of anger. There is no such thing as righteous anger. It is loss of control and an attempt to regain it. Arguing is a manifestation of the negative ego. It is never acceptable to attack one's partner. Never let attack come from you.

ᔕ It is never appropriate to judge or criticize. It is fine to have observations. Learn to have preferences instead of addictions and attachments.

- Preference: If you don't get what you seek you are still happy.
- Attachments or addictions: If you don't get what you seek you are unhappy.

꿍 Spiritual honesty is communicating what is appropriate and loving in a respectful manner.

**Love, Sondra**

*November 22, 2019*

## 꿍 DEFENSIVENESS

꿍 People who are ego sensitive will get defensive and insulted by just about anything you say to them no matter how lovingly it is presented. Defensiveness is really a way of blaming your partner. You are saying, in effect, "The problem is not me; it is you." One common form of defensiveness is the "innocent victim" stance which often entails whining and sends the message "Why are you picking on me? There is no pleasing you." Defensiveness in all its guises just escalates the conflict, which is why it is so deadly.

꿍 Criticism, contempt, and defensiveness function like a relay match handing the baton off to each other over and over again if the couple can't put a stop to it. ACIM says that defenses attract attack.

**Love, Sondra**

*November 23, 2019*

## 꿍 EVERYONE HAS A CASE

℧ Everyone has circumstances. It does not matter that they have a "case" but it does matter if they are willing to work on it.

℧ It is a big mistake to generalize based on yourself and assume or presume your partner is like you in terms of hurts, habits, preferences, hopes, and expectations. This kind of expecting the other to be a clone of ourselves is an emotional hangover from infancy where we were the center of the universe. Assumptions are negations of the other person's issues.

℧ The antidote? Inquire. Let curiosity be your guide to find out what your mate wants and needs from you. Expose yourself to the joy of knowing another soul in the truth and beauty of his or her own uniqueness.

℧ Your sweetheart should not be expected to be psychic. You yourself need to tell what you want and ask for what you need.

**Love, Sondra**

*November 24, 2019*

**℧ THE QUESTION OF SICKNESS**

℧ There is only one problem: separation. There is only one solution: forgiveness.

℧ We think sickness is of the body; that the solution then is of the body. But the mind is what makes us sick. Doing anything to heal the body is a form of magic. All sickness is guilt in the mind. Sickness will teach you that there is some problem of non-forgiveness so be grateful for the lesson. Behind every sickness is a person we are making responsible for it.

ℱ A traditional medical form of help is not a sin. Do not deny yourself the blessing of consulting a doctor if you need to. But you have to work on the mind that caused it and if you do, you may not need a doctor. You have to find the negative thought that caused the sickness.

ℱ Sickness is a way of punishing ourselves so God won't do it. "I will sacrifice myself to atone for my sins." When guilt rules, sacrifice must also be there. In death is sin preserved. The responsibility is only to heal your own mind.

ℱ Turn your mind over to the Holy Spirit. Whatever you ask in Jesus' name He will give you.

**Love, Sondra**

*November 25, 2019*

**ℱ GO FOR THE SOLUTION!**

ℱ I once took a course for new entrepreneurs. The teacher would write on the board GO FOR SOLUTION in big letters so we would never forget that. Here is what Esther Hicks has to say about it.

ℱ "The realization that something is not as you want it to be is an important first step, but once you have identified that, the faster you are able to turn your attention in the direction of a solution, the better, because a continuing exploration of the problem will prevent you from finding a solution. The problem is a different vibrational frequency than the solution, and ALL thoughts (or vibration) are affected by (or managed by) the law of attraction."

**Love, Sondra**

*November 25, 2019*

### ❡ HAVING FRIENDS IN BABAJI

❡ Here I am with one of my oldest of friends in Koh Samui, Thailand—Raghuvir Bol. He had us for dinner last night in his wonderful place, and we caught up with all the news. It is so fantastic to have "Friends in Babaji." Both he and I had many encounters with our master, and Raghuvir lived constantly with Babaji for a number of years. So our bond is very, very deep. And this is another Force which brings us to Koh Samui—one is Kamalaya, the wellness spa that John Kharku Stewart built, and the other is our dear Raghuvir Charan Chaudary Haidakhandi himself!

**Love, Sondra**

Sondra and Raghuvir

*November 26, 2019*

## ♫ AFFIRMATIONS I WROTE FROM ACIM

1. I pray to be awakened from the chaotic dreams that I have made. My goal is to come out of darkness into light.
2. I trade in fearful dreams for happy dreams. I trade in the pain and guilt for joy and freedom.
3. I remember my oneness and let go of all guilt, so I no longer use my body to punish myself. My body is innocent. I forgive myself for misusing my body.
4. My body is not for attack, nor does it need my constant attention and protection because I am not my body. I am a Light Being with all the safety of God since I am one with God.
5. I allow my body to be transformed in the Holy Instant. I desire the Holy Instant above all else.
6. Prayer: "I who am host to God am worthy of Him. There is no need to make it ready for Him, only that I do not interfere with his plan; I need add nothing to His plan, but to receive it. I must be willing not to substitute my own place of it. I am willing."
7. I forgive everyone who taught me heaven was somewhere else.
8. I forgive myself for believing it. I can have heaven right now by remembering perfect oneness and knowledge and that that is all there is.

**Love, Sondra**

*November 28, 2019*

## ♫ THE PATH OF POWER

♫ My last day here I was reading *Man Triumphant* by Annalee Skarin. Here are some high points:

❡ "The ecstatic vibration of praise love and gratitude which is the released Light of Christ, will exalt any individual and lift him above his present state of consciousness. The condition in which he lives will be changed into one of exalting progress and happiness and increased understanding and power.

No adverse condition can possibly continue to exist under God's eternal plan of perfect control as man uses that power aright. And all things become possible to him who uses these dynamic unspeakable powers righteously.

❡ The glory of praise and love and gratitude when released from a human heart IS LIGHT. As this is increased one becomes filled with light. Praise and give thanks without ceasing for he who is thankful in all things will be made glorious and the things of this earth will be added unto him one hundred-fold, yea, more. He shall have whatever he asks. The developed ability to give praise love and gratitude will purify one more speedily than any other vibrations."

**Love, Sondra**

*November 30, 2019*

❡ **LEAVING KAMALAYA**

❡ With my friend and Babaji devotee John Kharku Stewart, whom I have known for 42 years. This is the man who envisioned and built this Kamalaya. He took us out for a most exquisite dinner last night and flew back from USA a few days early just so we could meet up! We are really going to miss him and Kamalaya. It is like a heaven on Earth. See you next year dear ones!

**Love, Sondra**

Sondra and John Kharku Stewart

*December 1, 2019*

**♪ WHY I LOVE BALI SO MUCH**

♪ For one thing there are 10,000 temples on this island, and they are all used. Try to imagine this: every family sits down together every morning and weaves baskets and makes offerings. Then they put them up in the temple at home and take offerings to the workplace. Our driver is like a saint. He takes us to the holiest places and prepares the offerings.
♪ People are always bowing to you. The whole place feels like it is descended from another dimension. There are ceremonies going on all the time.

**Love, Sondra**

Our driver Agung who takes us everywhere sacred.

*December 1, 2019*

## ℘ THE FIRST TIME I CAME TO BALI

℘ I stayed at the Oberoi hotel the first night. For breakfast by the beach the waiters were all bowing to me, and I thought *Dear God, what has happened to the Western World*.

℘ I could only afford one night there and so I needed to find a place to stay. This was before computers, so I just started walking with my suitcase down a path wondering where I was going to go. A Balinese man stopped me on his motor bike asking me if I wanted a guide. Surely, I did! Babaji sent me everything I needed the whole time. He took me to Poppies Cottages where I stayed. Every single day the Balinese man would ride his bike over to my cottage and bring me an offering his family made for my altar. He always took me wherever I wanted to go.

℘ Now we are staying at beautiful Nefetari Villas in Ubud. We bring a group here every year. The place is gorgeous, and we all have our own swimming pool. The workers here have become another of our Balinese family. We are so at home here.

**Love, Sondra**

Our Balinese family who does our fire ceremony. Swasty, Wijaya, and a few of their seven children.

*December 2, 2019*

### ♫ ONCE HERE IN BALI

♫ Once here in Bali what I saw was amazing. Outside my window a hundred women were walking in a row, all dressed in their best batiks and all carrying a tall arrangement of fruits stacked upon their heads. I could not believe one fruit did not fall off. It was such a beautiful sight that I followed them wondering where they were going. They all went to the beach and kneeled down and put batik down to make an altar and then they offered the fruit. It was a most unusual, fantastic ceremony.

§ I kept trying to find someone who spoke English to explain it to me. I finally found one woman who told me how lucky I was to see this. She said this was the day that everyone came out to pray for families. She said everyone on the whole island would pray for families on that day. IMAGINE!

**Love, Sondra**

*December 3, 2019*

## § THE GANESH CAVE

§ The elephant cave, or Ganesh Cave, is where we start the Bali Quest. Ganesh is the remover of obstacles, so we have everyone decide what obstacle they would like to overcome before going into the cave, the Divine Mother's earthly regions.

**Love, Sondra**

Our Bali Quest group at the mouth of the elephant cave.

*December 4, 2019*

## ℐ THE FIRE CEREMONY

ℐ Today we are going to the fire ceremony with Swasty. We fell in love with the boy she adopted, and we help support him. He has "angel ears" and seems to be from another dimension. He was a high priest in past lives we found out.

Swasty and her son greeting us at the fire ceremony

¶ The fire ceremony is always very intense. The fire pit is decorated with paint and flowers and all the offerings of grains, fruit, and flowers are placed before us. Every time Swasty says deep mantras and then "swaha" we make an offering to the fire. Because of the deep mantras she does, one can burn up tons of karma. She always reminds us that Babaji is in charge of it all and that He wants us to do the mantra Om Namaha Shivaya which He says is the highest

172

thought in the world. The fire ceremony lasts about I-1/2 hours and it is very hot sitting next to it. Then they prepare our whole group a luncheon Balinese style. What a blessing!

**Love, Sondra**

A wonderful day at Swasty's for the fire ceremony.

*December 5, 2019*

### ꧁ GIVING HEALING SEMINAR THIS MORNING

꧁ "Sickness is a way of punishing ourselves so God won't do it. "I'll sacrifice myself to atone for my sins." Salvation thus becomes sacrifice. When guilt rules, sacrifice must also be there. In death is sin preserved. The belief in sin is a request for death. If we believe we are separate, we must eventually die. To the ego, your body establishes you as separate. To the ego the body is independent of the mind. But it is the mind that is the jail keeper. The body has not

power whatsoever. It merely does what it is told. To the ego the guiltless are guilty. You will see what you believe. The world keeps us guilty and in fear. But the problem is not in the world. The problem is in the mind. Guilt made the world and holds it in place. The only choice is the ego or the Holy Spirit."
(From A Course in Miracles)

**Love Sondra**

*December 6, 2019*

**♫ BALINESE DANCE**

♫ We went to the Balinese Dance last night. It activated some of us. But it's meant to, so it was doing its job.

**Love, Sondra**

Balinese dance

*December 7, 2019*

## ꧁ SELF HEALING

꧁ I read about a man who totally healed himself of cancer by saying the following: "The perfection of God is now being expressed through me. The idea of perfect health is now filling my subconscious mind. The image God has of me is a perfect image; and my subconscious mind recreates my body in perfect accordance with the perfect image held in the mind of God."

♪ It is a good idea prior to sleep to turn over a specific request to your subconscious mind and prove its miracle-working power to yourself.

**Love, Sondra**


*December 8, 2019*

**♪ TIRTA EMPUL – THE HOLY SPRINGS**

♪ For over 1,000 years Balinese worshippers have been drawn to this holy water temple whose sacred springs are said to have been created by the god Indra and possess curative properties. People from all over the world come to bathe in the blessed water temple situated just below the presidential palace of Tampaksiring. There are many waterspouts you bow under while standing in purification ponds. There are many lines you stand in waiting your turn.

♪ My friend Robert Coon said the ley lines of the earth are cleansed here and it is a place to charge up for physical immortality.

**Love, Sondra**

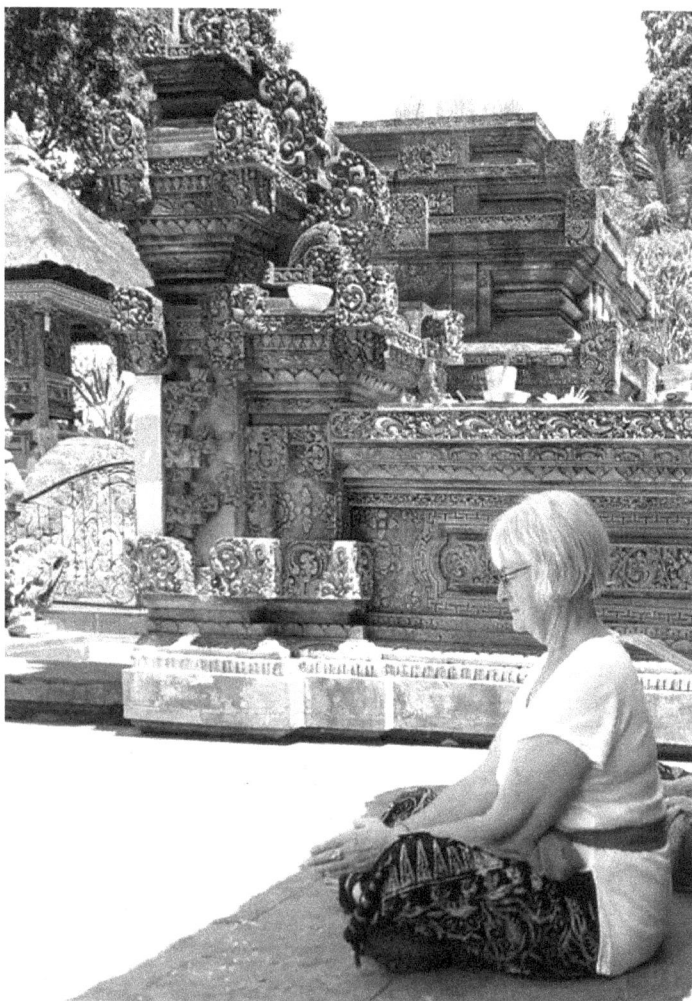

A quiet moment at Tirta Empul Immortality Springs with Dana in meditation

*December 9, 2019*

## ℘ ATTENTION TO THE UNSEEN WORLD

❡ The photo below shows the kind of intensity of attention the Balinese pay to the unseen world of "mythic reality." Carved in stone, the temple guardians of dragons give us a sense that even the scariest in life are all part of the Divine Dance of Creation.

❡ We are so blessed to be here amidst the ancient Balinese wisdom.

**Love, Sondra**

The guardians of Tirta Empul

*December 10, 2019*

## ❡ WE VISIT THE MAJESTIC MOTHER TEMPLE

❡ Besakih is the largest and holiest temple in Bali on the slopes of Mt. Agung. It has 23 separate but related temples and seven levels terraced up a slope. It dates back at least 2,000 years. There are many flights of stairs which ascend to courtyards closer and closer to the mountain which is considered sacred. In 1963 the mountain erupted, and the lava came right toward the temple but mysteriously split and went around it on both sides. The people consider that to be miraculous. There are at least 70 festivals there annually.

**Love, Sondra**

Mangku and Sondra at Besakih Temple

*December 11, 2019*

## ♫ THE DIVINE MOTHER TEMPLE EXPERIENCE

♫ On the trip to the Divine Mother temple, we all said the mantra Om Namaha Shivaya in silence. We met the priest, and he led me up all the stairs. On one level we got blessings from another priest, and we recited the 108 names of the Divine Mother. When we went to the highest level, the group took the vow for Physical Immortality. Each in front of the others. Then they read aloud ten reasons they want to keep living. This is the first time that 100 percent of the group took the vow. Often people say they are not ready. But this group went for it! Everyone loved the Mother Temple, which as the priest told me is actually 3,000 years old.

**Love, Sondra**

*December 12, 2019*

## ♫ REPETITION AND THE SUBCONSCIOUS MIND

♫ Suggestion: Repeat the words "Wealth, Success, Wealth, Success" for five minutes to yourself three or four times a day. These words have tremendous power. Your subconscious mind is like a bank, a sort of universal financial institution. I learned this from Joseph Murphy.

**Love, Sondra**

*December 13, 2019*

## ℐ YOUR SUBCONSCIOUS MIND

ℐ Your subconscious mind has the answer to all problems. Your subconscious mind is the builder of your body and can heal you. Your subconscious mind is your faithful servant and will obey you. You must give the right orders to your subconscious mind. It takes you at your word. You can do all things through its power. You have to believe it. According to your belief is it done to you.

**Love, Sondra**

*December 14, 2019*

## ℐ AFFIRMATIONS FOR TODAY

ℐ Today I choose happiness. Divine order takes charge of my life today and every day. All things work together for good today. This is a new and wonderful day for me. I am divinely guided all day long, and whatever I do will prosper. Divine love surrounds me, enfolds me, and enwraps me, and I go forth in peace. I am a spiritual and mental magnet attracting to myself all things, which bless and prosper me. I am going to be a wonderful success in all my undertakings today. I am definitely going to be happy all day long.

**Love, Sondra**

*December 15, 2019*

## ℐ COUPLE COUNSELING IS HARD

ℐ We used to have couples sit down with us first but then they would always have a fight and it was hard energy to process. So now we give a Liberation Breathing session to the woman first and find out her experience of the relationship, and then we give a session to the man, and then we see them together. Even that is tricky because sometimes one decides to tell the other they want to leave in our presence and we have to handle the aftermath.

ℐ Some couples we know have not slept in the same room for years. Some couples we know are not even speaking to each other except to deal with the kids.

ℐ I am glad we don't do couples therapy all the time. Of course, we ask each single client about their relationship and it is often messed up, but it is easier when they are not coming together. But it is important they both have sessions because breathwork really changes a person and if the mate is not getting breathwork, they end up at a totally different frequency. I must say I am always learning a lot by doing couples whether they come the same day or different days. Usually, I am pretty shocked to hear what goes on.

**Love, Sondra**

*December 16, 2019*

## ℐ STUDYING THE ISSUE OF FEAR

ℐ A Course in Miracles says there is only love or fear. That means that pain, suffering, sickness, conflict, depression, traumas, and so on are all due to fear.

◊ One may not be feeling the fear per se but it is there if one is not having perfection and happiness. Sometimes it is hard to admit that if you are not happy you must be in fear. The ego is always afraid of love because fear would leave and if fear leaves the ego leaves. If you see love, there is no fear. If you see fear, there is no love.

◊ ACIM says our real fear is the fear of redemption. The only way we can be free is if help comes from outside the system. The system is the ego. The only help will be from the Holy Spirit which is outside the system.

**Love, Sondra**


*December 17, 2019*

### ◊ A PRAYER FOR A RELATIONSHIPS

> *Lord, help us remember that our love for each other reflects your love for us.*
> *May we empower one another to fulfill our purpose in life.*
> *May our love be an example and model for all.*
> *May our experience as a couple give us a preview of the oneness we experience with you.*
> *Help us to see that everything is either love or a call for love.*
> *Help us to celebrate our similarities and honor our differences.*
> *Help us to accept our limitations and utilize our talents.*
> *Thank you for this opportunity in life and for my partner.*

**Love, Sondra**

*December 18, 2019*

## ♫ LETTER TO THE DIVINE MOTHER

*Dear Divine Mother,*
*I renounce my ego.*
*I give up my addiction to pain.*
*I deserve to be released from the hell I made.*
*I ask for forgiveness for blocking the solution.*
*I no longer block the light.*
*I give up my competition with God.*
*I accept the Christ Mind.*
*I command my whole body to live.*
*I release all fear and doubt to you.*
*I know you have no difficulty healing my problem.*
*I give this problem to you to be solved.*
*I know nothing is past the hope of healing.*
*I am ready to let this go.*
*I have no more need for this.*
*I am no longer afraid of the memory of God.*
*I join with you. I deny my ego.*
*Thank you for healing me.*

**Love Sondra**

*December 19, 2019*

## ♫ GUIDELINES FOR COOPERATION

1. Agree that there is no scarcity
2. Assume that a cooperative solution can be found
3. Go for the highest spiritual thought
4. Know all solutions are re-negotiable at any time
5. Equal rights + equal responsibility

6. Say 100 percent of what you want

7. No power plays

8. No rescues

9. Be willing to listen.

♩ The highest spiritual thought would be the one that is the most positive, the most loving, the most productive, and that feels the best in your body. You agree to go up to that thought no matter which person channels it.

**Love, Sondra**

*December 24, 2019*

♩ **THE SIGN OF CHRISTMAS**

♩ "The sign of Christmas is a star, a light in darkness. See it not outside yourself, but shining in the Heaven within, and accept it as the sign the time of Christ has come. He comes demanding nothing. No sacrifice of any kind, of anyone, is asked by Him. And you need but invite Him in Who is there already, by recognizing that His Host is One. No fear can touch the Host Who cradles God in the time of Christ, for the Host is as holy as the perfect innocence which He protects and Whose power protects Him. This Christmas give the Holy Spirit everything that would hurt you. Let yourself be healed completely that you may join with Him in healing and let us celebrate our release together by releasing everyone with us. Leave nothing behind, for release is total, and when you have accepted it with me you will give it with me. All pain and sacrifice and littleness will disappear in our relationship, which is as innocent as our relationship with our Father and as powerful. Pain will be brought to us and disappear in our presence, and without pain there can be no sacrifice. and without sacrifice there love MUST be. Let no despair darken

the joy of Christmas, for the time of Christ is meaningless apart from joy. Let us join in celebrating peace. What can be more joyous than to perceive we are deprived of nothing? Such is the message the time of Christ."
(From A Course in Miracles)

**Love, Sondra**

*December 25, 2019*

**ɠ CHRISTMAS DAY**

ɠ For Christmas Day we went to the Basilica which is the largest Catholic Church in North America—one of 10 largest in the world. It is dedicated to the Blessed Virgin. It has 80 chapels.

ɠ Actually I wanted to go to get some holy water, as it has been suggested to me that I need to spray holy water on myself between clients as a protection. So we did that and then decided to stay for the noon mass. I have never been to a Christmas mass at a Catholic Church so that was very interesting. The music was amazing, and the Christmas decor was spectacular. There was no way you could not feel good except when they got into the deal about SINNERS, and you are not worthy, etc. I did want to clear more of my church dogma, so it worked.

ɠ This Basilica took 40 years to build. Apparently, the difference between a basilica and a cathedral is that a basilica has special privileges granted by the Pope. I wonder what those privileges are. We even took communion which I did not think was allowed for me because I was raised a Lutheran, but Markus said he was baptized a Catholic, so it was okay. Besides, he told me I was innocent. I loved the hymns.

**Love, Sondra**

Basilica of the National Shrine of the Immaculate Conception, Washington D.C.

*December 27, 2019*

### ♫ BABAJI CAME IN A DREAM

♫ Last night in a dream Babaji came and hugged me. What a blessing! If you see him in a dream or vision, He actually

187

came. He said it is not possible to make that up. I wish that everyone could have a relationship with Him. You will find nothing but blessings near a true Master. Under His guidance you end up being a virtuoso. You cannot fall back into inertia. You are continually stimulated by a Master. You will totally advance in your spiritual life. Nothing can surpass receiving an initiation and wisdom from the Master. The Master will give you love you never found even in your own family. He will help you become beautiful. What He wants is the best for you. He wants you to be free. How else will you become liberated?

ᛘ If you don't have a teacher like that to guide you, you might get other tough lessons in the form of illness, misery, and difficulties. There would be a karmic reason. The Master lightens your karma. The Master will show you the highest ideal. The Master opens doors for you. It is because of Babaji I found Markus, the beautiful place in which we live, and the beautiful career we have.

ᛘ I want all of you to have what I have. So, won't you consider coming to India to Babaji's ashram with us in March? Don't let money stop you. The first time I went I had to borrow the money. (I paid it all back.) It was the best investment I ever made.

**Love, Sondra**


*December 28, 2019*

**ᛘ PREPARE YOURSELF FOR MIRACLES TODAY**

ᛘ "Hear Him today. Be still and listen to the truth. The bringer of all miracles has need that you receive them first and thus become the joyous giver of what you received.

❡ You do not want to suffer. It really makes no sense. Pain is purposeless, without a cause and with no power to accomplish anything. Your only function here is happiness. Love and joy are everywhere. God being love is also happiness. Joy and peace are your right yet must there be a place made ready to receive His gifts. You were not meant to suffer and die."
(From A Course in Miracles, p.193)

**Love, Sondra**


*December 29, 2019*

**❡ PROBLEMS**

❡ "You have no problems that He cannot solve by offering you a miracle. Miracles are for you. And every fear or pain or trial has been undone. Give the Holy Spirit everything that would hurt you. Leave none behind for release is total.
❡ Had you not lacked faith that it could be solved, the problem would be gone. There is no problem in any situation that faith will not solve. If you lack faith, ask that it be restored where it was lost. Your part is to offer Him a little willingness to let Him remove all fear and be forgiven.
❡ The Holy Spirit cannot take from us what we won't release to Him. He cannot remove our defects without our willingness because that would violate free will." (But the ego's resistance to change is very intense.
(From A Course in Miracles)

**Love, Sondra**

*December 30, 2019*

## ℐ MORE ON PROBLEMS

ℐ "The Holy Spirit offers you release from every problem that you think you have. He has not greater difficulty in resolving some than others. Every problem is the same to Him. One mistake is no more difficult to bring to truth than another. Every problem is an error. He does not judge whether the hurt be large or little. He takes the thorns and nails away.

ℐ Each time you keep a problem for yourself to solve, or judge that it is one that has no resolution, you have made it past the hope of healing. If God is just, there can be no problem that justice cannot solve. Think then how great your own release will be when you are willing to receive correction for all your problems. You will not keep one for pain in any form you do not want. What seemed to be an affliction without a cure has been transformed into a universal blessing."

(From A Course in Miracles)

**Love, Sondra**

*January 1, 2020*

## ℐ MAY BLESSINGS SHINE

ℐ May Blessings shine upon our nation from the Divine Father, Mother, and Child as ONE in this 2020 decade, and may Peace reign supreme and undo our differences, bring solace to our hearts, and restore harmony to our actions. May Truth, Simplicity, Love and Service be our only constitution of Immortal Justice, and Unity be the creed of all our declarations. May perfect happiness be our realization, and charity be our action in sharing our holy providence. Let wisdom guide us in our process of forgiveness, and reconciliation replace conflict and strife. May we join and not divide and have the strength to pause to correct our own errors before pointing the finger at others. May Blessings flow into us that we may rejoice in the delight of being Alive! (Written by Markus)

♪ HAPPY NEW YEAR OF 2020!

**Love, Sondra and Markus**

The Capitol, Washington, D.C., USA

*January 2, 2020*

## ♪ PROCESSING

♪ Recently I felt really grateful that I know how to process myself. Processing is a form of self-inquiry. To process means to examine deeply the nature of our conditioned ego patterning with the intention of finding the truth. We process our consciousness to become clear. We want to let go of extraneous baggage. A cleared consciousness is the most valuable asset in life.

꿋 It allows us to cope with life's challenges. It gives us creativity and increased energy. It creates balance in mind, emotions, and body. It is a very fast way to spiritual awakening. It prevents you from having clashes with others. It provides a healing of physical, mental, and emotional traumas. It gives you greater harmony and you feel less drained. It gives you a higher level of productivity.

꿋 It gives you better communication skills. It gives you the ability to resolve conflicts more easily. It helps you let go of self-destructive behavior patterns. It gives you greater tolerance, love, compassion, and appreciation of others. It gives you a greater flow of abundance and more!

꿋 I could teach you how to do this if you take one of our quests.

**Love, Sondra**

*January 6, 2020*

## 꿋 MORE ABOUT MIRACLES

꿋 You are entitled to miracles. You have been promised full release from the world you made. You are asking for what is rightfully yours. The Holy Spirit cannot but assure you that your request is granted. There is no room for doubt and uncertainty today. You have been assured that the Kingdom of God is within you and can never be lost.

꿋 Ask for miracles whenever a situation arises in which they are called for. You will recognize these situations. And since you are not relying on yourself to find the miracle, you are fully entitled to receive it whenever you ask.

ℌ Tell yourself this: "I will not trade miracles for grievances. I want only what belongs to me. God has established miracles as my right."
(From ACIM, Lesson 77)

**Love, Sondra and Markus**

*January 7, 2020*

**ℌ BELIEVING YOU ARE SEPARATE**

ℌ "Since you believe that you are separate, Heaven presents itself as separate too. Everyone has entered darkness. But he need not stay more than an instant. For He has come with Heaven's help within Him ready to lead one out of darkness into light any time. The time he chooses can be any time, for help is there awaiting but his choice.

ℌ The Holy Spirit offers you release from every problem that you think you have. He has not greater difficulty in resolving some than others. Every problem is the same to Him. One mistake is no more difficult to bring to truth than another."
(From A Course in Miracles)

**Love, Sondra**

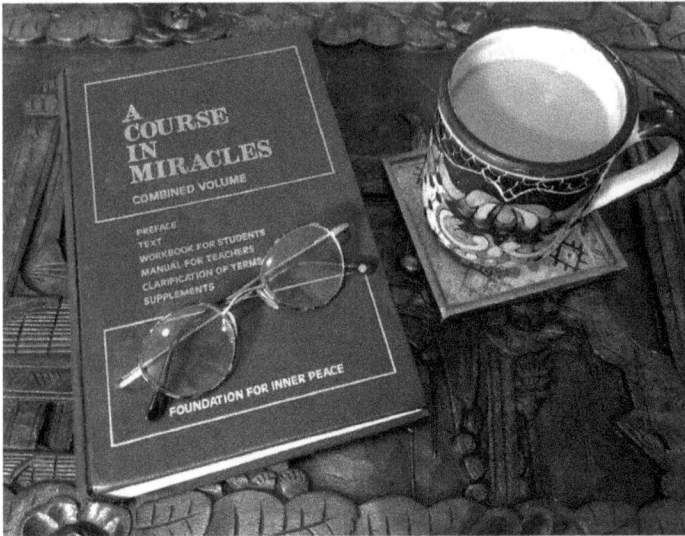

A morning ritual—coffee and A Course in Miracles

*January 8, 2020*

## ♫ GUILT IS NOT THE MIND OF GOD

♫ "Give no reality to guilt if you want to be healed. The end of guilt will never come as long as you see there is a reason for it. You must learn that guilt is insane and has no reason because it is not the mind of God. Whenever the pain of guilt seems to attract you, remember that if you yield to it, you are deciding against your happiness. No penalty is ever asked by God's son except by himself of himself. All salvation is the escape from guilt.

♫ Guilt is not only not of God, it is an attack on God. Guilt is seen as the sole cause of pain in any form. No one who sees himself as guilty can avoid the fear of God. Guilt demands punishment. Guilt asks for punishment and is granted. It is a sure sign that those who hold grievances will suffer guilt.

❡ Forgiveness will take away all fear, guilt, and pain."
(From A Course in Miracles)

**Love, Sondra**

Sondra at the Washington monument, Washington D.C.

*January 9, 2020*

### ❡ ON RELATIONSHIPS

❡ Frequently when you find something wrong with your mate, you are actually seeing your partner as your mother, father, or someone else in your past. Your mate actually then becomes that person to you because you make them into that person unconsciously. This is a very common phenomenon, and it is known as projecting. Because it is unconscious it may be a real trick to catch yourself doing it.

❡ Sometimes, because of your projections, you misinterpret your partner's behavior. Other times your mate will unconsciously act out that behavior in your presence. Because you are familiar with such behavior, you come to expect it and you may even draw it out of your mate. In other words, they might start behaving like someone in your past for you.

❡ I once created a very weird haircut. When I came home, my boyfriend said, "Oh my God, you look just like my mother now." I had never met her, nor had I even seen a photo of her. I became her for him!

**Love, Sondra**

*January 10, 2020*

### ❡ FROM MARKUS'S LITTLE GANESH BOOK

❡ "You remove me from my troubles. Without them I receive your Love upon the pages of my heart; on the pristine parchment the words flow into script to reflect Your presence in the Holy Book of appreciation that gathers in my chest. It lives and throbs on each leaf of words held to serve only You. My pen is the tiny tool transformed to record a poignant moment of deep listening. How can I love you more in this action of scribing my joy?"

**Love, Sondra and Markus**

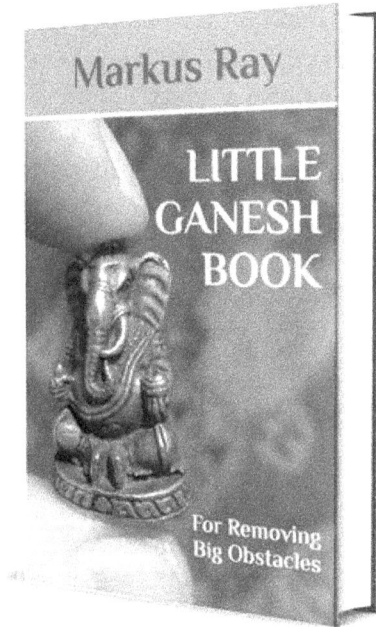

*January 11, 2020*

**ℐ IF YOU ARE SINGLE**

ℐ If you are single, accept that you have chosen solitude and realize that it was not forced upon you by bad luck, fate, lack of potential mates, or something being wrong with you. You are not a victim ever. For some reason your higher self has chosen to be alone for this period. Perhaps there is something you want to learn from this experience. Perhaps you fear being in a relationship. Perhaps you think you are not lovable or good enough. Whatever your reasons, you can "create a mate" whenever you are ready. You can process in yourself the fear of involvement whenever you are ready.

♫ It is not true you HAVE TO BE ALONE. Even A Course in Miracles says that when you are ready to join, others ready to join will find you. That is inevitable unless you are blocking it. If you are blocking it, it is helpful to get a Liberation Breathing session with us to find out what the block is and breathe it out!

**Love, Sondra**

*January 12, 2020*

## ♫ HOW LONG SHOULD A COUPLE STAY TOGETHER?

♫ In the book *Seat of the Soul*, author Gary Zukav says that the duration of a spiritual partnership is only as long as appropriate for the couple's evolution. How long is appropriate? He says it is appropriate for them to remain living together as a couple only as long as they grow together. In other words, couples in a new paradigm cannot say for sure that they will stay together forever. Their growth together may take a whole lifetime, or it may take only six months. Sometimes the Divine brings people together for a short time to grow and to clear karma. That is why I never used to beat myself up if a relationship I had ended in two years. In fact, I had to go through several of those before I found Markus, my true twin flame. I knew I had karma to clear with those guys.

♫ One has to have faith that when the other is taken from them, the situation was no longer best, and God is trying to give them something more appropriate. That is what always happened for me. Whatever happens is the perfect thing to happen. The length of "recovery" from change is dependent on one's level of trust in the universe.

❡ A relationship should always make you stronger, not weaker. You can pray for this relationship to be healed OR for something better for both of you. Then, either way it is a win.

**Love, Sondra**

*January 13, 2020*

### ❡ MY PRAYER TO THE DIVINE MOTHER

❡ I take refuge in your nurturing arms of compassion. My dear Mother, you are the rhythm of life, the ocean of bliss, the light of the sun and moon. You are the mystery of the universe.

❡ Oh gracious and compassionate Mother, please bless me with your vision in every minute of the day. Oh Holy Mother, Divine Mother help me be free.

❡ Everything I do is a result of your divine energy moving through me. You are the cause of all actions. I am simply your instrument. I am simply the manifestation of your never-ending flow of Divine Love. My wealth lies in your love. You are my only goal in life. I was born to serve you. I wish for all people to worship you.

**Love, Sondra**

*January 14, 2020*

### ❡ ANOTHER PRAYER TO THE DIVINE MOTHER

199

❡ May everything I do or experience bring me closer to you. Purify my aura and vibration. May I go beyond the mind to experience reality where quiet bliss reigns. Oh, please let your Divine Light shine in me. I want to experience your presence and let that light shine from me. Will you be the instrument of my healing? Mother of Immortal Bliss, hear my prayers. I accept your love. Oh transmit your pure vital energy to me. I know only a true master can heal my mind. I ask you, Jesus, and Babaji for this gift.

**Love, Sondra**

*January 15, 2020*

❡ **MANIFESTATION**

❡ "Now to the Great Law of Being, realize that it doesn't matter at all how small or big your desired manifestation may be. Do you have a goal that seems huge and unattainable to you? Accept the idea that the great miracles are not only possible but in fact operate by the same principle, and then move into acceptance that your desired demonstration is so. "Keep asserting the truth. To God, there is no big or small, no hard or easy. Divine law simply responds to your belief. Actually, if you want a miracle, you must have passion, determination, and strong feeling and only through this exalted conviction and trust can your miracles manifest in grace. But the feelings are joy, love, courage, and indomitable faith."
(From *Living the Miracle Consciousness* by Linda De Coff)

**Love, Sondra**

*January 16, 2020*

## ♪ HAPPINESS

♪ "The truth that is God and Life is sufficient in and of itself. We are not separate from that. We are happy only in ecstatic or self-realized Communion with That. To release the entire body-mind into Communion with the Radiant and unknowable Divine Reality IS happiness. It is not that the act of such release produces effects in us that are happiness. Rather, the sacrifice or Communion itself is happiness.

♪ "If you spend time in the company of what is lovable, then the emotional radiance of being will naturally come forward. Right association is the secret then. It is said that of all the things a person can do, association with the God-Realized personality, the Saint, the Spiritual Master, is best; simply to be in the company of one who is lovable in the highest sense, one in love with whom the very Force of God is encountered. The best Company in which to spend all of your time is the Company of God and the Spiritual Master." (From Da Love-Ananda)

**Love, Sondra**

*January 17, 2020*

## ♪ ANGER

♪ Guru Mai: "It is said that if you are a true ascetic, you are completely devoid of anger. If there is any trace of anger in you, you are called a scoundrel, not an ascetic. A great being will go to any extent to remove the fire of anger. The greatness of a Saddhu Monk is that he can drop something once he realizes he has it."

§ Dalai Lama: "We lose control of our mind through hatred and anger. If our minds are dominated by anger, we will lose the best part of human intelligence—wisdom! Anger is one of the most serious problems facing the world today."

§ Ammachi: "Try to make your own mind aware of the bad outcome of anger. When you are angry at someone, you lose all your mental balance. Your discriminative power completely stops functioning. You say whatever comes to your mind and act accordingly. You may even utter crude words. You lose a lot of good energy. This will only pave the way for your own destruction!"

**Love, Sondra**

*January 18, 2020*

§ **HEALING**

§ Thoughts on healing from my book *Pele's Wish*:

§ "The first step in healing is for the person to reduce his guilt complexes to the minimum and free himself of dogmatic religious beliefs. The kahunas think in terms of saying "Nothing gets hardening of the arteries as fast as religion."

§ The kahuna who maintained their original ways even after the missionary period in the island felt that religious fixations were frequently the cause of guilt and thus illness. The reason for this is that sin is always associated with intense guilt. And by its nature, guilt demands punishment. Dogmas that teach us that we are guilty or unworthy can block prayers of healing unless a clearing of those feelings is first performed."

**Love, Sondra**

*January 19, 2020*

### ⌡ INNER COMMUNION

⌡ Inner Communion is when you keep the Wine and Blood of Christ in your own inner sanctuary. This can be done through the spiritual life, i.e., not only through spiritual practices, but by remembering that all of life is an ashram and every moment is a spiritual opportunity. Pray to be purified by the Divine Love of the Christ. Meditate on this verse: "Be ye perfect even as your Father which is in heaven is perfect." Create the perfect life on earth by recognizing and knowing you are perfect. You were created perfect. You are one with God the Father. Raise your consciousness and partake of the bread of life knowing that you can even become so pure that you can master the very atoms which cause decay of the body.

**Love, Sondra**

*January 20, 2020*

### ⌡ BEING IN CONTROL

⌡ People are afraid to lose control but if you are out of control then nobody can control you. If you are in control, then you are using your ego to stop the Divine Energy—the flow of life or the Holy Spirit—from roaring through you. The reason it is harmful to be "in control" is you are using the ego mind against yourself, and this causes pain, sickness, accidents, and even death. In breathwork if you stay in control and stop the life force by hanging on to a negative thought with power you could go into temporary paralysis.

❡ People have the idea that if they let go, something terrible will happen. It is just the opposite. When you let go, you are just letting go of negative thoughts and the result will be more bliss. If you let the Divine control you, you will experience abundance, energy, love, joy, and more and more good things.

❡ An enlightened person is totally guided by Divine control. Then you get "God-intoxicated" and you become irresistible. This is why some people cannot stand to be in the presence of a guru for very long. The guru is under divine control. Your own ego control comes up in His presence.

❡ If you can take it, the guru will teach you to get out of ego control.

**Love, Sondra**

*January 21, 2020*

❡ **NOTES FROM JOEL OSTEEN**

❡ "When you connect with someone who is blessed, someone who is favored, as they increase, you will increase. Who you are connected to is extremely important. There are blessings that belong to you that are attached to the people God has placed in your life, and if you are not seeing any fish, you need to evaluate who you are connected to. You may need to disconnect from relationships that are not producing any increase and connect with people who are blessed, people who are seeing favor. You are going to become like whoever you are connected to! Look around and find the favor connections in your life.

(From Joel Osteen's book *The Power of Favor*)

**Love, Sondra**

*January 23, 2020*

**♪ AVOIDING INTIMACY**

♪ Harville Hendrix asked spouses this simple question: "What does your mate do to avoid you?" He came up with a list of over 300 different answers. Here are some of them:

- Reading romance novels
- Disappearing into the garage
- Facebooking, Tweeting, or Snapchatting
- Camping out on the phone
- Worshiping the car
- Being wed to the computer
- Spending time at her mom's
- Having an affair
- Avoiding eye contact
- Falling asleep on the couch
- Being a sports junkie
- Coming home late for dinner
- Fantasizing while making love
- Being sick and tired all the time
- Not wanting to be touched
- Having sex but not making love
- Living on the tennis court
- Jogging ten miles a day
- Going on weekend fishing trips
- Going shopping
- Playing video games
- Refusing to talk
- Picking fights
- Going to bars

♪ I kept wondering if there would be similar answers if they were not spouses. Is this just married life?

**Love, Sondra**

*January 22, 2020*

**♫ ASKING FOR DIRECTION**

♫ "This holy instant would I give to You. Be You in charge for I would follow You, certain that Your direction brings me peace." (ACIM, Lesson 360)

♫ The Holy Instant is a beginning in which the Christ's voice, the One of Love, directs my actions in all that I do. The day is a gift I give to God by asking for what He would have me do. I can be assured that guidance will be provided in His Name and that only happy outcomes will result. When I go astray, I can return to stillness and ask again, "Father, what would You have me do? Where would You have me go? What would you have me say and to whom?" And in what I hear would be the sound of His voice in me. I can decide for truth; it can be this simple. Direction is the way toward freedom from thought and judgements. All the lessons of ACIM are true and reinforce my understanding of myself. Being is the real step to take. Without taking this step, learning is pointless preoccupation. Now is the time to Love through complete forgiveness. By asking the Christ for my directions, I am accepting who I am as God created me. I am the Christ, and nothing less, by asking to be led by Him. Because to ask of Him is to ask of my Self. The results are Pure Joy only.

(From Markus' book *Alpha and Omega*)

**Love, Sondra and Markus**

*January 24, 2020*

**♫ DEVOTION TO GOD**

❡ Amma says: "Most do not feel this urgency to be devoted to God. We think that life is possible without devotion to God and live our lives depending on the world not on God. At present, God is the last item on our list. But He should be first. If we put God first, all other things will fall into proper place in our lives. Once we have God in our lives, the world will follow. But if we place the world first, God will not follow.

❡ To have God in us is a struggle in the beginning, but if we persist, it will lead us to everlasting bliss and happiness. All struggles will end. To embrace the world is easy and things go smoothly in the beginning, but this will culminate in never-ending sorrow and suffering. We are free to choose one or the other."

(From *Awaken Children*)

**Love, Sondra**

*January 25, 2020*

❡ **SPIRITUAL LOVE**

❡ Amma says: "Love is love, but the intensity is different, and the depth is different. Spiritual love is as deep as a bottomless pit. How deep and how expansive it is cannot be measured.

❡ Spiritual love is without limits or boundaries while worldly love is superficial and not very deep. The spirit of worldly love is not constant. Its rhythm fluctuates; it comes and goes. The beginning is always beautiful and enthusiastic, but slowly it gets less beautiful and less exciting until it ends up being shallow. In most cases it ends in an upset.

❡ Spiritual love is different. The beginning is beautiful and peaceful. Shortly after this peaceful beginning it becomes agony of longing. Excruciating pain will ensue, and this will

prevail until just before it leads up to unity with the beloved. This unity is beautiful. The beauty and peace of this unity never dries up or diminishes. Your whole being will be transformed into Love. Spiritual love culminates in unity, in oneness. Sometimes a relationship between two people, if it is pure, can reach that union."
(From *Awaken Children*)

**Love, Sondra**

Amma, the hugging saint

*January 28, 2020*

## ♪ EVOLUTIONARY RELATIONSHIPS

♪ "A couple must work together for something that brings greater love and care to the world. These partners impassion their vision. They see service as a sacred prayer, not simply as an act of charity. They see their relationship as a contribution to the transformation of the world—as a sacred act of communion. Both partners learn to embody generosity. By learning the essence of generosity through their service, they have so much more generosity to give to each other because passion is fed by generosity.

᛭ If we allow our personal problems in a relationship to become central, they overwhelm the relationship. However, when we are engaged in serving the world, we come into a deeper understanding and acceptance of our personal problems because we have a much bigger picture in which to hold them. Our engagement in the world changes the focus of our psyche. We move from the focus being on our overwhelming personal issues to what we can do for the world—how we are bringing love to the world. That shift allows a couple to be excited, thrilled, and enriched by something they are doing together for the world, rather than obsessing about their personal disappointments."
(From *Evolutionary Love Relationships* by Andrew Harvey and Chris Saade)

**Love, Sondra**

*January 30, 2020*

**᛭ "SHOULD" THINKING**

᛭ "Should" thoughts are not related to a constructive, responsive behavior. A "should" is not really a guide, it is a negative judgement. "Should" thinking not only expresses the belief that things are not okay but is coupled with a sense of personal condemnation. "Should" thinking is a tool of self-conformation. (Reality "should" conform to my particular views, terms, desires.) When people fail to fit in with our "should" we become upset and blame the people involved.

᛭ Marriage is the prime arena for "should" thinking, i.e., my husband or wife "should" meet my needs. "Shoulds" lead to interpersonal power struggles. In the *"you should, no, YOU should"* game, harmonious resolution is made impossible by the fact that the game requires a winner-loser outcome.

♫ "Should" thinking is the thought pattern belonging to ego-consciousness. "Should" thinking hurts. If we believe our "should," we are in big trouble.

(From *A Gift of Love: Marriage as a Spiritual Journey* by Ann Linthorst)

**Love, Sondra**

*January 31, 2020*

## ♫ WHEN ONE PARTNER IS "OUT OF WHACK"

♫ Most teachings would say you cannot rescue someone from his or her ego trip by joining with him or her. It is suggested that the other partner maintains a respectful distance giving the troubled one room and time to work it out with God. This shows love and respect by communicating "I know you are having a hard time, but I am confident you can resolve this problem. I am working prayerfully to support you." This is a good way to address the situation.

♫ I would say that the only exception would be if both are Breathworkers. One could give his or her partner a breath session. It has been extremely helpful for me at times when Markus gave me a session. He is then also channeling the good of God for me.

**Love, Sondra**

*February 1, 2020*

## ♫ AFFIRMATIONS I MADE FROM CHAPTER 12 IN ACIM

1. I confess I made up pain, misery, and death and this has not made me happy. But I am responsible. I did this (in the past).
2. I am willing to learn what freedom is.
3. I cannot be hurt unless I give something power to hurt me. Therefore, all blame is off the track.
4. I see my brother as sinless. I am committed to see him differently than I have in the past. I constantly appreciate the value he provides for me to see myself.
5. I pray that all my relationships become holy.
6. My partner and I dedicate our relationship to the Holy Spirit and share the light with the world. I allow the Holy Spirit to teach us the means.
7. I celebrate life and the resurrection.

**Love, Sondra**

*February 2, 2020*

## ♫ PAST LIVES

♫ Once I had a client who began remembering being in a war in Ireland. She suddenly began to speak with a perfect Irish accent during the session. She certainly was not Irish in this life. Later I asked her if she had ever been to Ireland in this life and she said no. After the session she did not even remember she did that.

꽃 For me, I did not begin to remember any of my own past lives until I started going to India. After that they came up for years. We do carry cellular memories over from past lives into this one. For example, if you were hung in a past life, you may create the cord around your neck at birth and you might avoid tight clothes and choker necklaces. If you were drowned, you could have an intense fear of deep water.

꽃 Many phobias come from past lives. Often, they won't appear until you reach the same age that you were when the trauma occurred in a past life. Birth marks can also be scars from past lives. If we can release the fears we have left over from past lives and realize that we are safe today, we can often eliminate the physical and mental symptoms that those memories cause.

**Love, Sondra**


*February 3, 2020*

**꽃 PAST LIVES AND ILLNESS**

꽃 "The body and its various aches, pains, and dysfunctions is a living psychic history when read correctly. Even though the physical ailment may have very specific origins in a person's current life, I have found more and more that there are certain layers to every major syndrome of physical illness, accident, or weakness. The existence of a past life level of physical problems has been confirmed over and over again in the cases I have seen."

(From Roger Woolger, Ph.D *Other Lives, Other Selves*)

**Love, Sondra**

*February 4, 2020*

## ∮ PHOBIAS

∮ "Although many phobias do indeed arise in this life, it seems to be the case that almost everyone has some particular deep fear that will not be explained. Whether it be fear of spiders, wild animals, fire, water, heights, crowds, knives, dark places, and so on, I have consistently found that behind that fear lies a specific and detailed story of a past life trauma. In sessions people remember deaths from poisonous insects, from spiders, snakes, sharks, and more. Men who fear heights recall deaths from being thrown off cliffs, falling from planes in recent wars, etc.

∮ The likelihood of cure depends on whether or not I am able to guide my client to the crucial or key story from his or her past lives. If we can reach such a story in an early session, cure will be correspondingly swift."

(From Roger Woolger, Ph.D *Other Lives, Other Selves*)

**Love, Sondra**

*February 5, 2020*

## ∮ CRISIS AND THE LAST EXPERIMENT

∮ In life it is not what happens to us, but how we respond, that is important. From this point of view, every crisis or misfortune is an opportunity. Contained within the crisis, is the power to turn it into a blessing. There is no crisis, no matter how tragic, which cannot be transmuted into honor and achievement. The only requirement is to accept it and offer it to God in praise and thanksgiving. Many times, man has made his greatest strides during times of crisis. Usually after people have exhausted every other approach to solving a crisis, they turn within to God. This is why turning to God as a final resort is often called the "last experiment."

𝕵 A man told me of a case where a beauty queen had a car accident and went through the windshield and her whole face was cut and destroyed. She had such severe depression she ended up in a mental ward. She got worse and worse, and her mother could not take it anymore to go see her. The girl was put even in solitary confinement. Her father's minister told him he should go anyway and give thanks about the whole thing. He just could not do that for months. One month he gave up and forced himself to try it. That day the girl called out to her father and got out to see him. She totally recovered and was released, and she got married and the father led her down the aisle.

**Love, Sondra**

*February 6, 2020*

## 𝕵 PROSPERITY THROUGH THE DIVINE PLAN

𝕵 "When you begin to dwell upon the divine plan, you will attract to yourself the ideas, opportunities, events, and people that are meant to be part of your life. When you affirm the divine plan, those people and situations that are NOT a part of it begin to move out of your life. Those people that are part of it find their way into your life easily. This is the easy way to live life successfully.

𝕵 The one thing you must be prepared for, when you start calling on the divine plan, is transition and change. Whenever you need guidance about people or events, declare that the divine plan is manifesting in these situations

or in the lives of those people. You will be amazed at how quickly things will right themselves. Say, "The divine plan is unfolding for me now. Nothing can hinder the divine plan of my life. No one can delay the divine plan of my life. What God has given me cannot be diminished."
(From Catherine Ponder)

**Love, Sondra**

*February 7, 2020*

**⅃ GETTING THE ANSWER**

⅃ American author Catherine Ponder writes that we contact universal wisdom by recognizing its presence and asking for its help and by affirming that it is showing us what to do and helping us do it.

⅃ To invite it in to solve any problem, say: "There is an answer. Divine wisdom now shows me the perfect answer. I relax, let go, and let it instruct me" OR say: "We invite divine wisdom into every phase of our lives. We invite divine wisdom into this situation now. Divine wisdom is opening ways, where, to human sense, there is no way."

⅃ So when you find yourself in circumstances over which you seem to have no control, instead of fighting to survive in those circumstances, it is time to call on divine wisdom. Developing the wisdom concept is easy, and its benefits are unlimited.

**Love, Sondra**

*February 8, 2020*

## ꝯ PERFECT SETTING

ꝯ I must say I am very happy to be once again in California where it all started (rebirthing that is). I feel like California gave me my original enlightenment. Now it is wonderful to be here at Jane's, our organizer. Jane is totally dedicated to ascension and being her higher self. She is totally dedicated to serving others. She and Ernie have a fabulous home and we are fortunate to have a healing room to work in where she has three of Markus' paintings of the Dream Team (Babaji, Jesus, and Ammachi). Doing sessions in that room is the ultimate. There is nothing like perfection.

ꝯ We are excited to be taking a trip to the Hoover Dam and then coming back to do the Miracle Consciousness Training.

**Love, Sondra**

*February 9, 2020*

## ꝯ FACTORS THAT RETARD AGING

ꝯ Here are several positive factors that retard aging:

- Happy marriage (or satisfying long term relationship)
- Job satisfaction
- Feeling of personal happiness
- Ability to laugh easily
- Satisfactory sex life
- Ability to make and keep close friends
- Regular daily routine
- Regular work routine
- Taking at least one week's vacation a year

- Feeling in control of personal life
- Enjoyable leisure time
- Ability to express feelings easily
- Optimistic about the future
- Feeling financially secure

(From Deepak Chopra *Ageless Body, Timeless Mind*)

ℑ I think that although these points are good, there is no mention at all about having the necessity of giving up thoughts like *I am aging* and *death is inevitable*. Until you handle those thoughts, the body will age.

**Love, Sondra**

*February 12, 2020*

**ℑ AN EXTREME DAY IN ARIZONA**

ℑ Perhaps you already know the earth is four billion years old and the rocks at the bottom of Grand Canyon are two billion years old and that it took 17 million years to carve out the canyon. But maybe you don't know about the Grand Canyon skywalk.

ℑ It is a horseshoe-shaped, cantilever bridge with a glass floor. You are standing over what is 4,000 feet below. It gives you the feeling you are walking on air. Many people hang on to the rails and shut their eyes. It is so extreme to look below that I could hardly stand it. The cost is extreme too at $90 per person. (The Hualapai Indians are recipients of the money.) But it is a once-in-a-lifetime experience. I could only look down at my feet X2. My eyes could not take it in, and my eyes were burning for two hours after that. They told us that big body builders have come and have fainted.

§ We are living out in the desert with the Joshua trees. It is extreme out here. Then we watched *Ford v Ferrari,* and that was so extreme I nearly had a heart attack.

**Love, Sondra**

Markus Ray at the Grand Canyon

*February 14, 2020*

## § KARMA SHOWS US WE ARE RESPONSIBLE

§ Pleasure and pain come from your own past actions. So it is easy to define karma in one short sentence: Act well and things will go well; act wrongly and things will go wrong. Bad karma can be weakened through repentance. The bad deed must be repented of, with the firm intention of not doing it again. We can be liberated from the incessant cycle of birth, suffering, death, and rebirth only when our entire negative karma has been extinguished.

ℊ The notion of karma especially shows us that we are responsible for our own fate and should take charge of our own lives. We believe that the intention is what primarily counts. Everything that individual beings experience depends on their good or bad motives.

ℊ Bad karma must be rendered ineffective through good deeds, through a good life. What do people understand a good life to be? It cannot be equated with a pleasant life in which all of our material wishes and dreams are fulfilled. Instead, it is a life lived in ethical responsibility. A life in which we do not think only of our own wellbeing but also serve others. Good karma is created only through good deeds.

**Love, Sondra**

*February 15, 2020*

## ℊ THE SUBJECT OF GRACE

1. Is your home worthy to be a home of the child of God?
2. Does it protect your peace?
3. Does it shine love on you?
4. Does it keep your heart untouched by fear?
5. Does it allow you to give without a sense of loss?
6. Does it teach that giving equals joy?

**Love, Sondra**

*February 16, 2020*

𝕵 **GIVING**

𝕵 "Wherever I go, whoever I encounter, I will bring them a gift. The gift may be a compliment, a flower, or a prayer. Today I will give something to everyone I come in contact with, and so I will begin the process of circulating joy, wealth, and affluence in my life and the life of others."

𝕵 Anything that is of value in life only multiplies when it is given. If through the act of giving, you feel you have lost something, then the gift is not truly given and will not cause increase.

𝕵 If you want joy, give joy to others; if you want love, learn to give love; if you want attention and appreciation; learn to give attention and appreciation. The easiest way to get what you want is to help others get what they want."
(From *The Seven Spiritual Laws of Success* by Deepak Chopra)

**Love, Sondra**

*February 17, 2020*

𝕵 **AFFIRMATIONS FROM CHAPTER 9 IN ACIM**

1.  I am neither alone, nor at the effect of something outside of me that can get me. God is real and available and always loves me. I am one with God.

2.  When my prayers appear to be unanswered, I am blocking. Either a) I have asked for something I am too afraid to receive or b) I am giving a double message and have a negative sabotaging thought in my subconscious that keeps me from receiving

or c) I may not want to receive because my need to stay angry for not receiving is stronger than my desire to have.

3. In healing my body, the first thing I do is pray for release of the fear of healing. It is safe to be without this defense mechanism. I am safer the healthier I am. I am safe with all the aliveness and energy I will receive as I give up this condition.

4. I believe in my sisters and brothers and I accept them, side with them, and value them. When they behave insanely, I see them as sane and do not make their errors real. I see beyond them. I see them as healed.

5. I devote my life to healing myself completely.

6. I accept my grandeur with confidence and maintain this self-esteem always. God is incomplete without me. I am immensely valuable.

7. In this Holy Instant I completely accept the Atonement for myself.

**Love, Sondra**

*February 18, 2020*

**ꟓ THE VIOLET FLAME**

ꟓ "The violet flame goes after the schisms which cause psychological problems that go back to early childhood and previous incarnations and that have established such deep grooves within the consciousness that in fact, they have been difficult to shake lifetime after lifetime." (Saint Germain)

ꟓ "In one moment you sit surrounded with every kind of negative thought in your aura. In the next, you decide to invoke the violet flame. And lo! the mighty power of the seventh ray, as a giant electrode of cosmic energy, begins to form around your person. The violet flame angels gather around you. With palms outstretched, they direct across your four lower bodies and your aura an arc of the violet ray. As that arc flashes across your being, it vaporizes the negative conditions. They literally disappear from heart and mind!" (Archangel Zadkiel)

**Love, Sondra**

*February 21, 2020*

**℥ THE INFINITE NOW**

℥ I am reading my friend Maile's new book *The Infinite Now*. She talks about the four elements of manifestation.

1. SET IT. Create an intention for the desired manifestation.
2. FORGET IT. Release the energy to do its thing.
3. KNOW. Don't just believe it. It is on its way.
4. TROUBLESHOOTING. Things to check if it did not come.

**℥ BLOCKS TO INTENDED MANIFESTATION**

1. The intention was not really wanted.
2. Subconscious thoughts are blocking intended outcome.
3. Desired outcome contradicts a spiritual lesson that cannot be removed until lesson is learned.
4. Desired outcome is in direct conflict with God's plan.

(From *The Infinite Now* by Maile Page)

**Love, Sondra**

*February 22, 2020*

## ♫ TRULY CREATIVE PEOPLE

♫ "Truly creative people in all fields can temporarily suspend their ego and simply experience what they are seeing, without the need to assert judgment, for as long as possible. They are more than ready to find their most cherished opinions contradicted by reality. They can embrace mysteries. This is called negative capability. This will be one of the most important factors in your success. You must develop the habit of suspending the need to judge everything that crosses your path. You must adopt a kind of humility toward knowledge.

♫ Mozart never asserted any particular opinions about music. He absorbed the styles he heard and incorporated them into his own voice. Einstein was fascinated by the paradox of two people observing the same beam of light. He was able to consider every possible solution. Negative capability is a tool you use in the process. It is not a permanent state of mind. Allow for serendipity . . . the occurrence of something you are not expecting.

♫ The brain becomes increasingly excited and stimulated by a variety of information. You must maintain an openness and looseness of Spirit. Engage in activities outside your work." (From *Mastery* by Robert Greene)

**Love, Sondra**

*February 23, 2020*

## ♫ SPECIALTY OR FOOD SECURITY SOLUTION?

♫ Last night our friends took us to a very high-end Mexican restaurant. On the menu as a recognized specialty were grasshoppers for an appetizer. In Mexico it is a long-standing tradition to eat them, so Markus ordered them. They were smoked and served on guacamole. He told me to try them, so I did. They weren't so bad but the yuck factor got to me and kind of ruined my meal. Markus had no sympathy for me about that as he reminded me, I was the one who encouraged him to order them!

𝔍 I found out they have an extraordinary protein rich factor and have more protein than beef, chicken, or pork. The U.N. published a whole book in 2013 promoting edible insects as a solution to global food insecurity. Apparently in Mexico in any market there are piles of them for sale and catchers sneak out before dawn in the alfalfa fields to get them. But I probably won't eat them again.

**Love, Sondra**

*February 24, 2020*

## 𝔍 ATTAINING MASTERY

𝔍 "Mastery is not a function of genius or talent. It is a function of time and intense focus applied to a particular field of knowledge. But there is another element, an X factor that masters inevitably possess that seems mystical but that is accessible to us all. Whatever field of activity we are involved in, there is generally an accepted path to the top. It is a path that others have followed, and because we are conformist creatures, most of us opt for this conventional route. But masters have a strong inner guidance system and a high level of self-awareness. What has suited others in the past does not suit them, and they know that trying to fit into a

conventional mold would only lead to a dampening of spirit. So, they decide to forge their own route."
(From *Mastery* by Robert Greene)

**Love, Sondra**

*February 25, 2020*

### Ꝙ GIVING A DOUBLE MESSAGE

Ꝙ Very often we have asked for God's help in removing a problem. Help never came and we became disappointed and thought maybe there was no God. It is not that God was not there or that God refused our request, however we did not ask clearly. While we were asking for a problem solved, the ego's voice was urging us to hold on to it. In other words, we were giving a double message.

Ꝙ Example: You may have prayed for something you deserve but at the same time you had a thought in your subconscious such as *I can't get what I want,* or *I am not good enough.* That thought was so strong it sabotaged your receiving anything. If your fear of letting go of those thoughts is too great, God will wait. The Holy Spirit will not add to your fear.

Ꝙ I once had a student whose dominant thought was *Nothing works*. He kept proving that by not allowing things to work. Then he was more and more convinced. I chided him and told him if he did not watch out, I would meet him in 25 years and he would tell me the same. Guess what! I actually met him 25 years later and he told me "Nothing works!" True story.

**Love, Sondra**

*February 27, 2020*

## ꙮ RULES FOR DECISION

1. Today I will make no decisions by myself. With this outlook, you are not the judge of what you do. When you are called upon to make a response, you do not judge the situation.
2. Tell yourself the kind of day you want, the feelings you want to have, the things you want to happen, and what you want to experience. Then realize: This is the day that will be given me if I make no decisions myself.
3. If something occurred in your day that is not what you wanted, realize that you have asked a question by yourself in the ego. Then say: "I have no questions. I forgot to decide."
4. If you cannot let your questions go, begin to change your mind with this: At least I can decide I do not like what I feel now.
5. Having decided that you do not like the way you feel, the next step is easy: I hope I have been wrong (This reminds you help is what you want and need.)
6. You can now say this in perfect honesty: "I want another way to look at this."
7. The final step is acknowledgement of your lack of opposition. It is a statement of an open mind: "Perhaps there is another way to look at this. What can I lose by asking?"
(From A Course in Miracles)

**Love, Sondra**

*February 28, 2020*

## ₰ DEVELOP A CONSCIOUSNESS

₰ When you develop a consciousness of the things you seek, they will appear in your presence. God meets you on the level of your consciousness. If your consciousness of need is greater than your consciousness of God, then need will expand. When you love God more than your problem, you will be healed. You must re-dedicate yourself. You must develop the state of mind through which you can receive God.

₰ Prayer is a method to clear the way for your acceptance of your oneness with the Source. (The stream has the quality of its Source.) You must pray from the standpoint of already having what you ask for—knowing there is no spiritual lack. Prayer is the practice of the presence of God.

**Love, Sondra**

*March 1, 2020*

## ₰ HUNA PRAYER PROCESS

₰ I really support the Huna teaching of Hawaii and hope you will take a class in Ho'oponopono. (Google: IZI LLC) The process of prayer to the high self involves raising the vital force (mana) up from the middle self to the next voltage. The aspect that is unique to the Huna teachings is that it is the low self that takes the prayer to the high self. If the low self has a complex of sin, unworthiness, guilt, or doubt, it will not deliver the prayer. The low self uses the mana the middle self has raised and sends that vital force up the aka cord with the prayer.

꿏 Huna teaches that the high self cannot manifest a prayer unless it receives the needed mana from the middle and low selves. Thus, it is essential to accumulate a surcharge of vital force before beginning to pray to the higher self. You do this with a breathing exercise. What is so great is that there is a clearing of the path. This means removing all thought forms that could sabotage the prayer. Ordinary prayers in churches do not do that. So, you are removing any negative thought forms in the middle and low self that would prevent the low self from taking the prayer to the high self.

꿏 It is magic!

**Love, Sondra**

*March 2, 2020*

꿏 **FROM AMMA**

꿏 "Just what do you think of yourself? Do you think that you are a perfect soul? No, you are not. You are just a limited ego. You CAN attain perfection, but for that to happen, you need guidance. You need to be corrected. You need to be disciplined. That is what a disciple must undergo. If you do not allow somebody (and this somebody means a Guru) to work on you, then it is difficult for you to be transformed.
꿏 The Guru's scoldings are actually blessings. When the guru scolds you, that means his Grace and compassion have started flowing towards you. He has set his eyes on you. He wants to save you. He wishes to free you eternally. The Guru cannot hurt anyone. The river cannot hurt you. The Guru sheds light. There is only consciousness in the Guru. Consciousness cannot hurt anyone. Whatever comes out of the Guru is for your own good."

(From *Awaken Children Volume IV*)

**Love, Sondra**

*March 3, 2020*

### ❧ MAINTAINING PEACE AND CONTENTMENT

❧ "You may feel peaceful, happy, and content when you are alone or in favorable company. But if you cannot maintain that peace and contentment while you are in the midst of people whom you do not like or while you are in a tempting situation, that peace or contentment is not genuine. To maintain that peace and contentment in all circumstances is our goal. Your calmness will disarm other people.

❧ If you have any complaints, write a letter to Amma but do not get angry, do not speak roughly, or use harsh words. If anger arises in you, do not express it immediately. Go and sit somewhere by yourself. Contemplate and meditate. You will find that the cause of your anger is not the other person, but within you. It is your past. Someone accidentally touches the anger in you, and you erupt. Anger is like an infected wound."

(From Amma's *Awaken Children Volume IV*)

**Love, Sondra**

*March 4, 2020*

### ❧ WORDS OF WISDOM

❧ When someone is supporting you and you don't think it feels like support, perhaps you have them set up as your obstetrician. You can say, "This feels like an attack. Maybe I am projecting onto you."

❡ Never perceive yourself as unjustly treated. Remember you are creating every reaction you get from someone. Consider that this reaction may be a result of your karma.

❡ Do not give your power away. Know that your opinions count. The other person's opinions count as well. Space must be created for both opinions.

❡ Know whether you are into "victim consciousness" or your God power. You must know the difference. If you stay connected to love and the Source, you will be able to think from your center and for yourself.

❡ Mean what you say at all times. Do not give double messages or withhold information. Your actions should match your words.

❡ Know that the key to vitality is to stay in the present. Give up your fear of being out of control.

**Love, Sondra**

*March 5, 2020*

### ❡ A PRAYER FOR ANY SITUATION

1) I place this situation of _____ in the hands of infinite love and wisdom. 2) Divine Love and Wisdom are united in this situation expressing through it perfectly now. 3) I cast this burden on the Christ within. 4) The light of Christ now streams through this _____. 5) I ask for a definite, unmistakable lead as to what to do. 6) Infinite Spirit, reveal to me the way, let me know if there is anything for me to do. 7) This _____ is a perfect idea in the Divine Mind.

**Love, Sondra**

*March 6, 2020*

### ❡ TRAVEL RESTRICTION TO INDIA

❡ We received word that we may not be allowed to go to India because of the COVID-19 virus. We had 20 signed up and paid with tickets going this month. So this is a HUGE deal and I am processing this right now. Babaji has trained me to let go quickly so I can do it; however, it is very complex to handle, and we must be very careful not to go into fear.

❡ I have not been listening to the news on purpose, so I did not realize how bad things have become. All I can say is I feel fortunate to have Babaji in my life and if He does not want us to come to India with a group then so be it.

**Love, Sondra**


*March 7, 2020*

### ❡ COVID 19 MAKING ITSELF KNOWN

❡ Spoke to India last night. Impossible to go now. Even Ammachi has stopped giving darshan!

❡ Went to the store and tried to buy disinfectant wipes as I usually carry them routinely. I was not thinking of the virus then. But they are all gone. Many shelves are bare. Really shocking. Now I know how they felt during the plague.

❡ I would have a drink, but I am not drinking anymore. So I have been eating a lot of chocolate! I must have been a bit nervous as I accidentally deleted all my inbox emails.

**Love, Sondra**

*March 8, 2020*

## ♫ MISSING INDIA AND POSSIBLY EUROPE

♫ So far everyone scheduled for India with us took the cancellation really well. The only time I have missed going since 1977 was the year after my mother died so it is strange for me. Now the next hurdle is going to be our European tour in May and June. We had Italy scheduled so I doubt we can go. A lot of our income comes from traveling in foreign countries so this will be an interesting challenge.

♫ Israel says they will have a vaccination in several weeks, but then it will take 90 days to clear. So if that is true it will be marvelous, but it will still be AFTER the time we are to go to Europe.

**Love, Sondra**

*March 9, 2020*

## ♫ WORKING CLOSER TO HOME

♫ We have been holding a 5-Day Intensive Liberation Breathing training here at our apartment. It has turned out really great. We will have to do more of these now. Babaji wants us to apparently work in our own countries. We are open to work anywhere in the USA now.

♫ I am still collecting personal lies and am always amazed when I get a new one, as I have already got 350 for our book on that subject (*Liberation*)! Here I found one: "I am not noticed." It is slightly different from the one "I am invisible."

♫ If you have not read that book, you would be surprised how important it is for your life.

**Love, Sondra**

*March 10, 2020*

## ꠦ THE AARTI AND INDIA

> ꠦ *Thou art a constant spring of bliss, the infinite essence of truth.*
>
> *Thou art form and the base of everything pervading the whole material world.*
>
> *Thou art worthy of being served by Lakshmi and Vishnu, yet Thou art their selfless servant.*
>
> *The reward of divine love comes to those alone, who always repeat Thy name.*
>
> *Have mercy, have mercy*

(From the Aarti which we sing to Babaji in the temple)

ꠦ I can hardly believe that I cannot go this year. It has not totally sunk in yet. Of course, we can sing the Aarti here. From the 25th to the 31st will be the exact time of the ceremonies to the Divine Mother. Tune in.

**Love, Sondra**


*March 11, 2020*

## ꠦ THE INTERRUPTION OF ABUNDANCE

ꠦ It really got to me today that my supermarket had bare shelves. Usually everything is totally abundant. Now there is no toilet paper, there are no disinfectant wipes, there is no hand soap, there is no dishwasher soap, etc. It made me depressed. It is feeling like America's Great Depression.

ꠦ I am asking Babaji for a direct sign as to whether we can go on our European tour in May and June. The media said that Israel had an inoculation and now they are saying it is not true.

**Love, Sondra**

*March 12, 2020*

## ♪ PREVENTION

♪ As soon as the pandemic was declared, Babaji came and told me what to do. He said the only hope was going to be the reciting of the mantra OM NAMAHAA SHIVAYAA. One should say it out loud and get it into the lungs. If for some reason you cannot say it out loud, then whisper it. Singing it is ideal.

♪ Chanting is one of the most powerful things you can do for yourself (we recommend Om Namaha Shivaya by Robert Gass) and it is recommended you immediately get mala beads. You should recite ten rounds of 108 daily (there must be 108 beads on the mala, and it is best if there are knots between the beads). The best of all would be ten rounds upon waking and ten rounds before going to sleep.

♪ Babaji always said this is the highest thought that there is. It has many meanings: It means: "Oh Lord you are my refuge, thy will be done." It means: "Infinite Spirit, Infinite Being, and Infinite Manifestation." It means: "I bow to God within."

♪ I strongly recommend that you take heed and listen to Babaji asap.

**Love, Sondra**

*March 13, 2020*

### ֍ REPEAT GOD'S NAME

֍ Babaji said, "Always repeat God's name (Om Namaha Shivaya) whatever you do, wherever you are. It is the original mantra. The mantra is the nectar nourishing you. It is like plugging you into the Source. It charges you up. It leads to remembering your total union with God (which is what we need right now). It enlivens the inner consciousness and helps overcome suffering. It provides protection and brings inner peace. Behold the glory and power of the Divine Name! God's name is the greatest treasure on earth. You can achieve all things with it.

֍ The name of God is also a cure for all diseases. (This is called Divine Namapathy.) You can take this medicine for curing anything. You can also administer it to others. The only real doctor is God. When you are in gloom, despair, or have low energy, it is also the supreme pick-me-up. We need this now. You know that.

**Love, Sondra**

*March 14, 2020*

### ֍ COPING WITH THE PANDEMIC AND STAYING STRONG

֍ My friend Jane tells me that the Italians are singing from their balconies! Sounds right to me. Have you recited or sung the mantra in the last few days?

ℐ I also recommend you read our book *Physical Immortality* which will strengthen your life urge a lot. You can order it on Amazon.

ℐ My clairvoyant recommends ascorbic acid powder (Vitamin C) drunk in water. I will give you the dosages tomorrow. I still find it hard to go to the supermarket.

**Love, Sondra**

*March 16, 2020*

ℐ **AMMA RECOMMENDS A MANTRA**

ℐ This is what Amma recommends. Listen to this or sing it 9X
https://www.youtube.com/watch?v=Rn1JJb5N9cY&feature=youtu.be.

ℐ Mantra chanted by Tavamithram Sarvada. I pray that those of you afflicted by disease receive proper medical care and take the help of this powerful mantra to develop sheer mental power to cure you of your illness. Please note that the mantra helps in removing fear from one's mind and strengthening it in order to promote the healing process. Along with chanting this mantra, following a pure VEGAN diet, i.e., consuming animal-products-free food and receiving proper medical care are of utmost importance. Translation of the mantra: I bow down and pray to the Lord Dhanvantari, the incarnation of Bhagavan (Lord) Vishnu and known as Sudharshana Vaasudeva Dhanvantari (The Lord of Ayurveda). You hold in your hands, the Kalasha (a pitcher) filled with the nectar of immortality. You can remove all fears and cure all diseases. You are the protector and well-wisher of the three worlds. O manifestation of Bhagavan Vishnu. O

Bhagavan Dhanvantari. You are the ultimate healer. I pray to you to keep me in your ring of protection.

**Love, Sondra**

*March 18, 2020*

ℭ **CREDO**

ℭ "The goal is God. God I am united with universal life and power and all of this strength is focused in my entire nature, making me so positive with God Perfect energy that I send it out to every form and I make it so positive that all may be transformed into harmony and perfection. I know that they are all in accord with infinite life and God freedom and peace.

ℭ My mind is fully polarized with Infinite Intelligent Wisdom. Every faculty of my entire body finds free expression through my mind and all humanity does express the same.

ℭ My heart is filled to overflowing with peace, love, and joy of the conquering Christ. I see in every face that conquering Christ. My heart is strong with God love and I know that it fills the heart of all humanity. God life fully enriches my entire blood stream and fills my body with the purity of Divine Life.

ℭ God is all life. I am inspired with life with every breath and my lungs take in life with every breath and it fills my blood stream with vitalizing life."

(From *Life and Teachings of the Masters* - Volume 5 by Baird T. Spalding)

**Love, Sondra**

*March 20, 2020*

**♪ A POEM GONE VIRAL**

♪ "In the Time of Pandemic"

And people stayed home
And they read books and listened
And rested and exercised
And made art and played games
And learned new ways of being and were still.
And they listened deeper
Some meditated
Some prayed
Some danced
Some met their shadows
And the people began to think differently.
And the people healed.
And, in the absence of people living in ignorant,

Dangerous, mindless, and heartless ways,
The earth began to heal.
And when the danger passed,
And the people joined together again,
They grieved their losses,
And made new choices
And dreamed new images
And created new ways to live
And heal the earth fully
As they had been healed.
(Written by Kitty O'Meara, Madison, WI in March 2020)

**Love, Sondra**

SONDRA RAY

**March 20, 2020**

**🎵 FROM MARKUS'S NEW BOOK**

🎵 *The Second Coming: You Are The Christ*, coming April 1, 2020.
🎵 "A Meditation for Times of Trouble: 14—MAR—2020
I call upon God's Name and on my own. ACIM, Lesson 183.

1.  May the Power of Christ blanket you.
2.  May the Blanket of Christ protect you.
3.  May the Protection of Christ calm you.
4.  May the Calmness of Christ still you.
5.  May the Stillness of Christ awaken you.
6.  May the Awakened Christ bless you.
7.  May the Blessed Christ give you peace.
8.  May the Peaceful Christ give certainty.
9.  May the Certain Christ resolve all things.
10. May the Resolute Christ help you.
11. May the Helpful Christ give you solutions.
12. May the Solution of Christ bring you joy.
13. May the Joyful Christ uplift your hearts.
14. May the Uplifted Christ shine on you.
15. May the Shining Christ brighten you.
16. May the Brightened Christ show you.
17. May the Showing Christ lead your way.
18. May the Leading Christ simplify your life.
19. May the Simple Christ solve your problem.
20. May the Solution of Christ bring clarity.
21. May the Clear Christ show you the way.
22. May the Way of Christ be your rock.
23. May the Rock of Christ give you strength.
24. May the Strength of Christ make you mighty.
25. May the Mighty Christ give you relief.
26. May the Relieving Christ help you relax.
27. May the Relaxing Christ descend upon you.

28. May the Descended Christ engulf your being.
29. May the Engulfing Christ surround you fully.
30. May the Surrounding Christ shelter you."

**Love, Sondra and Markus**

*March 22, 2020*

### ♪ A PLAN I COULD NOT MATERIALIZE

♪ Because I was a nurse, a Peace Corps Volunteer, and now a Babaji devotee, I really wanted to help people in this building. I wanted to tell them about the mantra as a protection from the virus. I even wrote up something I was going to put under everyone's door. (There are 140 apartments here.) I had a fantasy of getting everyone in the building to do the mantra!

♪ But in reality, it became clear I would have to get permission from the front office. It was obvious they would not let me do this because they would say I was promoting myself and probably we were a cult. Furthermore, some people in the building would be offended by such a thing and might complain to the office, even if I did have permission. So because of this and other reasons, I had to scrap the idea and throw away the papers. My clairvoyant said our energy is already helping them and I certainly do hope so.

**Love, Sondra**

*March 23, 2020*

## ℘ FASTING FROM THE NEWS

℘ I have started fasting from the news and now I feel so much better. For about a week I was obsessed with what is going on in the news. People sent me all kinds of stuff like conspiracy theories, and I got way too involved. So I stopped. Now I feel so much better.

℘ I feel so lucky we have such a beautiful space to live in and such a wonderful relationship. I can't help wondering how some people are doing staying home all the time. What if their living space is not nice? What if their relationship is a disaster and now they have to tolerate it 24/7? It is really a chance to clean up everything. Cleanliness is Godliness.

℘ We are available for sessions if anyone needs help.

**Love, Sondra**

*March 24, 2020*

## ℘ WHAT TO DO?

℘ What to do with my time? We deliberately do not have TV, so I can't do binge watching. I have not felt like reading for some reason, so I have been watching Ted Talks. I recommend this one: "The Next 100 Years of Your Life" by Pedro Domingos. At night we have been watching Woody Allen movies—the funny ones so we can laugh.

℘ One has to keep putting the situation into the hands of Infinite Love and Wisdom. I am asking for a definite, unmistakable lead as to what to do.

**Love, Sondra**

*March 25, 2020*

**♪ NAVARATRI – DAY 1**

♪ Today is the first day of Navaratri (Divine Mother Festival) when we are usually in India. So we have started fasting, chanting the Aarti, and we are also speaking about the Divine Mother at 1PM EST.

♪ In India they say there is nothing higher than worship of the Divine Mother so that is the obvious thing to do if you want to stay high. Sri Aurobindo also said worship of the Divine Mother is the final stage of perfection in a soul.

♪ Posted on our March 25, 2020 Facebook page is a video "The Divine Mother Celebration: Day #1" duration 30:24 (30 minutes 24 seconds).

**Love, Sondra**

*March 26, 2020*

**♪ NAVARATRI – DAY 2**

♪ Posted on our March 26, 2020 Facebook page is a video "The Divine Mother Celebration: Day #2" (duration 30 minutes 22 seconds).

**Love, Sondra**

If you see Him who has not been born of a woman,
throw your face to the ground and worship Him –
He is your Father.

Gospel of St. Thomas

*March 27, 2020*

**ॐ NAVARATRI – DAY 3**

℣ The below photo of Babaji is very powerful to meditate on. It was taken soon after he materialized in the cave. He went on top of the mountain above the cave and sat like this for 45 days and 45 nights without sleeping, eating, or even drinking. He had to keep his eyes closed because he was such pure Spirit that if he opened them people would faint.

℣ Posted on our March 27, 2020 Facebook page is a video "The Divine Mother Celebration: Day #3" (duration 34 minutes 33 seconds).

**Love, Sondra**

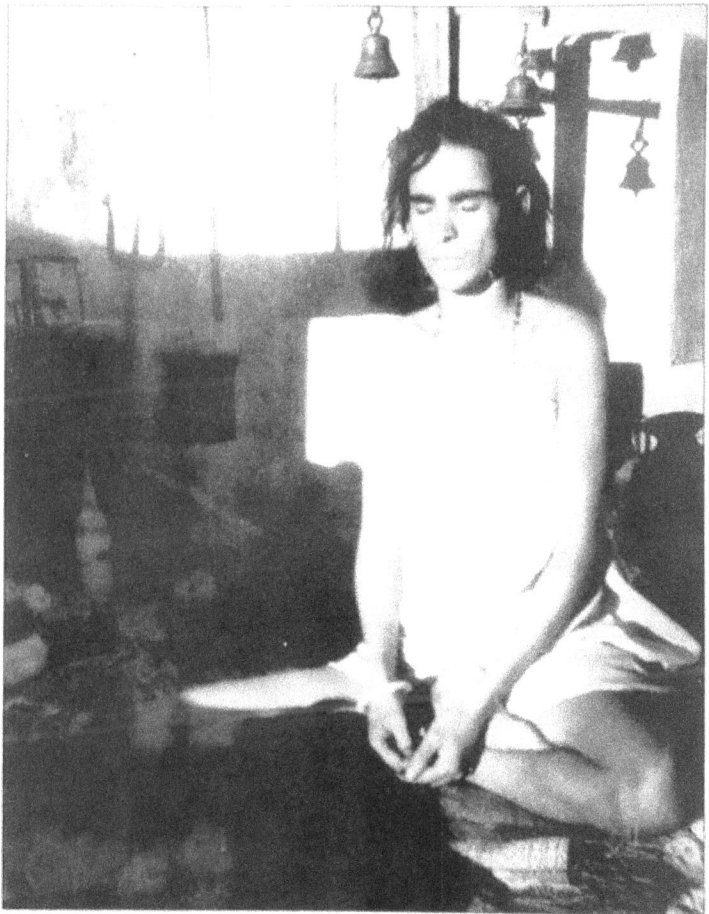

In the beginning was Brahman,
With whom was the Word.
And the Word was truly the Supreme Brahman.
> Rig Veda 12th Century BC

And the Word became flesh,
And dwelt among us...
Full of grace and truth.
> John 1:1, 1:14

**March 28, 2020**

## ꒰ NAVARATRI – DAY 4

꒰ Lesson 264 in the ACIM Workbook says the following: "I am surrounded by the Love of God. Father, You stand before me and behind, beside me, in the place I see myself, and everywhere I go. You are in all the things I look upon, the sounds I hear, and every hand that reaches for my own. In You time disappears, and place becomes a meaningless belief. For what surrounds Your Son and keeps him safe is Love itself. There is no Source but this, and nothing is that does not share its holiness; that stands beyond Your one creation, or without the Love which holds all things within itself. Father, Your Son is like Yourself. We come to You in Your Own Name today, to be at peace within Your everlasting Love. My brothers, join with me in this today. This is salvation's prayer. Must we not join in what will save the world, along with us?" Babaji said the same!

꒰ Posted on our March 28, 2020 Facebook page is a video "The Divine Mother Celebration: Day #4" (duration 41 minutes 24 seconds).

**Love, Sondra**

We are all one with each other and with God.
BABAJI

*March 29, 2020*

**ॐ NAVARATRI – DAY 5**

℈ Hi everyone, we are having connectivity problems today. Very sorry. We will try tomorrow. 1 pm EDT.

℈ Read your Divine Mother Names and we will see you tomorrow on Monday.

**Love, Sondra**

*March 30, 2020*

## ℈ NAVARATRI – DAY 6

℈ Below is a picture of Babaji when He first manifested in 1970. We will see you all at 1PM Eastern . . . God Willing the internet is OK.

℈ Posted on our March 30, 2020 Facebook page is a video "The Divine Mother Celebration: Day #6" (duration 21 minutes 23 seconds).

**Love, Sondra**

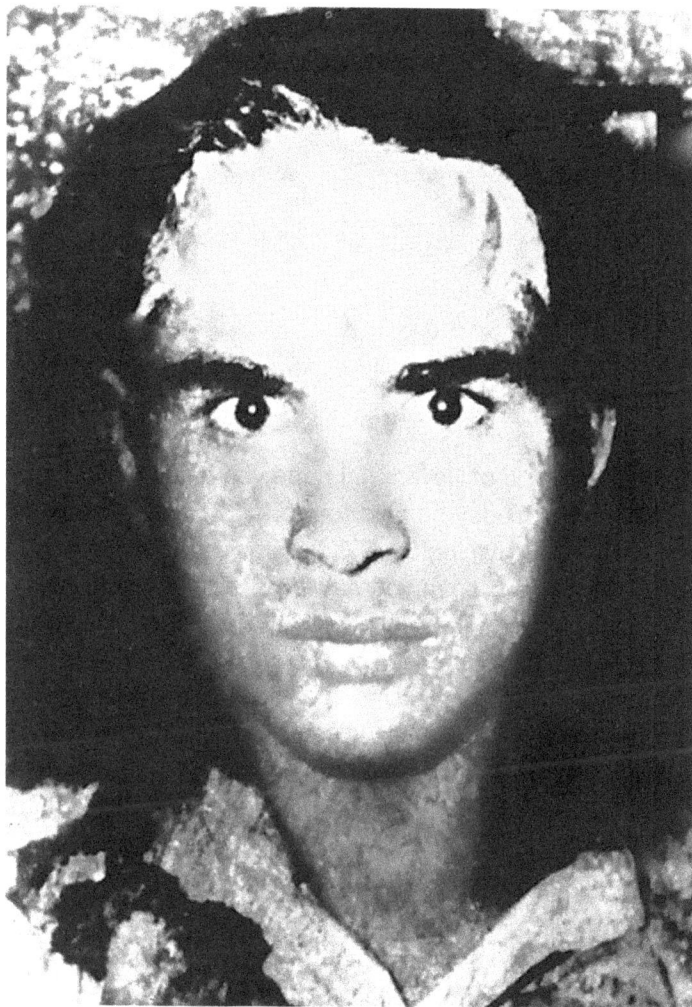

Babaji when he first manifested, 1970

*March 31, 2020*

ꢀ NAVARATRI – DAY 7

ᵍ Posted on our March 31, 2020 Facebook page is a video "The Divine Mother Celebration: Day #7" (duration 37 minutes 33 seconds).

**Love, Sondra**

*April 1, 2020*

**ᵍ NAVARATRI – DAY 8**

ᵍ Today is day 8 of Navaratri. I hope you enjoy the photo of Babaji below. Today he said to me: "Now you know why I moved you to Washington, D.C. Your mantras and chanting are helping everyone in your building and the whole city." I was always asking Babaji what it was He wanted us to do in Washington, D.C. It seemed so odd we could be of help here because we were gone so much on tours. Now we are going nowhere, and I am so glad we can be of service this way.

ᵍ Posted on our April 1, 2020 Facebook page is a video "The Divine Mother Celebration: Day #8" (duration 32 minutes 03 seconds).

**Love, Sondra**

I AM the Way and the Truth and the Life.
John 14:6

*April 2, 2020*

## ℐ NAVARATRI – DAY 9

ℐ Today is the last day of Navaratri. May you all be newly blessed.

♫ Posted on our April 2, 2020 Facebook page is a video "The Divine Mother Celebration: Day #9" (duration 35 minutes 55 seconds).

**Love, Sondra**

To Him who has the highest love for God, and for Guru as God,
To that great soul the truths taught here shine forth in all their glory...
OM Shanti Shanti Shanti.

Svetashvatara Upanishad VII-VI24

*April 3, 2020*

## ♪ CLEARING BODILY PAIN AND SYMPTOMS

♪ I was judging myself for not handling this whole crisis better. This was causing some pain in my cranium. I was rebirthing myself about all this and trying to let it go. Babaji came to me and told me to stop judging myself because it was keeping the pain in place. Then I remembered ACIM lesson "Today I will judge nothing that occurs." Then He told me to love the pain. I knew that was the right answer, but I did not know how to do it. I asked Markus, "How do I love the pain?" Markus told me that admitting that I did not know was the first step and then the second step was to turn it over to the Holy Spirit.

♪ Then I remembered ACIM again which said that unless we work with the Holy Spirit in healing, the results will vary. So I turned it over and told the Holy Spirit I did not know how to love pain. This started working. I understood then that pain is the ego, and that the ego cannot stand love. So if I were to love it, the pain (ego) would leave. This made sense to me, and I knew it should be applied to any symptom or disease in the body. I thought if I had the virus, I would have trouble loving it, even if I understood the principle. So then one would definitely have to turn that over to the Holy Spirit.

♪ "Holy Spirit I don't know how to love these symptoms I have. Please show me how to do it. I turn it over to you for healing."

**Love, Sondra**

*April 4, 2020*

## ♪ WORRY AND FEAR

253

᛿ I think the worst part of having a condition in the body is the worry that you won't get over it or it will get worse. That thought *What if I never get over this?* comes up and haunts you. Or *What if this gets worse?* I was reading that Chris Cuomo was having these very fears today. He is stuck in the basement (in quarantine).

᛿ Of course, fear makes the thing worse. The condition is started by fear and then one adds this extra fear and so you get more stuck. Or maybe you have no symptoms, but you are stuck in fear that you will get the virus. Fear is a low frequency and makes you more susceptible. Once again, this is when you have to turn that fear over to the Holy Spirit. It is not easy to think it away by oneself. The minute you catch yourself with some fear like this, you need to remember the Holy Spirit. Everyone is coming to a place of helplessness, and it makes one panic. The Holy Spirit is the answer.

᛿ P.S. Markus and I have been happily married 11 years today!

**Love, Sondra**

*April 5, 2020*

᛿ **BUILDING IMMUNITY**

᛿ What are you doing to build your immunity? We are taking Vitamin C powder (working up to 12,000 mg per day) plus homeopathy, plus Manuka honey, plus zinc. But the main thing is ten rounds (108 = 1 round) of the mantra Om Namaha Shivaya morning and evening.

᛿ You have to be disciplined. You have to decide you won't miss doing this. Students of ours who are doing this mantra are feeling strong and not afraid. It is like taking a medicine

254

that prevents sickness. This name of God is the greatest treasure on earth. It is like nectar nourishing you. It charges you up. I keep saying this to remind you if you have not started it . . . why not today?

**Love, Sondra**

*April 6, 2020*

ℐ **TRUST THE HOLY SPIRIT**

ℐ "The only way we can be free is if help comes from outside the system, i.e., via the Holy Spirit. The Holy Spirit lifts us out of quicksand. He (She) is not of this world. He (She) acts in our minds."

ℐ Some people don't trust that the Holy Spirit can heal us. You have to trust that the Holy Spirit can solve the problem and bring us along. You have to invoke the Holy Spirit and trust. If you cannot have complete trust, you say to the Holy Spirit, "I offer you the trust I do have. I have done what I can." The Holy Spirit says you need just a little willingness.

ℐ ACIM says there is only one problem: the belief that we are separate. This causes all our troubles. Now is the time to accept that you are one with God which is true because there is no separation. Say, "I am united with Jesus and Babaji and the Divine Mother." Saying this will strengthen you.

**Love, Sondra**

*April 7, 2020*

ℐ **FOCUS ON THE FATHER**

255

☙ Now is the time for me to stop looking at all the videos people are sending me about what is going on behind the scenes. It does not help my mood.

☙ So instead let's focus on ACIM, Lesson 264:

☙ "Father, You stand before me and behind, beside me, in the place I see myself, and everywhere I go. You are in all the things I look upon, the sounds I hear, and every hand that reaches for my own. In You time disappears, and place becomes a meaningless belief. For what surrounds Your Son and keeps him safe is Love itself. There is no source but this, and nothing is that does not share its holiness; that stands beyond Your one creation, or without the Love which holds all things within itself. Father, Your Son is like Yourself. We come to You in Your Own Name today, to be at peace within Your everlasting Love."

**Love, Sondra**

*April 8, 2020*

## ☙ WIRED TO THE DIVINE MOTHER

☙ I had a dream that an immortal came to find me. He was approximately 145 years old, and he hugged me and kissed me so much. I don't know who that was; could have been Babaji who appears in so many forms. After the hugging he told me "I am wired to the Divine Mother." I thought that was perfect because in India they say only the Divine Mother can grant the boon of physical immortality. That always made sense to me because the original spark of creation is a feminine aspect they say. So when you worship Her, you are worshiping the life force and all.

❡ This dream also inspired me to start reading the book *The Mother* by Sri Aurobindo. I have not been able to read a book this whole month for some reason. I finally broke through.

**Love, Sondra**


*April 9, 2020*

❡ **FAITH RISES ABOVE FEAR**

❡ Babaji always told us "Faith is everything." At a time like this, it is more important than ever. When we have any fear, we are not in faith. He also reminded us that "God's will is Perfect Happiness." (ACIM) God is going to lead us to more happiness, never more catastrophe. In the Old Testament catastrophes like this were considered punishment from God. That is not what is going on. They even say this virus is man-made. I don't want to debate that, but I do know it is not God's will.

❡ Most people only see the fear of all the problems they are going to have. Markus tells me we are into the unknown. He said to me that one should not fear the unknown. In the unknown new solutions can come. We have to have faith that God is going to solve this. Lack of faith is saying that we don't have an answer and God is not helping us at all. God is going to lead us to the solution. You have to stay STRONG. Faith makes you strong. Fear makes you weak. Give up all worst-case scenarios.

**Love, Sondra**

*April 10, 2020*

## ♫ FORGET ALL THOUGHTS OF DEATH

♫ "The Holy Spirit bids you bring each terrible effect to Him, that you may look together on its foolish cause and laugh with him for a while. Bring all forms of suffering to Him. All of them are easily undone. (You would not react to all figures in a dream you knew you were dreaming).

♫ What would you choose: life or death? Death is the opposite of peace because it is the opposite of life. Life is peace. Forget all thoughts of death and you will find you have the peace of God." (From ACIM notes)

**Love, Sondra**

*April 11, 2020*

## ♫ THE VISION OF HOLINESS AT EASTERTIME

♫ "This Easter, look with different eyes upon your brother. There is no fear in love. The Song of Easter is the glad refrain the Son of God was never crucified. Let us lift up our eyes together, not in fear. Easter, in which we join in glad awareness that the Son of God is risen from the past and has awakened to the present. Now he is free, unlimited in his communion with all that is within him.

♫ It is almost Easter, the time of resurrection. Let us give redemption to each other and share in it that we may rise as one in resurrection not separate in death."
(From A Course in Miracles)

**Love, Sondra**

*April 12, 2020*

## ❦ EASTER IS THE SIGN OF PEACE

❦ "For Easter is the sign of peace not pain. A slain Christ has no meaning. But the risen Christ becomes the symbol of the Son of God. Join now with me and throw away the thorns, offering the lilies to replace them. This Easter I would have the gift of your forgiveness offered by you to me. But let the whiteness of your shining gift of lilies speed him on his way to resurrection. The time of Easter is a time of JOY and not mourning. Look on your own risen friend and celebrate his holiness along with me. For Easter is the time of your salvation."

(From A Course in Miracles)

**Love, Sondra**

*April 13, 2020*

## ❦ THE BEAUTY OF ACIM LESSON 165

❦ "LET NOT MY MIND DENY THE THOUGHT OF GOD."
"The thought of God created you. It left you not, nor have you ever been apart from it an instant. It belongs to you. By it you live. It is your Source of life, holding you one with it, and everything is one with you because it left you not.

❦ The thought of God protects you, cares for you, makes soft your resting place and smooth your way, lighting your mind with happiness and love. Eternity and everlasting life shine in your mind, because the thought of God has left you not, and still abides with you." (ACIM, Lesson #165)

**Love, Sondra**

*April 14, 2020*

## ♫ WORSHIP ALL OF LIFE

♫ If we worship a person, we see no wrong in him whatsoever. We open ourselves completely to him and become his willing servant. If we worship our teacher, we will learn very quickly and completely from him, for we will be open and receptive to all he has to say. Worship, however, is invalid unless we worship ALL OF LIFE, for equality is the only Truth. (Notes from an old book called *Being the Christ*)

♫ By worshiping you will gain the most out of life. By worshiping you will feel the best you can feel. By worshiping you will contribute to a more advanced civilization. Not to worship is unnatural.

♫ Chanting is a form of worship. We hope you are chanting the mantra these days. Gratitude is, of course, a form of worship. I am once again going back to my gratitude journal. Spiritual poetry is worship. Send Markus your mobile number in an email if you would like that. ManMohan1008@gmail.com. You will get high hearing him recite these. A very high vibration!

**Love, Sondra**

*April 15, 2020*

## ♫ HEAVEN IS YOURS FOR THE ASKING

♫ "Deny not Heaven. It is yours today, but for the asking. Who would deny his safety, his peace, his joy, his healing, and his peace of mind, his quiet rest, his calm awakening, if he but recognized where they abide? Would he not instantly prepare to go where they abide? Would he not instantly go where they are found, abandoning all else as worthless in comparison with them? And having found them, would he not make sure they stay with him, and he remain with them? ♪ Nor need you perceive how great the gift, how changed your mind will be before it comes to you. Ask to receive, and it is given you. Conviction lies within it. Till you welcome it as yours, uncertainty remains. Yet God is fair. Sureness is not required to receive what only your acceptance can bestow. Ask with desire!" (From a Course in Miracles, Lesson 165)

**Love, Sondra**

*April 16, 2020*

### ♪ WORSHIP TO THE DIVINE MOTHER

♪ Oh Shiva, You are the embodiment of ultimate bliss and conscious Energy. You are supreme knowledge of the Absolute. You are the image of infinite compassion, unfathomable as is the deep sea. Oh Durga, Goddess of the universe, I prostrate before you.
♪ Oh Universal Mother, you give me shelter. In truth, You are the One who gives life to all the beings of this world. You are the physician who cures the fevers of life and death cycles of this wheel of life. You are the source of life and liberation to all living beings. We pray to that timeless Energy which resides as Mother Goddess of Haidakhan.
♪ Remembering You is to crown the life with success, to attain liberation."
(From the Aarti)
♪ Remember that worship is the highest form of love.

**Love, Sondra**

*April 17, 2020*

## ❡ SOMETHING CAME UP FOR ME

❡ I really had to look at myself yesterday as my charge card was hacked for the second time since we have been under lockdown. How did I create THAT? I said to Markus, "I must be feeling insecure." Not that I walk around feeling that all day nor do I walk around feeling fear. But I had to face the fact that it must be going on in my subconscious. Fortunately, Capital One caught these hacks and notified us both times so we did not lose any money.

❡ But since we do not have a regular income like we did before, it is rather disconcerting. In other words, I was apparently having some CONCERN in my subconscious. What we did for an antidote was read ACIM, Lesson 47 – "God is the Strength in Which I Trust." It says right in there "Now try to slip past all concerns related to your own sense of inadequacy."

❡ I never thought of that. *I don't feel inadequate* I thought to myself. But the next line was this: "It is obvious that any situation that causes you concern is associated with feelings of inadequacy for otherwise you would believe that you could deal with the situation successfully." Wow. This lesson put me in a process and was very healing for me. I shifted AND stopped judging myself for it all.

**Love, Sondra**

*April 18, 2020*

## ❡ SOLITUDE

❡ Solitude is one of the best ways to be spiritually nourished. It is very different than be lonely, although many people are afraid of solitude because they are afraid of being lonely. If you are one of those who are living alone right now, I honor you. You are truly learning to live with yourself. One has to be good at that before one can expect a partner to live with you. So in a way, solitude can be the end of loneliness. When you master solitude, many people will want to be with you because you have learned to love yourself.

❡ In solitude you can clear the thoughts that make your life difficult. People are often afraid of solitude because they are afraid of their own thoughts! But once you are enlightened and you know for sure you can change any negative thought at any time to positive thoughts, there is nothing to be afraid of. You can be in charge of your own mind and your feelings. You are having the opportunity, like never before, to observe your mind. This is an exquisite opportunity to remember your connection with God. That is why this whole thing (the virus) can be the Great Awakening! You may finally begin to listen to the voice of the Holy Spirit, that voice that knows your highest good, that voice that guides you perfectly. That voice that leads you back to joy. It is tempting to keep the TV going now, but please don't rip yourself off.

❡ We have the chance now to get new ideas, new ways of clearing problems. Use this time to raise your self-esteem.

**Love, Sondra**

*April 19, 2020*

### ❡ MY CURE FOR TENSION

❡ I awoke at 2 AM with some tension in my shoulders. I asked Markus to massage them which he did, and then he surprised me with a better cure. He suddenly started reciting a poem he wrote to the Divine Mother which he knew by heart. If you read it, I think you will get high like I did.

♪ "Make me the vessel of Your Love. Open my mind to receive the gift of all-pervasive Presence that is the essence of You everywhere. In all situations and places I can turn my attentions to You and surrender my senses to a different perception, one of gentleness and peace, one of beauty and grace, one of harmony and aliveness. I am but the container of what cannot be contained. Every instant of every day is a moment of Your timelessness. Forever do You go on extending Yourself to all living creatures, all elements in all galaxies, all atoms and all molecules making up matter itself.

♪ "What could I add to the great writings of this world that have not already been written? What praises could I sing to You that have not already been sung? My pen is still and my voice is mute. Yet You direct the thoughts that arrive in my mind as I am open to receive Your words of beatitude. Guide my hand as I scribe only what comes from You. Otherwise let my mind be silent and my hand cease all its meaningless movements.

♪ "This urge to express Your grandeur, I can hardly contain, yet I will hold myself in waiting, knowing You will always breathe the firmament of inspiration into me. Then it will be You who fills my sky with gladness and extends the very essence of creation into these songs. You are the great poet of constellations. How could I approach Your compositions so vast except with the same core of interstellar possibility?

♪ "I write to touch Your stars that are the pigments in my palette of divine possessions."

(Ode #57 from *Odes to the Divine Mother* by Markus Ray)

**Love, Sondra**

*April 20, 2020*

## ♪ TODAY IS THE BEGINNING OF OUR NEW LIFE

♪ "Today is the beginning of our new life!" That is what Markus wrote on my computer last night after I was asleep. I was stunned to find it this morning. It really got me thinking. It was so refreshing to see that and read that. It made me feel younger. It was such a surprise. Most people over 60 don't think like that.

♪ I was rebirthing with Babaji yesterday and I did in fact get the message that I could write several books at once. In other words, I don't have to limit myself to one book at a time. Why be bored? I can switch back and forth. So this is a time we can all get more creative. Some days I just did not feel like writing the book I was writing. So I could just start a different one and go back to that one. What a revelation!

**Love, Sondra**

*April 21, 2020*

## ♪ A NEW LIFE

♪ Well, we truly did start a new life yesterday. Babaji rebirthed me again. This went on for three hours. We received a new book to write together. It is kind of like the thrill of getting pregnant. We also got a new direction for our work.

♪ It is a good practice to start your life over and re-invent yourself. I have had to do that many times; it keeps you young. I am also thrilled because Markus is memorizing his poems to the Divine Mother, so I get to hear those praises throughout our abode.

**Love, Sondra**

*April 23, 2020*

## ♫ DOING WHAT WE CAN

♫ Today we are speaking with Estonians and the Spanish. Doing what we can.

♫ Markus has put up a site called SPIRIT PANTRY where we put up all our work for free and he is excited about that. We are starting a book called THE SUPERMARKET FOR A MEANINGFUL LIFE. The title seems so appropriate for these times since about the only place we can go is to the supermarket. Even that is precarious. Sometimes I use InstaCart which is a very fast delivery.

♫ My friends in Georgia are not too happy with their governor. I keep telling people this all is an opportunity for ascension. Last night we did 10 rounds of Om Namaha Shivaya and one round of another mantra for healing and another round of the anti-death mantra which is very long. We did this for a friend who is having a health matter. It works telepathically.

**Love, Sondra**

*April 25, 2020*

## ♫ TOO MUCH EMPATHY

♫ The trouble with me is I am too much an Empath. When the Texas massacre was on TV (and the place we were staying had the TV running all day) I developed a nosebleed that lasted 12 hours! I ended up in the emergency room as it would not stop. It was like a stigmata my guides said.

❡ Yesterday I started crying. I cried a lot for the world and for myself and for friends who are freaking out. (We get calls about family members going nuts.)

❡ Last night I dreamed people were going CRAZY. It was a rough night but at 4 AM I heard my husband chanting the mantra out loud in the living room. It was so comforting. So I got up and put my head in his lap.

❡ Okay today. We started the SPIRIT PANTRY which has a lot of our materials on it. Hope you like it.

**Love, Sondra**

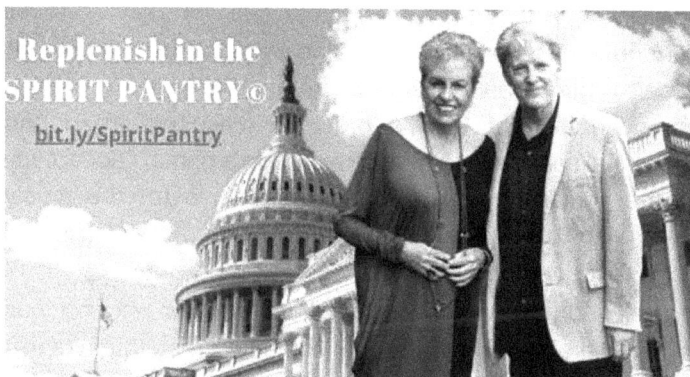

Replenish in the
SPIRIT PANTRY©
bit.ly/SpiritPantry

*April 26, 2020*

## ❡ DISCOVERING PAST LIVES

❡ A client we had recently did not understand what her personal lie was. It was all related to a very deep past life and that explained everything. She did great in the session; what a strong session we had.

❡ Dr. Roger Woolger says, "I have found more and more that there are certain layers to every major syndrome of physical illness, accidents, or weaknesses. The existence of a past life level of physical problems has been confirmed over and over again in the cases I have seen."

**Love, Sondra**

*April 27, 2020*

### ♫ EXAMPLE OF A PRAYER FOR MONEY

♫ "I hereby ask and humbly pray with all my heart and soul for Divine Abundance made manifest through personal fortune and success. I am willing to move beyond fear in order to fulfill God's Plan on earth and beyond. I am willing to move beyond fear in order to fulfill my group and individual service commitments. In God's name, I accept my divine heritage right now and thank thee for the timely answer to this prayer. God's will be done. Amen." (Repeat this prayer out loud X3.)

♫ "Beloved Presence of God: Oh, my beloved unconscious mind, I hereby ask and lovingly command that you take this thought form prayer to God along with the mana and vital force needed and necessary to manifest and demonstrate this prayer. Amen." (Breathe the prayer to God X4.)

♫ Lord, let the rain of blessings fall.

(From my book *Pele's Wish*)

**Love, Sondra**

*April 28, 2020*

### ♫ EXAMPLE OF PRAYER FOR RELATIONSHIP

♪ "Beloved Divine Mother = Ammachi, Babaji, Jesus, kahunas, all angels, and all good forces necessary: I come before you this day and pray with all my heart and soul and mind to request humbly that I now receive into my life the mate to whom my love belongs, the mate of my being.

♪ "Bring forth anything that I have not looked at in myself that would prevent me from receiving this now. Bring it all forward and let me work on it now. I call forth all my unfinished business so that I may finish it, so I will be ready to meet the mate of my being.

♪ "I ask for this Divine Dispensation in the name of Christ, and I accept this as done, as is thy will.

♪ "My beloved unconscious mind, I hereby ask and command that you take this thought form prayer with all my mana and vital force necessary to demonstrate this prayer to God the Source of our being. (Breathe three deep breaths.)

♪ "Beloved presence of God, Assembled Masters of God, let the rain of blessings fall. Thank you." Best to do for thirty days.

**Love, Sondra**


*April 29, 2020*

**♪ PRAYER USING OUR PALMS**

♪ Begin by placing your palms down as a symbolic indication of your willingness and desire to turn over any concerns you may have to God. The following are some examples:

- Lord, I give you my anger at . . . (palms down)
- Lord, I would like to receive your divine love for . . . (palms up)

- Lord, I release my fear of never being healed of . . . (palms down)
- Lord, I now receive certainty that I can be healed of . . . (palms up)
- Lord, I surrender my anxiety about my . . . (palms down)
- Lord, I receive your peace about . . . (palms up)

♫ Do not rush the process.

**Love, Sondra**

*April 30, 2020*

## ♫ FAMILY LOYALTY

♫ You may think you do not want to copy your parents, especially not their ailments. Of course, none of us WANTS to do that. But we feel a deep loyalty to our parents even if we are not close to them. In breathwork, we have seen family loyalty take an unconscious form of copying not only parental behavior, but also copying parental illness and death patterns. It is an unhealthy form of "loving" them. People that are natural conformists manifest these patterns frequently. Rebels, on the other hand, are less likely to manifest them.

♫ You might be in trouble when you reach the age that your parents died. You could unconsciously go into agreement and start killing things off. Don't kill off your body!

♫ The affirmations to use are these:

- I disconnect from my mother's mind.
- I disconnect from my father's mind.
- I disconnect from the family mind.

**Love, Sondra**

*May 1, 2020*

## ⚡ GETTING YOURSELF UNSTUCK

⚡ Are you feeling unhappy and isolated?

- Are you feeling anxious or moody, rarely feeling joy?
- Are you feeling helpless, can't move forward?
- Are you sick, in pain, or is your vital energy blocked?
- Are you feeling an urge to attack?
- Are you not able to get your personal relationship clear?
- Are you feeling financial traumas?

⚡ It is probable during this crisis you feel some of these things. If so, you need to give yourself more special attention. The situation is calling for spiritual purification. Don't stay stuck. Get a Liberation Breathing session or do some chanting or do A Course in Miracles lesson. AT LEAST write down your negative thoughts, look at them, and turn them around into affirmations. Or you can write a letter to the Dream Team (Babaji, Jesus, and Divine Mother) and express everything. Then put it under your altar cloth. (You should have an altar.) That technique ALWAYS works for me.

**Love, Sondra**

*May 2, 2020*

## ⚡ BLESSING INSTEAD OF JUDGING

⚡ The kahunas in Hawaii teach that even mentally criticizing others affects your body. Criticism of the self or others causes stress and inhibits awareness and energy flow, making you weaker and more susceptible to illness.

❡ The Bible teaches us that someone who is thankful for ALL things will be made glorious and that attitudes of love, praise, and gratitude fill one with the incomprehensible power of the Spirit. These are called "ascension attitudes."

❡ To break the habit of judging a person, try blessing the situation instead. Support the person who is moving through the offensive pattern, bless them, see them as healed of it, and honor and respect their God Self. Blessing what you want daily and focusing on PRAISE as a habit will create a safe space in your primary relationship. Your partner will become more willing to work out issues and their dark shadows.

**Love, Sondra**

*May 4, 2020*

## ❡ HANDLING CHANGE

❡ We are all in a huge change. Many people are afraid of change. Perhaps we fear it because the first big transition we experienced—from a liquid environment in the womb to the atmosphere—happened very quickly and we got hurt. Our birth trauma hurt us. So we unconsciously think change can hurt.

❡ Our fear also comes from a need to control everything with the mistaken idea that we can. Right now, we feel out of control, and this is uncomfortable. Control leaves us feeling rigid. So now if we don't change when our environment is changing, we will feel even more uncomfortable. We cannot hang on to the old when the new is arriving.

♪ So how do we handle the chaos that comes with change? With fear or with creativity? Let's have the thought that change is fun and exciting. A friend taught me this: "All losses are gains not recognized." We are losing our old life but maybe our new life will somehow be better.

**Love, Sondra**

*May 5, 2020*

## ♪ LEARN FORGIVENESS

♪ Have you forgiven everyone 100 percent? The unforgiving mind is full of fear and offers love no room to be itself. The unforgiving mind is sad without hope of respite and release from pain. The unforgiving mind is torn with doubt, confused about itself and all it sees. The unforgiving mind is afraid to go ahead, afraid to stay. The unforgiving mind does not believe that giving and receiving are the same.
♪ Forgiveness must be learned. Forgiveness is the key to happiness. It is not that you can't forgive; it is that you won't, so it is a stubborn refusal. Forgiveness is a decision. You have to decide to do it. If you want peace, you can only find it through forgiveness. The holiest of all spots is where an ancient hatred has become present love.

**Love, Sondra**

*May 6, 2020*

## ♪ DO YOU HAVE A LOVE OF CORRECTION?

♪ It is a great thing to have. The art of giving and receiving feedback occurs most successfully between couples who have agreed to make it happen between them. This should be established at the beginning of a relationship. You can begin this agreement by saying, "You always have my permission to point out things that I do that do not work for you, or that you believe could be detrimental to myself or others. Do I have the same permission from you?"

❡ I personally like feedback. It is one of the reasons I am where I am today. Decide how you can give feedback that is supportive, tender, and sweet. One agreement you can make is to give feedback on feedback. Such as, "I can hear you when you say it like this, but when you have a rough tone like that, I cannot hear you well and I shut down."

❡ Also try asking someone why they are doing something the way they are doing it BEFORE you criticize their action. Sometimes they have a very good reason. Be curious.

**Love, Sondra**

*May 7, 2020*

**❡ FIND THE PRESENT**

❡ Once I heard a minister say, "Let us keep no records of wrongdoing." I thought that was amazing advice for couples. ACIM says we must perceive our brothers (or partners) only as we see him NOW. We should find the present. We should see him without his past. We should perceive him born again. His errors are all past, and by perceiving him without them, we are releasing him and ourselves.

**Love, Sondra**

*May 8, 2020*

## ℐ SIGNS WITHIN RELATIONSHIPS

ℐ How do you tell if your relationship is really good? Well, are you getting stronger or weaker? If you are getting weaker (and giving your power away) you are on the wrong track. Also, a negative, unholy relationship feels depleting, like a depressing burden.

ℐ But a healthy, holy relationship is a whole different game. It nourishes each mate's individuality, strength, power, creativity, and productivity in the world. Each partner considers their spirituality the top priority. There is spontaneity and joy. Each partner feels safe to give feedback that produces movement within the relationship. There is no fear of communicating ANYTHING. Each person easily maintains a high degree of self-esteem. Each supports the other in getting into his or her power. Each knows how to process family patterns that come up without getting stuck. Everything they do is life-enhancing and harmony abounds.

**Love, Sondra**

*May 9, 2020*

## ℐ RESCURERS AND CARETAKERS

ℐ Are you a "rescuer" or a "caretaker"? These are the moves:

- Doing something you really don't want to do
- Saying yes when you mean no
- Doing something for someone although that person is capable and should be doing it for themself
- Meeting people's needs without being asked

- Doing more than a fair share of work after your help is required
- Consistently giving more than you receive in a particular situation
- Fixing people's feelings
- Doing people's thinking for them
- Speaking for another person
- Suffering people's consequences for them
- Solving people's problems for them
- Putting more interest and activity into a joint effort than the other person does
- Not asking for what you want, need, and desire

(Inspired by the book *Codependent No More* by Melody Beattie

**Love, Sondra**

*May 10, 2020*

**ᔕ GET OUT OF MISERY**

ᔕ There is no longer any reason to be sick, depressed, or miserable. We have all the techniques available to get out of misery. The only question is whether you will take advantage of them. You have to use them to get unstuck. To create misery takes a lot of effort, strain, and hard work indulging in negativity. Letting it go is always easier than hanging on to it.

ᔕ Some people say they don't have time to do the techniques of spiritual purification, and yet you can get more done in a shorter period of time if you are clear. Your work will improve, and you will make more money. When you are totally committed to your own spiritual enlightenment, then you learn how to master life. If you love life, it will begin to work for you.

¶ But some people have negative thoughts about life itself. That won't work because whatever you believe to be true, you create. So if you think life is hard, then it will be. We see what we expect, and we expect what we invite.

**Love, Sondra**

***May 11, 2020***

**¶ BABAJI'S MESSAGE**

Love and serve all humanity.
Help everyone.
Be happy. Be courteous.
Be a dynamo of irrepressible happiness.
Recognize God and good in every face.
There is no saint without a past and no sinner without a future.
Praise everyone. If you cannot praise someone, let him go out of your life.
Be original. Be inventive.
Be courageous. Take courage again and again.
Do not imitate. Be strong. Be upright.
Think with your own head. Be yourself.
All perfection and every divine virtue are hidden inside you.
Reveal them to the world.
Wisdom too, is already within you – let it shine forth.
Let the Lord's Grace set you free.
Let your life be that of a rose – in silence, it speaks the language of fragrance.

**Love, Sondra**

*May 12, 2020*

### ℐ WHEN RESPECT DISAPPEARS

ℐ When respect disappears from a committed relationship, the couple often gives up and looks elsewhere. To keep your partner's respect for you, you don't have to be perfect. It is better to see your shadows and be willing to work on them. Your partner will respect you for being willing to work on yourself. And anyway, shadows are not the real you. They are like cobwebs covering up your Real Self.

ℐ The Real Self is your oneness with God. If you choose to disrespect someone because of their shadows, you are making their shadows real and you are re-enforcing them. You have to be looking at your own shadows.

ℐ Maintaining respect for someone when they have a money problem can be tricky. You might blurt out something horrible like, "What is wrong with you? Can't you even make a decent living?" But you need to look at how you attracted that situation in your own life. YOU ARE THE ONE YOU LIVE WITH.

ℐ You have to solve this problem together. You have to see that if your mate has that problem, you BOTH have that problem. Always respect your mate for being your mirror.

ℐ In some cases, one may have to leave the relationship to maintain their self-respect. But it is important to always follow up with self-analysis of one's own personal agenda.

**Love, Sondra**

*May 13, 2020*

### ℐ SIX BIGGEST MISTAKES WOMEN MAKE WITH MEN

1. Women act like mothers and treat their men like children.
2. Women sacrifice who they are and put themselves second in importance to the man they love.
3. Women fall in love with a man's potential.
4. Women cover up their excellence and competence.
5. Women give up their power.
6. Women act like little girls to get what they want from men.

(From *The Barbara De Angelis Show 1991*)

**Love, Sondra**

*May 14, 2020*

## ♪ SOME REALLY IMPORTANT LINES IN ACIM

♪ "You will attack what does not satisfy you to avoid seeing that you created it."

♪ "Beware of the temptation to perceive yourself unfairly treated."

♪ "Only you can deprive yourself of anything."

♪ "There is nothing that happens to you without you calling for it or asking for it."

**Love, Sondra**

*May 15, 2020*

## ♪ ASK YOUR PARTNER QUESTIONS

◢ Let's say your mate says something that bothers you. Shelf your desire to snap back. The most important part of this process is to ask your partner questions about his upsetting statement so you can follow his line of reasoning. If, for example, he says, "I wish you wouldn't spend so much time with that friend of yours!" Try asking a question like, "Oh, don't you like her?" Keep asking questions until something opens up. Try using your intuition to find out what really lies behind that statement. For example: "Do you feel I spend too little time with you?" Even if the answer is no, he will appreciate your concern. Tell him how you heard his statement and what you thought it meant. This way he can correct or confirm your understanding.

◢ And if your mate does something you don't like, I recommend the same thing. Ask them why they are doing it the way they are doing it! Try that.

**Love, Sondra**

*May 16, 2020*

## ◢ BEHAVIORS THAT WEAKEN ONE IN A RELATIONSHIP

◢ If one ends up weaker in a relationship then it is not a good relationship. Here are some types of destructive behaviors:

- Making the relationship top priority over everything else and neglecting other parts of life.
- Making your mate more important than God, yourself, and everyone else. Idolizing or worshipping this person.
- Assigning the relationship over to a priority other than spirituality.

- Attempting to become just like your mate and losing your individuality in the process.
- Being afraid to communicate your own ideas.
- Being afraid to confront your mate on weak areas and stuffing resentment about those areas.
- Protecting one's mate from productive feedback.
- Becoming insular by not having enough exposure to new friends and creative outlets. Getting into ruts.
- Giving your personal power away to your mate.
- Adopting the tendency to assume a set "role."
- Sinking into old family patterns.
- Lacking self-esteem.

 Indulging in these habits can make you very stuck and can lead to destruction of the relationship.

**Love, Sondra**


*May 17, 2020*

 **NOT OUR JOB**

 It is not our job to change our brother but accept him as he is for "his errors do not come from the truth that is him." We need to take a good look at where we invest our valuable energy. When we react to our brother's errors as if they are real, we MAKE them a reality. In confirming that our brother's sins are real, we condemn ourselves—for all of us comprise the Sonship. When we accept our brother unconditionally, on the other hand, we open the door to loving all humanity.

 Correction, however well intended, can also be a form of attack: "The choice to judge rather than to know is the cause of the loss of peace . . . You have no idea of the tremendous release and deep peace that comes from meeting yourself and your brothers totally without judgment. In the presence of knowledge all judgment is automatically suspended. When a brother behaves insanely you can heal him only by perceiving the sanity in him." (From A Course in Miracles)

**Love, Sondra**

*May 18, 2020*

### ꙮ DIVINE SUBSTANCE

ꙮ John Randolph Price, author of *The Abundance Book*, explains that God does not provide us with money or homes; He give us Himself. He gives us DIVINE SUBSTANCE and substance is molded by our thoughts. The substance becomes money and homes. This substance, or creative energy, flows through the mind of human beings and externalizes itself as a mirror of our thoughts and convictions. Money, he explains is an EFFECT, a by-product of this process. When we concentrate on the effect, we often forget the cause. As we lose sight of the cause, the effect begins to diminish. When we focus on GETTING money, we actually shut off the supply.

ꙮ Money is not your support. God is! You have to have a relationship with this substance God gives. You do that by having deep, profound gratitude.

**Love, Sondra**

*May 19, 2020*

### ꙮ BOOMERANG KARMA

❡ "John hurts Mary, and Mary (in a future existence) meets John in a new body, with a different name (sometimes a different sex) and hurts John back, through a dim subconscious awareness that he formerly hurt her. Then comes a new lifetime for both, and now it's John's turn to hurt Mary again, then Mary's to hurt John, with each becoming the channel for the other's boomerang karma in a chain of dreary, seemingly endless incarnations." (Linda Goodman)

❡ What a boring cycle of existence! Especially when it is so clear that this chain can be broken if either of them get enlightened and FORGIVE.

**Love, Sondra**

*May 20, 2020*

**❡ THE JOY OF GIVING**

❡ What has brought us joy during this sequester is GIVING a lot. We have been doing so many private sessions for free and so many group sessions for free. We have also been giving away books. It is not only a nice idea, but it also makes me feel more prosperous somehow. If you give more and more love, you will also notice changes in your feelings and your health.

❡ Do you know someone who is having a hard time right now? Why not send them a book; one of our books or perhaps the book *Power* by Rhonda Byrne. It is a supreme pick-me-up.

❡ So if you feel a bit down, start giving more.

**Love, Sondra**

*May 21, 2020*

## ℐ RECOGNIZE THE EGO

ℐ Since one of the main purposes of life is to substitute the ego with the truth, then it is important to recognize the ego.

- The ego is a false self you made up to replace God.
- The ego is the belief that you are separate from God.
- The ego is the belief you are guilty and deserve punishment.
- The ego is fear and terrified of love.
- The ego is idolatry.
- The ego is a sign of the limited self.
- The ego sees the will of God as the enemy.
- The ego sees strength as weakness and life as death.
- The ego is in competition with God, thinks it is victorious.
- The ego dreams of punishment.
- The ego feeds on exclusivity.
- The ego nourishes deep distrust.
- The ego manifests itself through pride.
- The ego makes important that which is unimportant.
- The ego seeks to fortify itself through acquisitions.
- The ego wants to be superior or inferior.
- The ego is like an iceberg, the major portion submerged.
- The ego says that what opposes God is true.
- The ego is separation, limitation, fear, guilt, hate, pain, misery, suffering, disease, depression, and death.
- The ego is an illusion as there is no separation.

**Love, Sondra**

*May 22, 2020*

## ♪ THE WORLD IS A CLASSROOM

♪ The world is a classroom and other people are your assignments. Sometimes things that happen are "universal lessons" we are assigned to go through. Gabrielle Bernstein gives this prayer:

♪ "Thank you, Universe, for presenting me with this divine assignment for spiritual growth and healing. I am ready and willing to show up for this assignment with love. I welcome your support. Show me where to go, what to do, and what to say. I trust I am being guided."

♪ You need to have the willingness to accept the assignment, show up for it, and pray to be healed.

**Love, Sondra**

*May 23, 2020*

## ♪ ACHIEVING ENLIGHTENMENT

♪ The old way of achieving enlightenment is to simply let life itself process you. By going through the "school of hard knocks" and by experiencing life after life of numerous incarnations, the soul is finally forced to achieve enlightenment. The problem is that this approach is incredibly slow, and often one isn't even conscious of what the goal is.

♪ Hopefully one wakes up and makes a conscious choice to commit to self-analysis and spiritual purification on a regular basis—dissolving and being reborn each day. We can help you with this and teach you how to do it faster. Having a conscious relationship helps as your mate becomes your teacher. Having a guru makes things move even faster up the scale of enlightenment.

ʃ What is your commitment?

**Love, Sondra**

*May 24, 2020*

## ʃ ENERGY EXCHANGE

ʃ Relationships are about energy exchange. When we meet someone for the first time, we are either attracted, repelled, or indifferent. A healthy relationship is one in which the energy exchange is mutually beneficial to the participants. That would be called a STRENGTHENING RELATIONSHIP in which both parties are stronger because of the relationship than they would be without it. A WEAKENING RELATIONSHIP would be one in which the energy exchange is destructive to the health and wellbeing of the partners.

**Love, Sondra**

*May 25, 2020*

## ʃ OPEN YOUR RELATIONSHIP

ʃ Never hesitate to open your relationship to a qualified person who is more enlightened or clearer than you. Don't be embarrassed; your willingness can save you years of hassle. I know couples who won't tell anyone they are having problems because they want to "look good." These couples cheat themselves. I've met other couples who were told by parents to never "air dirty laundry." They then feel it is improper to expose anything. But there are times when we cannot solve our problems by ourselves. We need support and we need someone then who is not emotionally involved in the dilemma. An enlightened friend or counselor can be a relationship saver. Not only may they offer an unexpected solution, but they may also guide you to an appropriate Breathworker who can give you a session. Everyone has problems. Don't get upset by yours, just seek solutions.

℥ The dynamic we use for problem solving and achieving solutions is enjoyable and invigorating. There can be a win for you and your partner. Recently we gave sessions to a couple who were really struggling under lockdown. They were very grateful.

℥ There is always this one issue: "Truth cannot deal with errors you want to keep." Some people actually want to keep their errors. If that is the case, nobody can help them.

**Love, Sondra**

*May 26, 2020*

**℥ WAYS TO KILL OFF A RELATIONSHIP**

℥ There are several ways people "kill off" their relationships:

- Not being in present time
- Not being spiritually awake or spiritually nourished
- Buying into prophesies of doom
- Failing to express one's creativity - being lazy
- Expressing constant negativity, put-downs, disapproval
- Failure to forgive
- Stuffing feelings

- Addictions
- Stuffing food, getting fat, smoking
- Control and dependency
- Giving away one's power
- Shutting down
- Staying depressed
- Staying angry
- Creating a lot of pain and sickness
- Withdrawing
- Having an affair

**Love, Sondra**

*May 27, 2020*

## ॰ GUILT AND SICKNESS

॰ Guilt demands punishment. One of the ways we punish ourselves when we feel guilty is to get sick. We attack our bodies with an illness, pain, or injury that we make up.

॰ ACIM says that guilt is not only not of God, it is actually an attack on God! It says that it is a sure sign that your thinking is unnatural. It also says that if you have guilt, you are walking the carpet of death! (That means that we think we must eventually die as a form of punishment for our guilt, especially if at some point we bought into the idea that we were sinners.)

॰ "Death is not your Father's will nor yours. The death penalty is the ego's goal, for it truly believes that you are a criminal deserving death. The death penalty never leaves the ego's mind, for that is what it always reserves for you in the end. It will torment you while you live, but its hatred is not satisfied until you die. As long as you feel guilty, you are listening to the voice of the ego, which tells you that you have been treacherous to God and therefore deserve death." (From A Course in Miracles)

**Love, Sondra**

*May 28, 2020*

### ℐ CLEARING KARMA THAT CAUSES DISEASE

ℐ There was a man who contracted a rare disease for which there was no cure. He was told he would eventually become paralyzed by it. What this amazing man did was take responsibility for his karma. He realized in a former life he must have caused someone or several people to be paralyzed. He may have caused this by being a hit-and-run driver or deliberately injuring someone in a sport or whatever.

ℐ Upon facing his karmic debt, he resigned from his high-paying job and offered his service for a very modest salary to a crippled children's hospital. He read aloud to the children, assisted them in physical therapy, and even performed unpleasant janitorial tasks. Three months after taking that job, he noticed he was better. Later after he returned to the original doctor, the doctor was amazed to find that all signs of the fatal disease had disappeared.

**Love, Sondra**

*May 30, 2020*

### ℐ MONEY CONFLICTS

ℐ Where do we begin by solving money conflicts in a relationship? Each person must start by handling their own "money case." That includes all negative conditioning about money—conditioning that has affected everything from a lack of money to addiction to greed and overspending.

ℐ You can take all kinds of seminars on money and read any number of books and learn a whole range of coping methods, but if you don't "process" your own emotional blocks about money, even the most refined tools and techniques will not work. Or if they appear to solve your present problem, chances are you will later sabotage your financial plans.

ℐ Some people actually have a "money rejection complex" which could stem from the belief money is somehow sinful and bad. Money itself is just paper and energy; therefore, it is innocent. What is your most negative thought about money? It has to be cleared. You clear it by breathing it out and changing it to a positive affirmation.

**Love, Sondra**


*May 31, 2020*

### ℐ YOU ARE AT CAUSE OF RECEIVING

ℐ Money is like love in that the amount you have is determined by how much you are willing to receive. You will have only as much as you feel comfortable having. Therefore, don't blame others for what you don't have. Only you can deprive yourself of anything. Money is energy and you control the flow.

❡ The same is true for food. In fact, if you were not breast-fed adequately when you were an infant, you may be run by the idea *I can't get enough* or even *I can't get any*. The baby wants the breast. If bottle fed, one might have the thought *I can't get what I really want*. So as an adult your subconscious interprets that as *I can't get enough love,* or *I can't get enough money*.

**Love, Sondra**

*June 1, 2020*

**❡ STAYING TOO LONG**

❡ Staying in a relationship that you secretly know is over, just because you are too afraid to leave, is neither kind nor virtuous. It is unfair to you and your mate. If you find yourself in this situation, get someone to help you process your fears. These fears can be erased. Ask yourself this: "If I had no fear, no guilt, and I did not care what anyone said, would I stay or leave?" "If I knew I could find someone else, would I stay or leave?" If the answer is "I would leave" then you are out of integrity for staying. When you do leave, there may be some discomfort, but you will respect yourself more.

❡ Don't go into the thought *There is nobody else out there*. That is not true. You will automatically find someone with the same good qualities of your mate as you know how to do that. And then you must consciously work on finding someone who does NOT HAVE the bad qualities.

❡ There are plenty of potential mates for everyone everywhere. Use the Cosmic Dating Service where you ask God to bring you the right mate and say, "If I am not ready, make me ready."

℈ Of course it is important to purify yourself first, so you won't make the same mistakes again. I married too young in my first marriage, and I was not enlightened. If I had forced myself to stay in that marriage, I would have gotten very sick.

**Love, Sondra**

*June 2, 2020*

### ℈ PRAYER TO DIVINE MOTHER FROM THE AARTI

℈ "Oh Universal Mother, you give me shelter. In truth, You are the one who gives life to all beings of this world. You are the physician who cures the fever of the life and death cycles of this wheel of life. You are the source of life and liberation to all living beings. We pray to that timeless Energy which resides as Mother Goddess of Haidakhan (Babaji's home). Remembering You is to crown this life with success, to attain liberation. You are the embodiment of divine speech and hidden supreme knowledge. You are the embodiment of the initial seed of "OM" and are rooted therein. The whole of Your appearance has the softness of a budding orange blossom."

**Love, Sondra**

*June 3, 2020*

### ℈ UNITED IN OUR GRATITUDE

℈ "We are united in our gratitude for each other, not by our criticisms and grievances. It is better to appreciate than to attack. There may be qualities and behaviors of another that we do not like but dwelling on them promotes hard feelings and resentments that only accumulate and fester.

⚶ "People need to be acknowledged for their strengths, not constantly reminded of their weaknesses. Gratitude and praise lift the soul to higher realms of being, especially when the attributes being praised are true and universal. This is real unity."

(From *Little Ganesh Book by* Markus Ray)

**Love, Sondra`**


*June 4, 2020*

**⚶ AFFIRMATIONS FROM CHAPTER 31 IN ACIM**

1. I learn the lesson now that I am not guilty.
2. The more I see my own innocence and that of others, the more I am free of fear and see a friendly world.
3. If I see sins in others, they are mine.
4. My body does not think. If it gets sick and dies it is because my mind is sick.
5. I can change what I believe, and my body follows.
6. I do not find happiness by looking at the world. The world does not offer me salvation, so I stop looking there.
7. I choose not to see myself or others as a body.
8. I am Spirit and deathless (since Spirit is that which cannot be destroyed).
9. I choose Heaven, knowing it is a decision I must make.
10. I am as God created me, perfect like He is.

**Love, Sondra**

*June 5, 2020*

## ♂ EVERYTHING IS A MIRROR

♂ Everything is a Xerox of your mind. All of life becomes a kind of Rorschach Test. It is actually fun to look at this feedback from the universe, and one can do it with one's mate:

♂ "I got a parking ticket today."
(How did I create that?)
♂ "The boss really disapproved of me today."
(How did I create that?)
♂ "I lost everything I was working on in my computer today."
(How did I create that?)
♂ "Nobody would pay any attention to what I was saying today."
(How did I create that?)

♂ A sensitive and enlightened mate helps his or her partner look at how he or she creates situations without adding to his or her feeling of guilt. Together they figure out how to turn the situation into a win. "Getting the lesson" can prevent one from repeating it. After they have done self-analysis to discover the consciousness factors that caused the situation, they clear it through spiritual purification techniques, such as Liberation Breathing.

**Love, Sondra**

*June 6, 2020*

## ♂ GIVING FEEDBACK

1. The giver shall first get "permission" to do so unless there is a prior agreement. Example: "Do you mind if I share with you my feelings about . . .?"
2. The giver shall not speak from anger or harsh tones. His heart shall be open as if he were speaking to a best friend with great respect.
3. The giver shall remember that the issue at hand could also be his projection. For example: If the giver says, "It feels like you are way too bossy" maybe the other person isn't bossy, but the giver imagines it because his own parents were bossy, or he is himself.
4. The giver should say, whenever possible, "What I feel is . . ." and what I would like is . . ." Speaking in terms of how you feel or what YOU want is much better than an accusation.
5. What would really work is something like this: "How am I creating it sounding like a bossy energy? It makes me feel like a child. What I need is a different tone."

**Love, Sondra**

*June 7, 2020*

### ꒰ RECEIVING FEEDBACK

1. The receiver shall keep his or her heart open and not become defensive. If the feedback is accurate, then one should be grateful for it. If the feedback is a projection, then it should not bother the receiver anyway.
2. The receiver shall pay particular attention if he or she gets this feedback from more than one person. If so,

then one should take actions quickly to change the habit.

3.  The receiver shall thank the giver and not debate the topic. Perhaps one should say, "How do you suggest I alter this behavior?"
4.  The receiver may act by asking others to help with clearing this problem more quickly. Example: "So and so says I hang up the phone too quickly and cut people off. I don't want to do that. Please support me by telling me whenever I do that with you."

♪ Gentle feedback is a huge benefit. One can advance rapidly if one handles it. It is called having "The Love of Correction." Feedback that is too critical, hurtful, or heavy can be destructive, however. Remember how you speak to your best friend whom you adore.

**Love, Sondra**

*June 8, 2020*

**♪ WHEN SOMEONE HAS DONE YOU WRONG**

♪ "When you recognize that those people you hold grudges against are actors in your own creation, they are easy to forgive. It gives power to a mistake that anyone could do harm to you without your consent. You need to think *I have made a mistake in my thinking to allow you to seemingly hurt me. I recognize you are merely doing what I invited, and that in reality neither you nor anyone can hurt me.*
♪ "I send you love from my heart (name) _____ and I forgive you, knowing it is impossible for you to infringe on my perfection."

(From *Unified: A Course on Truth and Practical Guidance from Babaji*)

**Love, Sondra**

*June 9, 2020*

**❡ EXERCISE EFFICIENT ACTION**

❡ I caught myself worrying about stuff yesterday and this created a lot of tension in my body, so I had to snap out of it.

❡ If you notice thoughts of lack, snap out of it! Think abundance. Count your blessings. Dwell on all the things you do have. Feel affluence. Only with these thoughts can the experience of wealth manifest. Keep a gratitude journal.

❡ If you notice ANY thoughts of failure, snap out of it! It is crucial for success that you think success. Whatever you are doing now, make it successful. Every little thing, do it well and that is a success. Complete everything perfectly. This is called the principle of EFFICIENT ACTION. Then you build a success consciousness.

**Love, Sondra**

*June 10, 2020*

**❡ THE PEACE OF GOD**

❡ Someday when you are confused or upset, try this simple experiment. Sit down quietly and say:

- "The peace of God is at the center of my being.

- I am conscious of this peace.
- I enter into this peace.
- I am surrounded by this peace.
- This peace moves out from me in all directions.
- It calms the troubled waters of my experience.
- It heals everything it contacts.
- There is nothing but peace.
- I rejoice in this peace.
- I permit this peace to enter my soul, to fill me with calm, to inspire me with confidence.
- I know that this peace goes before me and makes perfect, plain, and straight my way."

(From *The Science of Mind* by Ernest Holmes)

**Love, Sondra**


*June 11, 2020*

## ☙ SCIENTIFICALLY DEMONSTRATED

☙ "You do not have to grow old. It is now psychologically demonstrated that the mind does not grow old. We are just as young mentally at ninety as we were at nine. It is now scientifically demonstrated, according to some of the world's leading physicists, that our physical body renews itself each year. It is now scientifically demonstrated that love may rise triumphant over hate. It is now scientifically demonstrated that most of our physical ailments are results of negative use of the Power that is within us. It is now scientifically demonstrated that at least a large portion of our accidents are "unconsciously invited."
(From *The Science of Mind* by Ernest Holmes)

**Love, Sondra**

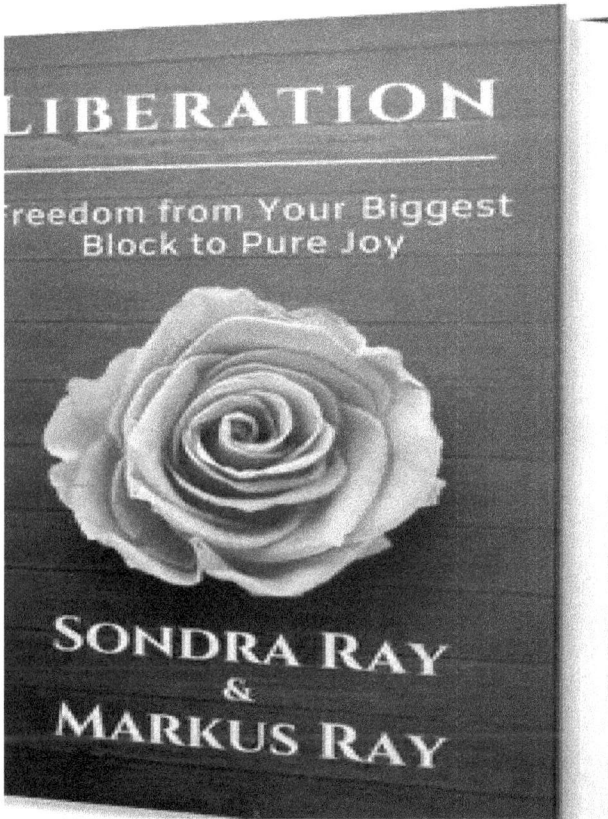

This is our book on the "personal lie," and how to get over it.

*June 12, 2020*

### ℐ A SIMPLE PROCESS ON GUILT

ℐ During this sequester I discovered I had some suppressed guilt. I was guilty of not working. I was guilty about some other stupid stuff in the past. Markus and I did a verbal process back and forth out loud. "Something I am guilty about is . . ." "Another thing I am guilty about is . . ." We were surprised what came out. We had no idea we were guilty about some of those things! Then we turned it all over to the Holy Spirit to be released. I recommend you try this process with someone. You can also write it out if you are alone.

♫ I can't believe I never did that before. The big problem with guilt is that it demands punishment. The way I was punishing myself was through having some tension. So here is another process you can do: "A way I am punishing myself for this guilt is . . ." Very revealing!

♫ A Course in Miracles says guilt is not only not of God, it is an attack on God!

**Love, Sondra**

*June 14, 2020*

**♫ A GREAT AFFIRMATION**

❡ I found a great affirmation in the book *The Universe Has Your Back* by Gabrielle Bernstein. "Universe (or God), thank you for helping me to find joy in this situation." I gave it to Markus for the tons of work he does on the computer, and it really helped.

❡ Another thought: "What if I chose for this (name the situation) to be fun." The whole point is when we commit to joy, we increase our chances for success.

**Love, Sondra**


*June 15, 2020*

❡ **REACTING**

❡ Amma says that when you react to someone, you are probably wrong, and they are most likely right. He or she, who is in a better state of mind, has the clarity to observe the situation. "Reaction makes you blind. Your reactive attitude does not help you see others or consider their feelings."

❡ Before reacting to a particular situation, can you pause and say to the other person, "Give me some time before I answer you. Let me contemplate what you said. Maybe you are right, and I am wrong."

❡ If you have the courage to say this, you are at least considering the other person's feelings. This will prevent many unpleasant events that could arise later.

**Love, Sondra**

*June 17, 2020*

## ꟿ ALONENESS AND LONELINESS

ꟿ There is a great difference in aloneness and loneliness. Amma says: "Aloneness is inner solitude and helps you relax. Aloneness has nothing to do with loneliness.

ꟿ "A lonely person is agitated and cannot feel peaceful and happy. Aloneness is something that happens deep within, and it makes you feel contented and at peace in any situation. A person who has developed this inner aloneness cannot be overpowered by emotions.

ꟿ "You feel lonely when you are enslaved by the mind. Aloneness is a state you enter when you become the master of your mind. Loneliness is the outcome of attachment. Aloneness is the outcome of detachment. Loneliness plunges you into a state of darkness and sorrow. Aloneness brings light and love into your life. You feel lonely when you are tense and agitated. Aloneness is experienced when you are relaxed and free of tension. Loneliness is the sign of a person who is bound by the world and its objects and desires. Aloneness is the sign of a soul who is free from all desires and the pleasures of the world.

"With aloneness the interferences of the past and future stop. To be content in one's own Self, by the Self, and for the Self, is what is known as inner Aloneness."
(From *Awaken Children Volume VIII*)

**Love, Sondra**

*June 18, 2020*

## ꟿ YOUR LOVE LIFE

❡ If you are worried about your love life (not liking it or not having one), you might be thinking *I am afraid that . . .* or *I am worried that . . .*

❡ Now instead of worrying, change to wondering. *I wonder how I can go about finding the right lover* or *I wonder how my partner and I can go about generating abundance.*

❡ This habit will take away the unpleasant sensations. Wonder is a positive feeling. Wondering breaks you free from the prison of your old thinking. You get a clear space. (Summarized from *Spirit-Centered Relationships* by Gay Hendricks and Kathlyn Hendricks)

**Love, Sondra**


*June 19, 2020*


**❡ MAJOR BARRIER**

❡ The major barrier that stands in the way of establishing a truly intimate relationship with another person is an "unloved" part of yourself—something you have never fully accepted. Even if you could attract someone anyway, this unloved part of yourself would prevent you from enjoying and keeping the relationship. The unloved part of yourself acts as a repellent.

❡ If you don't love yourself completely, you will always be looking for someone else to do it for you, and this never works. People who don't love themselves attract other people who don't love themselves. If you love yourself completely you will attract people who love and accept themselves the same way. This is what works.

❡ When you have an unloved part of yourself, your hope is that another person will give you enough love and that part of yourself will go away. It never does. You have to confront that unloved part of yourself. It might be a fear of abandonment. In that case you will either keep people distant, so they won't leave you or you'll cling to them dependently. Maybe it is a fear of being smothered. Then you worry that your freedom will be lost, so you stay at arm's length.

♪ You have to love yourself through your fears and of course we would recommend a Liberation Breathing session to heal them.

(Summarized from *Spirit-Centered Relationships* by Gay Hendricks and Kathlyn Hendricks)

**Love, Sondra**

*June 20, 2020*

## ♪ FORGIVENESS MEDITATION

1. Sit comfortably. Breathe ten deep breaths. Recite silently or audibly, "If I have hurt or harmed anyone knowingly or unknowingly, I ask their forgiveness now."
2. Notice what comes up.
3. Next, offer forgiveness to those who have harmed you by saying, "If anyone has hurt or harmed me, knowingly or unknowingly, I now forgive them."
4. As feelings, memories, or images come up, recite "I forgive you."
5. Turn your attention to yourself and say, "For all the ways I have hurt or harmed myself, knowingly or unknowingly, I offer forgiveness to myself."

**Love, Sondra**

*June 21, 2020*

**₰ AMMA'S WORDS ON RELATIONSHIPS**

₰ Once I went to a special outing with Amma and someone asked her this question: "Why is it so easy to have a relationship with a friend and so difficult with a lover?" Her answer was simply this: "EXPECTATIONS and CRITICISM."
₰ She has also said that a true relationship is possible only when one is able to let go of all one's preconceived ideas and prejudices and when one stops being possessed by the past. She said we should stop clinging to the past and we will be free and peaceful. To cling to the past, she said is like living in the dark.

**Love, Sondra**

*June 22, 2020*

**₰ GOING OUT FOR FUN THE FIRST TIME**

₰ Yesterday our friend Patty came to visit us. I spontaneously hugged her, realizing how much I missed that! Then we went to lunch at a restaurant by the river and sat outside. This was SO MUCH FUN after all this time. I could not believe how much I missed it. People are finally out and about in our neighborhood. Everyone was in really high spirits. It is hard to believe what has happened all these months. I realized I had been fairly tense at times because I felt so different after having some fun! Even talking to the waiter through masks was delightful.
₰ I remembered Dolly Parton's song "When Life Is Good Again."

**Love, Sondra**

*June 23, 2020*

**ℑ COMPANIONATE LOVE**

ℑ If your mate says "I love you" is that backed up with action? If they truly love you, then every day he or she should make decisions with your needs in mind, make plans with your interests in mind, and prepare his or her schedule with you. The same goes the other way. You love your mate if your daily ACTIONS and choices reflect an obvious concern for your mate's happiness and fulfillment. It is said "Love is as Love does."

ℑ Companionate love is the ACTIVE commitment you make to fulfill each other's dreams, goals, and values. You know someone loves you when he or she both desires your well-being and is willing to work for it daily.

(From *For Better Forever* by Dr. Greg and Lisa Popcak)

**Love, Sondra**

*June 25, 2020*

**ℑ SEXUAL ATTRACTIONS**

ℑ "In the course of this lifetime, you will meet dozens of people you have been married to in past lives and with whom you have had sexual relations. These energies naturally take place because there is an energy to be balanced between the two of you. Meeting them is not necessarily a sign of an enduring alliance with a constructive purpose.

ℑ "An instant attraction does not automatically mean that now you've met your twin flame or your soul mate. Rather, you might just have karma to balance. We may have sexual

attractions to people even when we realize they are not good for us! An attraction might be so overwhelming that we feel we cannot fight against it. Such an attraction may begin in appreciation and care, but it may end in anger or aggression because we have not grown enough to heal the relationship. ♫ "The sexual interchange does not necessarily balance karma. It is the heart's love that balances karma."
(From *Finding a Higher Love* by Elizabeth Clare Prophet)

**Love, Sondra**


*June 26, 2020*

## ♫ CONSCIOUS UNCOUPLING

♫ One has to take personal responsibility for one's part in what happened.

- You must let go of being a victim and craft a breakup narrative that starts you on a path of peace.
- Reflect on yourself as the source of your experience in a way that feeds you power and supports you to grow.
- Release unconscious and habitual patterns of people pleasing, self-abandoning, over-giving, and tolerating less than you deserve.
- Learn how to make amends to yourself in a way that frees you from resentment.
- Evolve beyond the person you were when you created that relationship.
- Discover you can trust again and love again.

(Summarized from *Conscious Uncoupling* by Katherine Woodward Thomas)

**Love, Sondra**

*June 28, 2020*

## ℘ AFFIRMING DIVINE ORDER

℘ "I do not depend upon persons or conditions for my prosperity. God is the Source of my prosperity and provides His own channels of supply to me now."

℘ "Christ in me manifests my true place with the true people and the true prosperity now."

℘ "Everything and everybody that are no longer part of the Divine Plan for my life now releases me. Christ in me reveals, unfolds, and manifests the divine plan of my life now."

℘ "I am in Divine Order. My world is in Divine order now."

℘ "I am beautifully and appropriately housed with the rich substance of God."

℘ "The success power of Jesus Christ is in absolute control of this day, producing perfect results here and now."

(Quotations by Catherine Ponder)

**Love, Sondra**

*June 29, 2020*

## ℘ BENEFITS OF THE PATH OF DEVOTION

- It gives much contentment
- It gives enthusiasm and vigor
- Everything that happens becomes a gift
- You get a compassionate heart
- You get a child-like innocence
- You get a pleasing nature
- It calms you in adversity
- It gives you unshakable faith

- It feeds your potential
- It makes you relaxed and optimistic
- You become cheerful in all circumstances.
- You gain strength and courage
- You develop fearlessness

**Love, Sondra**


*June 30, 2020*

**₰ SURROUNDED BY GOD'S FAVOR**

₰ Joel Osteen says that in Psalm 5 it says that God's favor surrounds us like a shield. It surrounds us; it is with us everywhere we go. You have favor at work, at the grocery store, favor at the gym, favor in traffic, etc. The more you are AWARE of this favor, the more conscious you are that God wants to assist you, the more you will see His hand at work.
₰ We should be in the habit of declaring, "Lord, thank You for Your favor. Thank you that I have favor with my clients and with my boss, etc."
₰ When you acknowledge God, He will crown your efforts with success. When something good happens, recognize that it's the favor of God and then learn to thank Him for it. What would happen, he asks, if you get up each day and pray this simple prayer? "Lord, thank you in advance for assisting me."
(Summarized from *The Power of Favor* by Joel Osteen)

**Love, Sondra**

*July 1, 2020*

## ℐ HAVING A GURU

ℐ Many people are OPPOSED to having a guru. I happen to be extremely grateful to have Babaji, Ammachi, and Jesus of ACIM. I totally trust what Amma has to say about this issue.

ℐ "The state of perfection cannot happen without his grace. Soon the way becomes complex, and guidance is required. The road to liberation is a maze of intricate paths, a labyrinth. Without a Guru, the path can be compared to sailing alone in the ocean in a tiny boat that is not equipped, without even a compass. Self-realization is very narrow. One walks this path alone if he does not have a Guru.

ℐ "As we walk the spiritual path there is a light that can guide us That light is the Guru's grace. Sometimes the path becomes very narrow. If it becomes too narrow and you slip off the path, it is necessary to have a guru pull you back on. The Guru encourages you; he instills more faith and confidence in you to try and try again. You cannot cross the final barrier by your own effort alone. Your effort is nothing. From the other side, the Guru extends his hand and pulls you through. Without the Guru, you may turn back and stray from the path."
(From *Awaken Children, Volume V*)

**Love, Sondra**


*July 2, 2020*

## ℐ TALK ABOUT WHAT YOU LOVE

⚚ You have to talk about what you love, to bring what you love to you. "When you talk about any difficulties with money, a relationship, an illness, or even that the profits of your business are down, you are not talking about what you love.

"When you talk about a bad event in the news, or a person or situation that annoyed or frustrated you, you are not talking about love. Even talking about little negative things will bring more struggle.

⚚ "Every time you talk about what you don't love, you are adding another bar to the cage, and you are locking yourself away from all the good."

(From *The Power* by Rhonda Byrne)

**Love, Sondra**

*July 3, 2020*

**⚚ THE PATH OF A RELATIONSHIP**

⚚ "Relationships offer you a profound spiritual path. Your partner is not only your friend, your lover, your companion, but also your teacher. She or he reflects to you all the beauty that lies within you, as well as all of your fear, doubt, and ambivalence that lies buried deeply within your soul. There is perhaps no more rapid path to psychological wholeness and spiritual awakening than the path of a relationship.

⚚ "There may be fun but just as many times when one of you is wounded and defensive. The great accomplishment is the ability to move through your pain together without making the other person responsible for it. Can you do this and hold onto joy and reverence?"

(From *I Am the Door* by Paul Ferrini)

**Love, Sondra**

*July 4, 2020*

## ♉ THE PATH OF A RELATIONSHIP CONTINUED

♉ "The truth is that you can be only as happy with another person as you can be with yourself. If you like who you are, being with your partner can be an extension of your happiness. But if you do not like yourself, being with your partner can only exacerbate your unhappiness.

"Your decision to enter into a partnership should not be based on a desire to avoid looking at yourself, but on willingness to intensify that process. When you live with other people, you are likely to trigger their unhealed wounds and they are likely to trigger yours."

(From *I Am the Door* by Paul Ferrini)

**Love, Sondra**

*July 5, 2020*

## ♉ CHOOSING A PARTNER

♉ "Choose your partner well. If you choose one who dances too slowly, you may be held back. If you choose one who dances too fast, you may break your ankle trying to keep up with him or her. Find a partner who dances at the same speed as you, one who will compliment you and help you realize your potential. Find one who can empower and assist you.

♉ "Most relationships fall apart as soon as people reveal themselves. For this reason, couples should live together successfully for three years before considering marriage. Many relationships will not survive this three-year period of exploration."

(From *I Am the Door* by Paul Ferrini)

**Love, Sondra**

*July 6, 2020*

## ℐ THE DURATION OF RELATIONSHIPS

ℐ I have always said you should not judge yourself if a relationship lasts a short time. Maybe you had karma to clear and that is all you are supposed to be together.

ℐ Ferrini says people come together because they have important things to learn together. When those lessons are learned, they might move on to other teachers. The key is not to worry about how long a relationship lasts, but to give it your best energy and attention. Experience as much joy as you can with your partner. Learn as much as you can from painful times. Do your best to be honest and clear with each other.

ℐ "No other area of your life offers you as many opportunities to understand your wounds and heal them. Your partner is your mid-wife to your birth into your full potential."

(From *I Am the Door* by Paul Ferrini)

**Love, Sondra**

*July 8, 2020*

## ℐ A WORLD OF OUR OWN MAKING

꿍 I read the following statement: "God does not come from on high to free you from a world of your own making. Why would He take you from what you have chosen?"

꿍 This is a very profound statement. We want to say, "God get me out of this situation, this mess, this problem." BUT we have free will to create our own misery. We chose that situation, that problem. We probably did not create that mess consciously. That is the point. Our unconscious created the mess. But it still means we chose it. It is so important to know how to discover how the issue got created. We need to be able to see our subconscious.

꿍 That is what is so great about Liberation Breathing. It brings the unconscious to the conscious so you can change it.

**Love, Sondra**

*July 9, 2020*

## 꿍 FEAR OF BEING ABANDONED OR HURT

꿍 Many people are afraid of being abandoned or hurt so they are avoiding relationships. When you are afraid of being left alone, you will either keep people distant so that it won't hurt so much if they leave you, or you will cling to them dependently so they cannot leave without dragging you with them.

꿍 Sometimes people just need this affirmation: "Hurt no longer exists in my reality."

**Love, Sondra**

*July 10, 2020*

### ℐ APOLOGY VS. DEFENSIVENESS

ℐ Saying "I am sorry, you are right" differs radically from defensiveness. If you say "I didn't mean to do it" or "It's all in your mind" or "It was no big deal" you are becoming a lawyer for your own case. This muddies the emotional waters. It obscures your flaws and requires that we be loved at the level of self-deception.

ℐ "Defensiveness is a way of keeping the relationship problem going. That is the important thing to note.

ℐ "Apology gives closure, opening the path to forgiveness and a new beginning. Apology, when it comes from the heart, is one of the quickest healers of any rift. It is the perfect bandage for every wound in a relationship."
(From *True Love* by Thich Nhat Hanh)

**Love, Sondra**

*July 11, 2020*

### ℐ VIBRATIONS OF CONSCIOUSNESS

ℐ A lot of people still think that if they die, they will go to higher place and therefore they look forward to dying. But the book *The Door of Everything* explains this:

ℐ "When death does come, it releases the weight of gravity and temporarily frees the soul from earth. But it does not change the vibrations of consciousness from the human level. There is no escape from the vibration of yourself except by practiced change of thoughts and feelings. Nor does death cause the released consciousness to go directly

315

to celestial levels. Consciousness, when departing from the body, automatically seeks its own level of vibration."
(From *The Door of Everything* by Ruby Nelson)

**Love, Sondra**

*July 12, 2020*

## ꙮ ANGER HARMS A HUMAN BEING

ꙮ "At the slightest indication of anger drink a sufficient quantity of cold water. Anger harms a human being in every respect. It produces the action of poison in the body. Pray to God to preserve you from this mood. To criticize people or to feel hostile towards anyone harms oneself and puts obstacles into one's path to the Supreme.

ꙮ "If someone does something bad, you should feel nothing but affection and benevolence towards him or her. Think *Lord, this is also one of Thy manifestations.* The more kindly and friendly you can feel and behave towards everybody, the more will the way to the One who is goodness itself open out."
(From *Life and Teaching of Sri Anandamayi Ma* by Alexander Lipski)

**Love, Sondra**

*July 13, 2020*

## ꙮ CAST ASIDE THOUGHTS OF THE PAST

♪ Don't let the past disturb your mind. Amma says to see the past as a canceled check! There is no point in brooding over it. Don't ruin the present by dwelling constantly on the past. Strengthen the present and go forward.

♪ A traveler who is eager to reach his destination quickly does not look back to see by which road he has come.

♪ Strengthen the present. Forget about the past and the future or you will waste a pleasant occasion in the present.

**Love, Sondra**

*July 14, 2020*

### ♪ OPEN YOUR HEART

♪ Amma says, "Open your heart and tell everything to God." She says we need not hide anything from Him/Her. We should tell him everything. It is good to lighten the burden in our hearts by telling God all our sorrows. We should depend only on Him/Her in all our difficulties. The true devotee never tells anyone else about his troubles. God is his only real relation. God dwells within us, watching every movement. Our strongest relationship should be with God. If we decide to tell God about our sorrows, it should only be for the sake of getting closer to God."

♪ This is why I say, write out your problems and put the letter under your altar cloth. But it is important to write a responsible letter. Example:

1. I. This is my problem (write only about one at a time).
2. These are the negative thoughts I had that created this problem.
3. I lay them at your feet (meaning I am willing to give them up).

4. These are my new thoughts (write affirmations that are the exact opposite of negative thoughts in #2).
5. Please add energy to my new thoughts.
6. Thank you (add your signature).

**Love, Sondra**

*July 15, 2020*

**ʃ CHANGING YOUR FATE**

ʃ Sometimes people go to an astrologer and hear difficult things. They believe it is true and that there is nothing they can do about it. However, someone asked Amma if we can change our destiny. ʃ She said the following:

"Destiny can be changed through tapa and sadhana (spiritual practices). Even death can be averted. Anything in our fate can be transcended by performing actions with an attitude of total surrender to God. But we have to be ready to act, instead of just sitting somewhere. It is a sign of laziness to blame fate without doing any work."

ʃ One's effort will surely make a difference to change a horoscope.

**Love, Sondra**

*July 16, 2020*

**ʃ AMMA EXPLAINS KARMA**

ʃ "Death is not the end; it is the beginning of another life. As the circle of life turns around, the actions of the past bear fruit. We cannot say when the fruit will come, what the fruit will be, or how it will come. Whether you believe it or not, the law of karma operates. The cycle of karma is as mysterious as God. Do not try to analyze the cycle of life. It cannot be done.

ꣻ "Don't brood over the past or over past actions. Whatever is done is done. What is important is the present because your future depends on how you confront the present. This life of yours is the effect of the past. Therefore beware, your actions determine your future. If you do good, you will be rewarded accordingly, but if you perform bad actions, such actions will return to you with equal strength. Negative action committed in the past may not bear fruit in the immediate future.

ꣻ "You can raise a hundred objections to the theory of karma. But karma and its results must inevitably be experienced by every living being until the mind is stilled and one is content in one's own Self."

(From *Awaken Children, Volume VI*)

**Love, Sondra**

*July 17, 2020*

### ꣻ AMMA ON CLEARING KARMA

ꣻ "For one who does not have faith in a Supreme Power or ideal, there is no escape from the grip of karma. A believer, knowing that he has to reap the fruits of his actions, will perform spiritual practices like japa (repetition of the mantra), meditation, and prayer. These practices and the good actions which he performs serve as a neutralizer. The good actions in the present nullify the effects of past bad actions. Faith in God or the Guru gives a person immense strength to confront the inevitable karma. Faith in the Guru or God serves as an armor, a protective force.

ॐ "The true seeker will not want to turn away from his karma because he knows that it is a process of purification. A real seeker accepts the present circumstances without reacting to them. Any reaction will lengthen the chain of karma. But one can easily overcome one's karma through the Grace of the Satguru. If you follow the instructions of a Satguru, you will come out of such ordeals unscathed."
(From *Awaken Children, Volume VI*)

**Love, Sondra**

*July 18, 2020*

**ॐ AMMA ON FAITH**

ॐ "Look around. You can see that lack of faith is the cause of all the troubles. Without faith you have no feelings, no heart, no love. Without faith you will be full of fear. Fear cripples you; it makes you paralyzed. Placing much faith in certificates and qualifications, people have faith in a doctor's or scientist's words, though the doctor and scientist is stuck in the intellect and therefore limited. But because he has no impressive qualifications, they will doubt the words and authenticity of a Mahatma, one who has delved deep into the deepest mysteries of the universe and has unlimited wisdom and power.

ॐ "A person who has no faith will be unduly sensitive and fragile. Anyone and anything can hurt him. He cannot think or act with discrimination. Whereas a person with faith can keep in good spirits all the time. No matter what circumstances you find yourself in your faith protects you. Amma is of course talking about unshakable faith in God. A man without faith will likely have a dryness within him and will lack a zest for life. He will feel constant anxiety and will rarely be relaxed. He can be very narrow and loveless.

ᛃ "Life becomes full and complete only when the heart is filled with faith in a Supreme Power." Babaji also said that FAITH IS EVERYTHING.

(From *Awaken Children, Volume VI*)

**Love, Sondra**


*July 19, 2020*

### ᛃ AMMA ON CONTENTMENT

ᛃ "The path of devotion gives much contentment to the practitioner. A contented person will have enthusiasm and vigor. He will be very optimistic and endowed with an adventurous mind. His attitude is that life and everything that happens in life is a gift, and this gives him immense patience and strength. He does not believe that happiness is a right to which he is entitled. As far as he is concerned, there are not rights, there are only gifts. This attitude helps him accept everything as a gift, both good and bad, and also instills him with courage and faith.

ᛃ "Such a person will have a loving and compassionate heart, a child-like innocence, and a pleasing nature. Not wanting to injure anyone or hurt anybody's feelings, he cannot harm anyone. He will have the mental ability and balance to remain calm and quiet when adversity arises. He practices acceptance and such a person derives his power to be content and relaxed from his unshakable faith in and love toward the Supreme power. He knows that his Lord is always with him and protects him from all dangers, helps him be content, relaxed, optimistic, and cheerful at all times in all

circumstances. He must have the willingness to surrender to the Supreme Will. Only then will one be able to enter into that state of everlasting contentment."
(From *Awaken Children, Volume VI*)

**Love, Sondra**

*July 21, 2020*

## ♫ THE LAST JUDGEMENT

♫ "Peace be to you. There is no instant when you stand alone; no time when God will fail to take your hand; no moment when His Love does not surround you, comfort you and care, along with you, for every wish you have, each little joy or tiny stab of pain. At one with you forever, He remains your one relationship, your only Friend. You are the holy Son of God Himself. Peace be to you, for what is His is yours."
(From *The Gifts of God* by Dr. Helen Schucman, scribe of A Course in Miracles)

**Love, Sondra**

*July 22, 2020*

## ♫ PROGRESSIVE RELATIONSHIP COMMITMENTS

1. Preliminary commitment (1-3 months). Developing a friendship. I will make time in my life to get to know you. I will not be sexual with you or anyone else.
2. Intermediate commitment (6 months -1year). Friends becoming lovers. I will be sexual only with you. I will see you

322

twice a week. I will live separately and fully explore our relationship.
3. Advanced commitment (1-3 years). Lovers become partners. I will live with you and be faithful to you.
4. Lifetime commitment (lifetime). I am committed to living with you for the rest of my life. I will be with you no matter what happens.
5. At each level of relationship, the commitment can be completed, renewed, or extended."

(From *Creating a Spiritual Relationship* by Paul Ferrini)

¶ I think the preliminary commitment is especially good. One to three months without sex seems important.

**Love, Sondra**

***July 23, 2020***

**¶ SOLUTION**

¶ "The Holy Spirit is God's answer to the ego. He brings the plan of the Atonement and leads us back to our real Self. The Atonement is the complete removal of guilt. The holy instant allows the Holy Spirit's correction to occur. It is the miracle of instantaneous forgiveness.
¶ "To the Holy Spirit the world is a place that provides opportunities to forgive. People are seen as either acting out of love or calling for love. The Second Coming of Christ is the end of the ego's rule. However, right before the fear (ego) is transcended, the ego screams Stop! You do not want the separation healed! You must be vigilant against this temptation.

"In the Bible, Revelations says that Jesus stands at the door and knocks. Our fear is not that when we open the door Christ won't be there: our fear is that He will! For in His presence, the ego's world is dispelled. All fear and guilt are gone."
(From my book *Drinking the Divine)*

**Love, Sondra**

*July 25, 2020*

**℘ WHY PEOPLE STAY IN HELL**

℘ One can wonder why people stay in horrible relationships even those that are abusive. Perhaps the "victim" had a thought *I am bad* from a past life and so they unconsciously felt they deserved punishment. Or perhaps they hate themselves for another reason.

℘ The ego takes refuge in familiarity and is threatened by change. It defines the known as preferable to the unknown, even if the known sucks. The relationship, although painful, is at least predictable. The ego equates predictability with safety, even if the predictable is disaster! To the Holy Spirit, this is insane.

℘ The ego actively resists any attempt to alter the world it has created. What the ego does not tell you is that the world it has created is killing you. When something comes along that threatens the ego's world, it will do ANYTHING it can to keep you from stepping ahead to freedom. Often the bigger the change for the better, the bigger the drama and setback the ego manufactures.

℘ But the ego cannot stop you unless you let it. Just keep going despite the ego's attempts to sabotage your progress.

(Summarized from *A Course in Miracles Made Easy* by Alan Cohen)

**Love, Sondra**

*July 26, 2020*

### ♪ THE BODY AS A COMMUNICATION DEVICE

♪ ACIM says that the only purpose of the body is for a communication device to magnify the presence of love in the world. Your body shows you where you are in alignment with the flow of well-being, and where you have stepped out of alignment. Illness is an indication that there is a blockage in the current of life force. Your body is not the cause of your mind and emotions, it is their effect. Illness is a wake-up call to recognize where the flow has been obstructed.

♪ When your body is in alignment with Spirit, universal law will keep it well. No adverse physical condition need be permanent. Many people have healed every disease. When you shift the consciousness that brought about the illness, its cause is gone along with the effects. Your body is more liquid than solid, constantly re-creating itself according to the current stream of consciousness you are holding.

♪ Healing is the result of a shift in consciousness from separation to wholeness, a return to your true Self. (What is meant by a shift in consciousness is changing the negative thought that caused the illness.)

"Jesus Christ, like all agents of transformation, was able to achieve healing because his vision of his patient's wholeness was more powerful than their belief in disease."
(From *A Course in Miracles Made Easy* by Alan Cohen)

**Love, Sondra**

*July 27, 2020*

## ♪ ACIM AND PROSPERITY

♪ A Course in Miracles is the ultimate prosperity manual. It is uncompromising in its affirmation of your right to all the riches and wellness in the universe. It identifies you as heir to all that your heavenly Father is and owns. In the Workbook Lesson #343 it says the following: "And so all things are given onto me forever and forever...I cannot lose, for I can only give, and everything is mine eternally."

♪ It does not tell you how to get stuff. It teaches you how to get peace. God's blessings manifest on Earth as they do in heaven. When you are established in soul serenity, you are in the perfect position to attract all you need, supplied by grace.

♪ "Surely goodness and mercy shall follow me all the days of my life." (Psalm 23:6)

♪ "Remember that you are deprived of nothing." (T.4.IV 3:3)" (From *A Course in Miracles Made Easy* by Alan Cohen)

**Love, Sondra**

*July 28, 2020*

## ♪ LETHAL INTERACTIONS

♪ Dr. John Gottman (The Gottman Institute) calls these the *Four Horsemen of the Apocalypse:*

1. **Criticism:** When you criticize your partner, you are basically suggesting that their personality or character is the problem. (Whereas a complaint is an issue with the behavior not the person.)

2.	**Contempt:** It reveals your feelings of superiority over your partner. It shows up as sneering, sarcasm, cynicism, eye rolling, name-calling, mockery, and hostile humor.
3.	**Defensiveness:** It is a way of deflecting blame away from yourself and onto your partner.
4.	**Stonewalling:** Allows you to shut down and avoid responsibility altogether.

❡ These behaviors break down all intimacy and trust in a relationship.

**Love, Sondra**


*July 29, 2020*

## ❡ INITIATING RESOLUTION AND RECONNECTION

❡ Researchers have found that it takes five positive encounters between couples to counteract the impact of one negative encounter! And if they are dealing with a backlog of resentment and pain, neither is going to be motivated to initiate positive encounters. So then one needs to address any conflict right away. As soon as you can, reach out to initiate resolution and reconnection.

❡ There are ways to stop a full-blown fight. In the first place a couple should evolve to the point that they are free of anger altogether. Instead of yelling or even raising one's voice, one can say, "I am feeling activated. The negative thought that is making me feel activated is . . ." This makes one take responsibility. Besides, ACIM says you are never upset for the reason you think. It is likely to be some earlier similar thing from way in the past.

❦ Also, take a time-out instead of fighting. The moment you realize the conversation is going south, initiate a break. Don't allow stubbornness or pettiness to prevent you from healing any rift.

**Love, Sondra**

*July 30, 2020*

## ❦ THE **VIOLET FLAME II**

❦ "You have an opportunity to assist life or to place a burden upon it—either by interacting with the negative energy of your past karma cycling to the surface of your consciousness or by recognizing this energy as a challenge to your harmony and love and transmuting it.

❦ "The key to transmuting or changing past karma and fulfilling your mission with your partner is the violet flame, a spiritual energy given by God to man for his acceleration into the Aquarian age. This action of the Holy Spirit transforms negative energy: anger into love, irritation into peace, suspicion into trust, so that you can influence life positively as you move toward your ultimate victory on the spiritual path.

❦ "When you visualize this violet flame and call it forth into your consciousness, it instantaneously begins to change negative energy patterns accumulated over thousands of lifetimes. You begin to experience feelings of joy, lightness, and hope.

❦ "A simple but powerful violet-flame mantra is "I AM a being of violet fire. I AM the purity God desires."
(From Elizabeth Clare Prophet)

**Love, Sondra**

*July 31, 2020*

**❡ VULNERABILITY**

❡ In the dictionary it is defined as helpless, powerless, impotent, weak, and defenseless. In a relationship we want to be using the term defenseless but not weak. People are afraid to give up their anger because they feel they will be weak, and they won't be safe. But ACIM has a lesson that says, "In my defenselessness my safety lies." You are always safer without any anger in you. That is because anger is a defense and defenses attract attack. So if you keep your defenses up you attract attack.

❡ In our vulnerability we bring to the relationship our sensitivities, our feelings, and our ability to relate without protection. This gives the possibility of intimacy, depth, and warmth. In your vulnerability you pay attention to yourself, and you are attuned to what makes you feel good and what makes you feel bad. You are sensitive to the quality of interactions in your relationship. You can combine power with vulnerability when you figure out what you want to do about something in the relationship. So without the defense of anger, let's say you are at peace, and peace is power.

❡ So one can be vulnerable and still be in one's power.

**Love, Sondra**

*August 1, 2020*

**❡ CLEAR YOUR AURA OF UNINVITED INFLUENCES**

❡ Before meditation or whenever you go into crowds of people or are around sickness, etc. say the following: "I close my aura to all except my Higher Self.

꽃 "To all uninvited influences in my aura, I send love and light. You are each whole and healed. You are each created as love and light, and you are still love and light. You each feel no pain now, and you are not afraid. You each have a perfect place to go, and I ask my Higher Self to take you there now. Each of you go in peace."

꽃 When you have such an uninvited influence in your aura, you can feel moody, irritable, exhausted, pained, angry, or any other emotion and feeling that is inappropriate.

(From *Unified: A Course on Truth and Practical Guidance from Babaji* by Roger Lanphear)

**Love, Sondra**

*August 2, 2020*

## 꽃 TRUE FORGIVENESS

꽃 We are all actors for each other's script. We are the writer, director, producer, and lead character for our script. If we imagine that we have been hurt by anyone, it is only because that is what we, as creator, invited. It gives power to a mistake if we think that any could do harm to us without our consent. Here is what we need to think: *I have made a mistake in my thinking to allow you to seemingly hurt me. I recognize you are merely doing what I invited, and that in reality neither you nor anyone can hurt me. I send you love from my heart, and I forgive you knowing it is impossible for you to infringe on my perfection.*

(From *Unified: A Course on Truth and Practical Guidance from Babaji* by Roger Lanphear)

**Love, Sondra**

*August 3, 2020*

## ℥ SELF-INQUIRY

℥ It has been said that 75 percent of the spiritual path is self-inquiry. Self-inquiry is the process of monitoring one's thoughts, impulses, and desires and learning to discriminate between what is truth and what is illusion. You learn to discriminate between what is coming from the lower self and what is coming from the higher self; what is of Christ consciousness and what is ego consciousness. As stated in ACIM: "Deny any thought that is not of God to enter your mind."

℥ Keep your mind steady in the light. You have to be committed. Can you remain even minded no matter what happens in the external? Your mind can create bondage or liberation.

**Love, Sondra**

*August 4, 2020*

## ℥ COLOR HEALING USING CANDLES

℥ "If you want truth and purity, light a white candle. If you want to gain knowledge, light a yellow candle. Light a pink candle to send love. Light a blue candle for resolution of a spiritual problem. Green candles are good for all monetary and material concerns. Lavender candles are especially good for healing. Silver candles are good for protection.

℥ As you light the candle, say a prayer and state what you need. It is important to be specific. Thank God for granting you what you need. The candle and the color it is radiating

keeps your prayer manifesting that specific energy as long as the candle is lit."
(From *Hidden Mysteries* by Joshua David Stone)

**Love, Sondra**

*August 5, 2020*

## ♫ "I AM" AFFIRMATIONS FROM SAINT GERMAIN

♫ The affirmation becomes much more powerful when you use the words I AM.
♫ Be still and know I AM God!

- I AM God living in this body as (name).
- I AM a fully liberated God living in this body as (name).
- I AM the Mighty I AM Presence.
- I AM the resurrection and the life.
- I AM the truth, the way, and the life.
- I AM the embodiment of divine love.
- I AM the open door which no man can shut.
- I AM God in action!
- I AM the revelation of God.
- I AM the baptism of the Holy Spirit.
- I AM the ascended being I wish to be now.
- I AM the realization of God.
- I AM an open door to all revelation.
- I AM the Light that lights up every room I enter.
- I AM the Presence of God in action this day.
- I AM that I AM.
- I AM a perfect channel and instrument of God.
- I AM the presence filling my world with perfection this day.

- I AM an invincible body of light.
- I AM the victory into Light!
- I AM the cosmic flame of cosmic victory.

❡ Use every day! Whatever you say after I AM is instantly manifested.

**Love, Sondra**

*August 6, 2020*

## ❡ SPIRITUAL PRAYERS INSPIRED BY GODFRE RAY KING

❡ "Mighty I AM Presence! Charge my entire mind, emotions, and body with thy ascended master consciousness and keep it eternally sustained and all powerfully active.

❡ "Mighty I AM Presence! I call you into action to take dominion over my thoughts, feelings, emotions, body, home, world, and daily activities. Produce your perfection and hold your dominion!

❡ "Mighty I AM Presence! Take complete control of my being, world, and activity. See that I make my ascension in this embodiment, for I AM the resurrection, the truth, and the life! I AM the ascension in the light.

❡ "Mighty I AM Presence! Consume and dissolve in me all negative, egotistical qualities, their cause, effect, record, and memory and replace them with the fullness of the perfected spiritual qualities.

❡ "Mighty I AM Presence! Charge me so full of divine love that every person, place, condition, and thing I contact becomes instantly harmonious and obedient to the I AM Presence.

333

❡ "Mighty I AM Presence! Fill me with your divine love, power, and perfect intelligent direction.

❡ "Mighty I AM Presence! Charge me and my world with the violet consuming flame of divine love which consumes all that is undesirable and keep me clothed forever with thy almighty perfection."

**Love, Sondra**

*August 7, 2020*

❡ **SPIRITUAL HONESTY**

❡ Spiritual honesty in a mature form is different than inner-child honesty. A child may blurt out everything with no self-control or discernment. This can be hurtful and inappropriate. This is not honesty: it is oral diarrhea. Spiritual honesty, in its mature form, is communicating what is appropriate in a loving, respectful manner. Some things in life are better left unsaid.

❡ Some things are between oneself and God. Some things are better dealt with in your journal. Go within and soul-search as to what your true motivation is for wanting to say something.

(Inspired by Joshua David Stone)

**Love, Sondra**

*August 8, 2020*

❡ **THE FAST TRACK TO GOD**

℘ A committed relationship is the fast track to God. It is a spiritual training and the ultimate teacher for spiritual growth and self-realization. It is guaranteed to bring up all your stuff. Any dysfunctional pattern in your subconscious mind is guaranteed to be triggered. Anyone can be spiritual living in a monastery or in the Himalayas. The true test of being spiritual is living in the marketplace. If you can practice the presence of God in a romantic relationship, you can do it anywhere. Relationships are the ultimate teaching tool if you use them in this way. So use your relationships as a spiritual training course.
(Inspired by Joshua David Stone)

**Love, Sondra**

*August 9, 2020*

**℘ RICHNESS AND SUPPORT**

℘ What makes a committed relationship so wonderful is the richness and support that you bring to each other. Some people are afraid of commitment. Perhaps they don't want to be exposed. Commitment means not running away the minute you encounter difficulty, but instead working through problems and finding the solution at the highest levels of your being. It means considering your partner first before running off with friends. It also means knowing you can trust your partner on all levels and that your partner can trust you the same. Can you give 100 percent to the relationship and to yourself? If you cannot commit, why be in the relationship in the first place?
℘ Meanwhile, your intent should be to keep growing, keep evolving and keep moving forward on the path of ascension!

**Love, Sondra**

*August 10, 2020*

### ꧁ STAY ON TOP OF THINGS

꧁ In your relationship, don't let things build up too much. It is possible to communicate too little and it is possible to communicate too much. Some couples spend all their time processing, and they don't know how to let go of things.

꧁ I asked Markus's brother-in-law what the secret of his really good marriage was. He said three words: "Let it go!"

꧁ The reverse would be holding things in too much. This leads to volcanic eruptions. You need to stay on top of things. Never ever go to bed angry.

**Love, Sondra**

*August 11, 2020*

### ꧁ OUR RESPONSIBILITY AS LIGHTWORKERS

꧁ As lightworkers we should be much more concerned with working on ourselves than working on our partners. It is important to have an agreement that you can give feedback, but one must use nonviolent communication such as that below:

1. I observe . . . in our relationship
2. The way I feel about it is . . .
3. What I need or recommend is . . .

꧁ There is no attack. But what do you do when your partner won't take any kind of feedback on some very important issues? The best thing then is to pray about it and put it in

God's hands. What I do is write to Babaji about it. That works. It is also possible to do affirmations for your partner.

**Love, Sondra**

*August 12, 2020*

### ᛒ HAPPINESS IS AN ATTRIBUTE OF LOVE

ᛒ Happiness is an attribute of love and it cannot be experienced where there is no love. It has no limits, being everywhere, and therefore joy is everywhere. God being love is also happiness. God loves us with equal love in which we were created, smiles on us, and offers us the happiness we crave.

ᛒ Love asks only that we are happy and will give us everything that makes for happiness.

ᛒ The constancy of joy is a condition quite alien to us.

ᛒ We can ask easily for love and for happiness and eternal life in peace that has no ending. Ask for this and you can only win. There is no difference between love and joy. Whenever we are not wholly joyous, we have reacted with a lack of love to one of God's creations.

(Summarized from A Course in Miracles)

**Love, Sondra**

*August 13, 2020*

### ᛒ RELATIONSHIP PRAYER

⧉ "Lord, help us remember that our love for each other reflects your love for us.

May we empower one another to fulfill our purpose in life.

May our love be an example for our children and a model for all.

May our experience as a couple give us a preview
of the oneness we can experience.

Help us to see that everything is either love or a call for love.

Help us to celebrate our similarities and honor our differences.

Help us to accept our limitations and utilize our talents.

Thank you for this opportunity, this life, and for my loving partner. Amen"

(By Joshua David Stone)

**Love, Sondra**

*August 14, 2020*

## ⧉ FEELING REJECTED

⧉ "Feeling rejected is the negative ego's interpretation of a breakup, rather than the interpretation of the Holy Spirit and Christ consciousness. The negative ego always interprets everything in a win-lose manner. The Christ consciousness interprets everything in a win-win manner. The Holy Spirit says there is no such thing as rejection; there are simply relationships that are not meant to be. If someone does not want to be with you, it is not that you are bad or that something is wrong with you.

⧉ "The feelings of rejection are connected to an attachment and addiction to that person. The truth is that the relationship is not meant to be, and your God-selves have other plans for each of you. If you look at the situation this way, you can stay out of judgment and blame for yourself and the other.

❡ "Rejection will occur only if there has been an unequal sense of power in the relationship. There might be a far better person for you around the corner if you can surrender to God's wisdom.

(From *Ascension and Romantic Relationships* by Joshua David Stone)

**Love, Sondra**

*August 15, 2020*

**❡ ONE WITH CHRIST**

❡ We are giving our new "Miracles for You" training this weekend. It is all about A Course in Miracles. It is so good to be working with the frequency of Christ for the people. We came here to realize ourselves as the Christed Self. When you believe you are one with Christ, everything changes for you. And this is not just for Christians. When you align to this energy of Christ your frequency is adjusted to a very high vibration. Once the Christ is merged with your soul, miracles occur. You can transform any situation by bringing the action of Christ to it.

❡ When you go to bed, ask to be aligned to the Christ frequency.

**Love, Sondra**

*August 16, 2020*

**❡ ASCENSION AND THE ASCENSION BUDDY**

❡ You can invoke the divine presence of your master (such as Babaji, Jesus or Ammachi) to permeate your being, and thus making those extremely high energies available to you. If you and your partner join in this divine intent, a third entity is created comprised of yourselves, your I AM presence, and the master. This is a wonderful way to approach marriage.

❡ Your mate then becomes you "ascension buddy." The ascension buddy system will elevate any relationship. It is a wonderful tool for mutual support. Service work is at the fore of the relationship.

**Love, Sondra**

*August 18, 2020*

### ❡ WHEN SEPARATION IS THE BEST OPTION

❡ There are times in a relationship when separation is the best option. Following are several scenarios:

1. The "different elevator syndrome" has reached such proportions that the couple no longer sees eye to eye.
2. The karma between the two individuals has run its course and there remains nothing to bond them together.
3. There is either physical or psychic abuse.
4. The destiny of the couple seems to lie in completely opposite directions.
5. The particular work the two came together to do is at an end and both the ties of work and feeling of being in love seem complete.
   (Inspired by *Ascension and Romantic Relationships* by Joshua David Stone)

**Love, Sondra**

*August 19, 2020*

## ❡ RESISTANCE

❡ You can use your willpower to stop the energy flow, and this creates tension. Resistance is the ego trying to stop spiritual energy. It is a huge waste of energy. You might use your will to resist what has already happened or what has not happened yet. Think how much energy is wasted resisting what has already happened. If you are resisting what might happen, you are throwing away your energy. When you resist, your energy gets stuck, and this can affect you very badly. It blocks your heart and causes you to feel closed and less vibrant.

❡ If you let each moment just flow through you, you can be fresh. STOP RESISTING! Plenty of events move right through you. Why resist this particular one? Perhaps it is just your preconceived notion of how things should be. Let whatever happens move through you.
(Summarized from *The Untethered Soul* by Michael Singer)

**Love, Sondra**

*August 20, 2020*

## ❡ ALIGNMENT

❡ When you are aligned with the universal flow, horizons of creativity open to you. You get connected to infinite intelligence. You feel universal love. You no longer need to ask for love or crave love because you are love. You also get inner peace. When you wake up in the morning, simply align your consciousness with the highest possible frequency. Say, "I am now aligned with Christ consciousness." Say it as often as you remember. You will feel the power. The thoughts you think will be different. The actions you take will be different. Your sense of Self will shift. Keep doing this and you will get a sense of exuberance. You will feel "tuned up." ♫ You cannot help others by moving out of alignment and into a place of non-alignment in which others live. You can only help them by being vibrantly attuned. Remain attuned. You are then an invitation.

**Love, Sondra**


*August 21, 2020*

**♫ HOW TO FACE EXPERIENCES**

♫ Amma says there are 3 ways people face experiences.

1. I. We try to run away from situations.
2. We try to change the circumstances, believing that such a change will solve our problems.
3. We curse our circumstances and proceed somehow. We complain and go on.

♫ But, she says there is a fourth way and that is to change our state of mind. This is the only way to truly find joy. It is impossible to change the external environment completely to suit our needs. So, we need to change our state of mind to suit the environment. This is possible only through spirituality. If we transform our minds, we can face any situation with a smile.
♫ A Course in Miracles would have you say, "I am willing to see this differently."

**Love, Sondra**

*August 22, 2020*

## ꒰ INTERNALIZING THE BEATITUDES

ꭹ Peacemakers have internalized the seven steps to wholeness outlined in the Beatitudes:

1. They recognize their faults.
2. They long for what they need to change.
3. 3.They are gentle, unpretentious, and nonviolent.
4. 4.They pursue right livelihood.
5. 5.They have a compassion for others.
6. 6.Their motivation is pure.
7. They offer unconditional love.

**Love, Sondra**

*August 23, 2020*

## ꭹ THE PEACEMAKER

ꭹ Are you a peacemaker? If so, you are extending God's healing, comfort, and blessing into a world in need of purification. You are a teacher of forgiveness. You teach through example as well as words. You are willing to bring Christ consciousness into all areas of living. You spread a lighthearted and friendly atmosphere.

ꭹ People who are NOT willing to open themselves to the healing process are not the responsibility of the peacemaker. Where there is no openness to receiving healing, there is no real desire for peace. And this goes for someone you might be in a relationship with. ACIM says this: "TRUTH CANNOT DEAL WITH ERRORS PEOPLE WANT TO

KEEP." So, if you experience a setback, you do not get discouraged. You continue with the work in the world.

**Love, Sondra**

*August 24, 2020*

**♪ MY BIRTHDAY**

♪ On this day I was born at home on the kitchen table. My mom had been walking around the house while in labor, whistling when she had a contraction. My sister was disappointed that I was a girl. She did not want any competition so went to the window and said to her friends outside, "We had a boy, but it came out a girl." My Dad went out on the porch to have a cigarette and I was disappointed about that. My grandfather had been in the mental institution for depression but when he saw me, he was healed and never went back. I was born in a little town of 300 people, and everyone came over to see me, so I was a public figure right off the bat.
♪ Markus just gave me two exquisite perfumes!

**Love, Sondra**

*August 25, 2020*

**♪ CONTINUALLY EVOLVING BEINGS**

♪ People in a new paradigm relationship view their partners as continually evolving beings. They lovingly help each other in their pursuit to become the best possible version of themselves. This makes the relationship thrive!

℘ They also recognize that everyone evolves at their own pace. They know their partner's progress may be gradual.

℘ It is very important that a partner creates their own highest vision of themselves and not having the partner's vision imposed on them. In other words, it is important one does not insist that the partner be who you think they should be. If one is not sure of what the partner's highest vision of themselves is, one has to ASK. However, when two people are really tuned in to one another, they are often able to envision possibilities for their partner that their partner has not yet envisioned for themselves.

(Inspired from *The Soul Mate Experience* by Mali Apple and Joe Dunn)

**Love, Sondra**

*August 26, 2020*

℘ **WORKPLACE RELATIONSHIPS**

℘ We tend to think relationships in the workplace are only important to work and not to our personal growth. Unlike our personal relationships where we chose the people we relate to, our work relationships seem to be chosen for us at random.

℘ In truth, these relationships are no different than those in our personal life regarding their purpose and the impact they have on our growth. In ALL our relationships we have the opportunity to offer love and forgiveness or fear.

℘ We are just as responsible to keep our work relationships clear and loving. At work there is often the "invisible sibling syndrome" coming up. That is where you are in competition with someone at work, but you really have them set up as your sibling in your unconscious mind. Or you may have them set up as your parent (like your boss). Or if a co-worker never values your opinions and judgments, perhaps they are reflecting your fear that your opinions are of little value.

♫ No one is in our life by accident!

**Love, Sondra**

**August 27, 2020**

**♫ DIFFICULT RELATIONSHIPS**

♫ No one is in our life without a specific purpose and learning goal. Some offer major lessons and others minor lessons. But the lesson is always the same: to remove the fears and judgments that are in the way of loving each person unconditionally.

♫ There are only two forms of behavior: extending love or asking for love. When someone behaves badly, they are calling out for love. If someone is attacking us, they do not love themselves or feel themselves worthy of love and respect of others. People who love themselves and who feel worthy of the love and respect of others do not treat people unlovingly. By forgiving and loving them we are teaching love.

♫ Forgiving another does not mean allowing their fearful and upsetting behavior to continue. We may confront the situation, but we do it with an awareness of love and understanding. We may desire to remove ourselves from a close relationship with them. But resolving our bitterness and desire to attack back allows resolution. Then we have learned the lesson.

(Inspired by *The Spirit of Business* by Phoenix Jackson)

**Love, Sondra**

*August 28, 2020*

## ◊ THE PLANET AS A SCHOOLHOUSE

◊ "The planet is a one room schoolhouse where both first graders and college students attend together. These grades in no way correspond to our physical age. A child may be in a much higher grade than their parent. A physical adult may be a spiritual child and vice versa. We all enter the planet at a certain grade level due to our work before this lifetime. In truth all these differences are illusions since we are always totally whole. We are given many opportunities to work through all the grades and we can remain in any one grade for as long as we wish.

◊ "The curriculum in this schoolhouse is set and we cannot change it. The curriculum has only one lesson to teach, and that is unconditional love in all circumstances. We have free will to set the pace of our learning. We are here to remove the blocks to the awareness of love's presence. There should be no judgment attached to the different grades."
(From *The Spirit of Business* by Phoenix Jackson)

**Love, Sondra**

*August 29, 2020*

## ◊ TURNING OUR WILLS OVER

◊ The idea of turning over our wills to anyone or anything other than ourselves is seen as dangerous. It may even feel like a weakness. We have come to believe that there is no clearer authority than the human will. But if you look at the state of the planet in general that is proof enough that the use of our own will using our ego is unsuccessful in creating a peaceful world.

ᔓ We ask the Holy Spirit to undo our ego so that we can do things a better way. We ask to work with our Higher Self or Divine Self to dominate in our decision making. We are not asking for advice from something outside of ourselves, we are asking that our true nature, which is LOVE manifest in our lives. This is the only way to be truly at peace and joy. When we surrender our will to the power of the Universe, we receive miracles.

**Love, Sondra**

*August 30, 2020*

ᔓ **HOW THE WORLD WORKS**

ᔓ There are three models:

1. No Creator/Random universe
2. Things just happen. Lucky or unlucky. Lives have no purpose. No plan. No God. Chance events.
3. Created Universe/Punitive or indifferent planet
4. Model taught in most churches. View of punitive God. Belief in sin and punishment. When we do something wrong, something painful will happen. God is loving AND punitive. Fear is always in this model. God is separate from us.
5. Created Universe/Benevolent Creator and Planet
6. Divine Being created the universe intelligently and with a purpose. Universe is totally loving and safe environment. Everything is a blessing or gift. God designs lessons to aid our growth. Nothing is an accident or punishment.

♪ Hopefully you and your mate are living in the third model!

**Love, Sondra**


*August 31, 2020*

## ♪ THE ENTHUSIASTIC PERSON

♪ The enthusiastic person is high on any tone scale. He or she is eager, cheerful, and alive. They wake up with a sense of wellbeing. They are an active person who inspires others to action. They recognize and enjoy the good things in living. They do not need approval from others. (I often give this affirmation: "I rise above the need for approval OR disapproval.")

♪ The enthusiastic person can spend time with low-tone people without getting depressed. They have no need to control or dominate people to satisfy their own ego. Their tremendous personal power is a calming influence. They make themself understood easily. They can communicate deeply felt ideas and they listen to others and understand them easily. They are loved by almost everyone. (However, low-toned types may get upset around them.) They are alive and they like it. They are clear on their own worth.

♪ If you can find such a mate, go for it.

**Love, Sondra**


*September 1, 2020*

## ♪ WHEN DIVORCE IS THE BEST POSSIBLE OPTION

🎵 Several friends and clients are going through a divorce. There are times when it is the best possible option. This may be the case when the karma between the individuals has run its course and there remains nothing left to bind them together. It can also happen when the destiny of the couple seems to lie in completely different directions. Or maybe the particular work the two came together to do is at an end and feelings of being in love are over. Or when there is physical or psychic abuse.

**Love, Sondra**

*September 2, 2020*

🎵 **ARE YOU READY TO BE A SERVER?**

- Servers have transcended their preoccupation with personal issues to a degree where they are able to align their ideals, thoughts, and actions with a higher cause.
- Servers present purity of motive, sincerity, and an unconditionally loving attitude.
- Servers have a genuine urgent sense that they have some important duty to perform and that they are here to help.
- *Servers are by nature energy transmuters. They can sublimate gross energies.
- Servers can rise above most exterior harmful vibrations.
- Servers have attained the spiritual goal of unconditional love and spontaneity of service.
- Servers act as catalysts in relationships and interaction with them is often dynamic. They elicit in others that which needs to be recognized.

- Servers perform a kind mirroring function that allows others to become aware of their own psychological encumbrances. They have a purging effect.
- Servers have a kind of "white magic" that is a spiritual force of benefit to others.

(From the book *Servers of the Divine Plan* by Rudolph Berger)

**Love, Sondra**

*September 3, 2020*

### ℊ BENEFITS TO SERVERS

ℊ There are benefits to the servers of the divine plan. They may receive help from benevolent entities who reside upon higher planes. They will be provided with infallible spiritual guidance that will help them through earthly trials. They will be given assistance by other Divine Agents. Their own spiritual advancement will become enormously accelerated. Grace will be bestowed upon all servants of the Divine Plan as they proceed on their ministry of joy. His or her identity will expand to something infinitely more splendid.

ℊ The path of selfless service is by far the most easy, joyful, and quickest road leading back to the kingdom of God. Helping others is the way that leads to liberation!

ℊ Saint Theresa of Calcutta said this: "It is not the things that we do which count in the eyes of God, but how much love we put into them."

**Love, Sondra**

*September 4, 2020*

## ♫ WORLD SERVERS

♫ World servers, like all humanity, should do what they find uplifting, what gives them a sense of real purpose. They simply need to follow their joy, for in joy there is happiness and where there is happiness, spontaneous and spirited service will naturally flow from a full and loving heart. Let servers do whatever makes the heart sing. The true path is never dull, for as we serve, we also learn. The rate of learning is much enhanced upon the path of loving service.

♫ It is a blessed opportunity because you will raise your vibratory rate of consciousness and be emancipated from pain and suffering of the lower self. The rewards are going to be everlasting. Your light will inevitably be brighter.

(Inspired by *Servers of the Divine Plan* by Rudolph Berger)

**Love, Sondra**

*September 6, 2020*

## ♫ A LIFE WITHOUT FEAR

♫ "Fear is caused by blockages in the flow of energy. When your energy is blocked, it cannot come up and feed your heart. Therefore, your heart becomes weak and becomes susceptible to lower vibrations. One of the lowest of all vibrations is fear. The purpose of spiritual evolution is to remove the blockages that cause you fear. You have to decide not to fight with life; not to try to control things. You have to keep letting go." (Michael Singer)

♫ I would add that you have to give up your unconscious death urge. Death is the stronghold of all fear. If I processed each of your fears down to the bottom, the fear of death would be there. The more you get that you are in charge of how long you stay alive, the less you are threatened by death just "happening to you." The more you change your negative thoughts, the less fear you will have. It would help a lot to read our book *Physical Immortality*. Also, fear can be "breathed out" in a Liberation Breathing session.

֍ There is such a thing as life without fear. It feels really good. You have to keep your heart open, keep letting go, keep having the right thoughts, and keep evolving spiritually.

**Love, Sondra**

*September 8, 2020*

֍ **STAYING OPEN**

֍ We all want joy, enthusiasm, and love. If you can always feel this, what does it matter what happens on the outside? Michael Singer says we should not let anything that happens in life be important enough to close our heart over it. Say, "No I am not going to close. I am going to relax and let this situation take place." He says that no matter what it is that happens, let it be the sport of the day. No matter what anyone does, embrace life with all your heart. Once you attain this high state, your energy level will be phenomenal.

֍ If you want to stay open, pay attention when you feel love and enthusiasm and ask yourself why you cannot feel that all the time. The answer is obvious: it only goes away if you choose to close. By closing you are making the choice not to feel love. You can either choose to close because you don't like what happened, or you can keep feeling love and enthusiasm by not closing. The more you stay open the more the energy flow can build.

(Inspired by *The Untethered Soul* by Michael Singer)

**Love, Sondra**

*September 9, 2020*

**℈ LIFE WITHOUT STRESS OR TENSION**

℈ How do you learn to live a life without stress or tension? Stress only happens when you RESIST life's events. To resist you must first decide that something is not the way you like it. You carry around with you your own preconceived notions of how things should be. Let your spiritual path become the willingness to let whatever happens make its way through you. Begin dealing with each situation as acceptance. Acceptance means that events can make it through you without resistance.

℈ It is possible to never have another problem. This is because events are not problems; they are just events. Your resistance to them is what causes the problem. If you don't have fear or desire about an event, there's nothing to deal with. You do deal with things, but you deal with them as merely events.

℈ Allow life to unfold. It is all about no problems, no tension, no stress, no burnout. The way to work with resistance is by relaxing. The path of non-resistance is the path of surrender, the path of acceptance. You relax and release. Get to the point that nothing disturbs you.

(From *The Untethered Soul* by Michael Singer)

**Love, Sondra**

*September 10, 2020*

## ∬ THE UNTETHERED SOUL

∬ I have so enjoyed reviewing the book *The Untethered Soul* by Michael Singer. I have shared some of the highlights in case you don't have time to read it. One of the big things Singer stresses is the Path of Unconditional Happiness. He asks bluntly: "Do you want to be happy, or do you not want to be happy? Do you want to be happy from this moment regardless of what happens?"

∬ Your happiness is under your control. Are you willing to take the Vow of Happiness? That means you decide to be happy regardless of what happens You have to mean it. You don't let stuff "out there" ruin your day. You don't let your happiness be conditional upon the behavior of other people. The purpose of life is to ENJOY. You no longer say, "I'll be happy if this or that does not happen." Are you going to break your Vow of Happiness because certain things happen? You should be happy just be alive. Period! Try it.

**Love, Sondra**

*September 12, 2020*

## ∬ AN IMMORTAL ENCOUNTER

∬ I had a group in 1985 at Glastonbury once and the night before we began someone told me there was a ceremony at midnight on top of the Tor. I was determined to go. But then it started raining and only two came with me. At the top, a single man was sitting and making invocations. He looked like an Elizabethan poet with his long hair blowing in the mist. He was shouting invocations such as "I call for all the

Immortals of the world!" I was astonished. I went up to him and said, "Here I am," and kissed him on the cheek. Then I asked him to come and teach my class. What a miracle!

⁊ He told us that when he was 20 years old, he was meditating on his bed and Elijah from the Bible materialized floating in the air in front of him and stayed for four hours. Elijah telepathically transferred to him the knowledge of physical immortality and told him to move to Glastonbury, England. His name is Robert Coon.

⁊ Robert said, "Every exhalation of breath should send an expansive energy of gratitude outwards in all directions to bless all time and space. Every inhalation should condense and absorb the Divine Touch of Love that is offered to you at every instant, coming from every particle of the universe and enthrone this gift within your heart. At every instant, immortals are radiating gratitude for you."

⁊ Affirm: "At every instant the Divine touches me and fully awakens me to the uniqueness and beauty of my own immortality."

**Love, Sondra**

*September 13, 2020*

### ⁊ VERY INTENSE RELATIONSHIPS

⁊ Recently I came to understand at a much deeper level why some relationships are so much more intense. An old friend of mine was going through two major crises. Even though she lived far away and even though I had not seen her in years, I started feeling everything she was feeling. If she was sad, I started crying for no reason. I felt all her fear and that was really awful. If she had physical pain, I had it in the same place at the same time. This went on for several weeks. I could not seem to stop it. I mentioned it to another healer, and he told me that we had had 26 past lives together! I called her and told her this and together we came to understand which one was affecting us the most.

ſ I wrote to Babaji every day and started doing the mantra and Ho'oponopono. Things started clearing up then, thank God. If you are interested in this subject, I suggest you read the book *You Were Born Again to Be Together* by Dick Supton. He writes especially about relationships between couples, but it could apply to any relationship as I had been coupled with her in other lives.

**Love, Sondra**

*September 14, 2020*

### ſ WORDS FROM ROBERT COON, IMMORTALIST

ſ "The physical body is a temple of infinite potential and should be consecrated to serving the universal purpose. This purpose is the Great Work of overcoming all death, decay, entropy, and suffering throughout all realms. Absolute joy is yours when you raise the frequencies of your entire being—body, spirit, mind, and heart above the realm of mortality. We become perfect channels for the Will of the Divine when we become translated immortal beings. Thus, we become angelic in our nature.

ſ "Greet the dawn of each new day with Gratitude for all that that day shall offer thee. Affirm with joy: All that I touch becomes spiritual Gold. At every instant the Divine touches me and fully awakens me to the uniqueness and beauty of my own immortality."

(From *The Art of Everlasting Life* by Robert Coon)

**Love, Sondra**

*September 15, 2020*

## ℊ THE GREAT ASCENSION LAWS

ℊ Robert says that the great Ascension Laws are the Law of Divine Praise, the Law of Joyous Thanksgiving, and the Law of Love. Praise. Thanksgiving. Love. Together these three divine frequencies have the power to create physical immortality if operated by Divine Will. And, of course, thanksgiving for all experience in life is the key to abundance. Thanksgiving magnifies. That is why I started doing a gratitude book again. When I realized praise purifies, I decided to order a book of hymns of praise, and I plan to read one a day.

ℊ All this is marvelous, but I would add that one must work out the unconscious death urge also. This takes a real commitment, and it is important to know your programming and to BREATHE it out with Liberation Breathing. You just don't think your way to immortality. It requires a lot of cleansing. If one does not do that, one can end up getting old and sick. When that happens people come to me and say, "I wish I had listened to you 20 years ago and I wish I had done what you said and stuck with the work."

**Love, Sondra**

*September 16, 2020*

## ℊ WORKING ON YOUR RELATIONSHIP

ℊ Once I was in a relationship and a psychic told me to give it up because I was the one who would have to do all the work in the relationship. What he was saying was that my partner would not be willing to work on himself. After that I thought *I don't mind if a man has a "case"* (issues everyone has) *but I care about whether they are willing to work on their issues.* This proved to be super important.

♪ Some people resent having to do the work it takes to have a good relationship. Others say, "This is just the way I am, take it or leave it." That is a copout. It takes work to keep a relationship clear, but if you play it right, it is actually fun to keep your relationship rewarding and healthy. Fortunately for Markus and me we had done a lot of work on ourselves before we married as we each had tough gurus that blasted our egos. I would not say we have to work hard at our marriage. But even so, we keep clearing anything that comes up using spiritual purification techniques.

♪ Quite frankly, I don't know how people make it without a spiritual life and ways of clearing. They usually just fight and then they say, "Fighting is normal." That is no way to live, believe me.

♪ It is even possible to resurrect a bad relationship. But it would have to be totally reconceived.

**Love, Sondra**


*September 17, 2020*

♪ **TURNING THINGS OVER**

♪ During our devotions Markus and I were discussing the importance of turning things over to the Holy Spirit rather than figuring it all out ourselves. We realize we had to admit that our way was not working on certain issues, and we don't know the answer. Markus was saying we have to trust the unknown. That is where the answer is. We are not used to trusting the unknown.

❡ For the whole day I tried to turn things over to the Holy Spirit, but I was not sure I was really doing it. I felt like I had to repent before I could do it all the way. I went through all the things I wanted to repent about. That was a good process. I am really trying to find out what it is to be able to completely turn everything over to the Holy Spirit. It seemed too easy just to say it. I am asking for guidance.

**Love, Sondra**

*September 19, 2020*

## ❡ RUTH BADER GINSBURG

❡ Here in Washington, D.C. everyone is processing the death of Judge Ginsburg. There was a vigil at the Supreme Court building that started last night. It is sad and looks like there is a fight over it coming up. It is going to make our election even crazier! There is a real risk that a new appointee could undo her life's work.

❡ If you have not seen the movies about her, I highly recommend *RBG* and *On the Basis of Sex*. Every woman should see those no matter what country you are in. So inspiring!

**Love, Sondra**

*September 21, 2020*

## ❡ GOD BEING LOVE IS ALSO HAPPINESS

❦ We have been setting the timer on the phone and saying the lesson (ACIM, Lesson 103) every hour. This really feels good. Over the years when I studied ACIM, I did not repeat the lesson as often as was suggested. I would always forget to do it every hour. So it helps a lot to set a timer. I suggest you try it.

❦ "Happiness is an attribute of love. It cannot be apart from love. God, being love, is also happiness. And it is happiness I seek today. I cannot fail because I see the truth."

❦ It was not said like that when I was a child in church. We had a fear of God and we feared God was going to punish us. How great it would have been to have learned that God, being love, is also happiness. ACIM is a teaching on how to be happy.

**Love, Sondra**

*September 22, 2020*

❦ **UNDOING CHURCH DOGMA**

❦ I am stunned by the fact that my sub-conscious was still running me around church dogma. Because my husband is such a gifted Breathworker, he pulled it out of me. He was helping me complete my pattern of taking on stuff from people now and then. It has always been so automatic because in past lives I was a gifted healer who took through my body their disease. I wanted to eliminate this pattern completely and forever in this life.

❦ Markus was giving me a session on this and he came up with the notion that it had to do with the idea from church that suffering is holy. Every single church service said that Christ died for our sins. Markus said I wanted to be like Jesus so I would take on the suffering of others.

ᒑ In A Course in Miracles Jesus corrects all this and says that was NOT the purpose of the crucifixion. The purpose was to show that there are no victims, and he was not even a victim of that. He also demonstrated total forgiveness. The old idea of empathy is to join in the suffering of others. I must have had this pattern for lifetimes. The reason I could never clear this pattern until now is because I never ever went that deep in my process before.

**Love, Sondra**

*September 23, 2020*

ᒑ **WHAT ACIM SAYS ABOUT TRUE EMPATHY**

ᒑ "The capacity to empathize is very useful to the Holy Spirit. His way is very different. Healing pain is not accomplished by delusional attempts to enter into it and lighten it by sharing the delusion.

ᒑ "To empathize does not mean to join in the suffering. That is the ego's interpretation of empathy. The ego always empathizes to weaken and to weaken is to attack. You do not know what empathizing means. If you will sit quietly and let the Holy Spirit relate through you, you will empathize with strength.

ᒑ "All you have learned of empathy is from the past. There is nothing from the past that you should keep. Do not use empathy to make the past real, and so perpetuate it. True empathy is of Him (Holy Spirit) who knows what it is. You will learn His interpretation of it if you let Him use your capacity for strength, and not for weakness. Offer your empathy to Him for it is His perception and His strength that you would share. And let Him offer you His strength and His perception to be shared through you. Leave Him his function for He will fulfill it if you but ask Him to enter your relationships and bless them for you."

(This is summarized from ACIM Text, Chapter 16, Section I.)

❡ It also says to focus your mind only on this: "I am not alone, and I would not intrude the past upon my Guest. I have invited Him, and He is here. I need do nothing except not to interfere."

❡ So to summarize, lifting people up into your Divine Joy is more helpful than "sharing in their suffering." And if they cannot join you there, then trust the Holy Spirit is helping them through you by your being quiet and fully present for them. You need "do nothing" to empathize. All you need to do to truly empathize is ask the Holy Spirit, or the Divine Mother, or Energy of your Spiritual Master to enter into the situation and "take over the healing."

**Love, Sondra**

*September 24, 2020*

## ❡ RULES FOR DECISION IN ACIM

1.  Today I will make no decision by myself.

2. Tell yourself the kind of day you want, the feelings you want to have, the things you want to happen and what you want to experience. Then realize: This is the day that will be given me if I make no decisions myself.

3. If something occurred in your day that is not what you wanted, realize you have asked by yourself in the ego. Then say: "I have no question. I forgot to decide."

4. Say this: "At least I can decide I do not like what I feel now."

1. 5.The next step is easy: Say: "I hope I have been wrong." (This reminds you that help is what you need. Now you have reached the turning point.)

5. You can say now in perfect honesty: "I want another way to look at this."

6. The final step is an acknowledgement of your lack of opposition. It is a statement of an open mind. Perhaps there is another way to look at this. What can I lose by asking?

₰ Who is your advisor? Christ or the ego? If you oppose the Holy Spirit, you fight yourself.

**Love, Sondra**


*September 27, 2020*

## ₰ SUBCONSCIOUS NEGATIVE COMMITMENTS

₰ Whenever there is a discrepancy between what you say you want and what you are actually experiencing, it is due to an underlying commitment—a stronger negative commitment in the unconscious that was made out of fear which will override other desires you have.

❡ What you are receiving is always in perfect alignment with what you have been most committed to on the level of the unconscious. Let's say you say you want a relationship but then you do not have one. In your subconscious you probably have a commitment that goes like this: I have to make sure I do not have a relationship and that way I won't be hurt.

**Love Sondra**

*September 28, 2020*

## ❡ THE PURPOSE OF LIFE AND UNION

❡ Once you understand that the purpose of life is spiritual and the purpose of a union is to further spiritual expansion, you will have to re-evaluate the relationship on that basis. Clearly, if the partnership is making either of you more dependent, selfish, or rigid, you are on the wrong track. But if the union purifies your ego, making you stronger, more expanded, and more spiritual, you will very likely weather the hard parts and grow.

❡ I have seen many people use their mate to hold themselves back spiritually. Although they may be on an enlightened path, they are committed to someone who resists enlightenment. They stifle their own development to avoid threatening their mate. However, resentment smolders and later they wish they had had the courage to leave that relationship before so much time had been invested.

**Love, Sondra**

*September 29, 2020*

**♪ ACIM, LESSON 38**

♪ "There is nothing my holiness cannot do."

♪ It says your holiness is totally unlimited in its power because it establishes you as a Son of God, at one with the Mind of His Creator. Through your holiness the power of God is made manifest. Through your holiness the power of God is made available. And there is nothing that the power of God cannot do. Your holiness can remove all pain and end all sorrow and solve all problems!

♪ So look today what problem you want solved. Apply the idea for today like this:

- In this situation involving _____, in which I see myself, there is nothing my holiness cannot do.
- In this situation involving _____ in which _____ sees himself, there is nothing my holiness cannot do.

♪ It is good to do this every hour for five minutes each time, stating aloud what situations you have.

**Love, Sondra**

*September 30, 2020*

**♪ LEAVING A RELATIONSHIP**

♪ Once I was living with a guy for two years and we had a lot of fun and a great relationship. One day he came home and said, "I have to leave." I was shocked. I said, "Are you upset with me?" He said, "No." Then I asked, "Are you upset with this relationship?" He said, "No, I just have to leave." He gave no explanation. I was quite devastated, but then I realized I was going to India to meet my Master and I figured maybe I needed to let go of everything. But when I got to New Delhi I was walking in the park, and I was miserable and complaining about it all in my head. Suddenly I heard a voice in the air (this has only happened to me three times in my life). The voice said, "What if leaving could be a joy?" I said out loud, "THAT IS RIDICULOUS!" Then the voice said, "Just wait until you see what I have for you next!" I literally threw myself on the ground saying, "Pardon me for my lack of faith."

❡ Well, what Babaji gave me after that was so far beyond the life I had that you cannot even imagine. If someone leaves, they will be replaced by something better if you can trust.

**Love, Sondra**

*October 1, 2020*

## ❡ VISUALIZING WHAT YOU WANT

❡ Most people know that they should visualize the end state of what they want . . . see yourself having it. But people forget that they should simultaneously focus on the Source. As long as you are focused on the Source, the ego is in the back seat.

❡ You, yourself, are not manifesting your desired circumstances. Only Spirit has the sufficient energy to get the job done. It is a mistake to think you are doing the miracle work. Your mind commands a very small part of the power. The true power behind a miracle comes from the Source. The visualization only provides direction for the power. The act of seeing the final state opens the mind so that it can function as a directed channel.

❡ If you see you have doubt, calmly turn that over to Infinite Intelligence to be quietly deactivated.

(Summarized from *The Twelve Conditions of a Miracle* by Todd Michael)

**Love, Sondra**

*October 4, 2020*

## ❡ WORSHIPPING THE DIVINE MOTHER

❡ Today during the training we talked about the Divine Mother and the teachings of Ammachi. Shastriji (Babaji's high priest) said this: "The first element is Mother Earth. The definition of the element earth is smell, fragrance. That is why the first step to worshipping the Divine Mother is that we offer flowers full of fragrance, because with her grace, Mother Earth is producing beautiful fragrance, that is, flowers on earth. A man might dedicate his whole life to creating a flower, but even with total dedication, he cannot create a natural flower. When the Divine Mother has given us this gift through Mother Earth, it is our duty that we offer her own creation—the flowers. This is why we offer beautiful flowers to her as the first step to worship.

❡ "You fold your hands and meditate on the Divine Mother to call her. After that, you offer her a seat, and to give her a seat. You take a flower and put it there. Water too is the Divine Mother's grace. So then you offer her water five times. First to wash her feet; second, you offer water with your hands. Third, you offer her water to drink. Fourth, you give her a bath; fifth, you give her water to please her. We offer all this to show our gratitude for it is her grace alone that she has given us the element of water. Without water we would all have died of thirst."

**Love, Sondra**

*October 6, 2020*

♪ **ACIM, LESSON 152**

♪ Today we reviewed "The Power of Decision is my Own." The lessons says, "No one can suffer unless it be his own decision. No one suffers pain except his choice elects this. And no one dies without his own consent! In fact, nothing occurs but represents your wish." So there it is! Everything that happens to you that you don't like, you wished for. People do not want to hear this.

♪ It goes on to explain that when you choose these negative states for yourself, that is ARROGANCE. It is arrogance because you have created something in opposition to God. Chaos of any kind contradicts the will of God. True humility is accepting yourself as God created you.

♪ Every hour we are to say: "The power of decision is my own. This day I will accept myself as what my Father's will created me to be."

**Love, Sondra**

*October 7, 2020*

♪ **GUILT AND SICKNESS**

♪ Guilt always demands punishment. One of the ways we punish ourselves when we have guilt is to get sick. We attack our bodies with illness, pain, or injury that we make up. We may not even be in touch with the guilt, but it is in the subconscious. It could be:

- Past-life guilt
- Guilt about hurting our mother at birth

- Religious guilt thinking one is a sinner
- Guilt about anything we have done wrong in this life

❡ That is a lot of guilt! ACIM says that guilt is not only not of God, it is actually an attack on God. It says that it is a sure sign that your thinking is unnatural. This is all explained in the text under the section "Ego's Use of Guilt" if you want to look it up. Somewhere else in the text it says that if you have guilt, you are actually walking the carpet of death. (That means that we think we must eventually die as a form of punishment for our guilt, especially if we think we are sinners.) We therefore kill ourselves with our own thoughts by squeezing the life force right out of ourselves!

❡ Reading A Course in Miracles helps you become re-grounded in your innocence. It says you can have forgiveness in the "holy instant" because God does not make your sins real. That is because God knows that your mistakes were in your ego and your ego is not real. Your ego was made from the thought that you are separate from God, but that is not possible so therefore it is not real. Your ego is a nightmare that you are temporarily experiencing. When your child has a nightmare, for example, you do not make it real.

**Love, Sondra**

*October 8, 2020*

## ❡ FEAR AND SICKNESS

❡ ACIM says that all healing is essentially the release from fear. It says we only have two true emotions: love and fear. Love is God. That won't make you sick. Fear is ego. That will make you sick.

❡ Fear may seem beyond your control, but it is not. Fear is self-controlled. We are responsible for what we think, and fear comes from fearful thoughts. When we have fear it is a sure sign that we have allowed our minds to miscreate. When we have fear we have chosen wrongly. The correction of fear then, is our responsibility. So, we should not ask God to take away our fear, but we should ask instead for help in the conditions that brought about the fear.

❡ The main condition that brings about fear is the belief that we are separate from God. ACIM says an attempt to "master" fear is useless because that gives fear more power. The only way to overcome fear, it says, is to master love. By choosing loving thoughts, you are rejecting fear. These are the steps to the release of fear.

- Know first that this is fear.
- Fear arises from lack of love.
- The only remedy for lack of love is perfect love.
- Perfect love is the Atonement.

❡ With the Atonement you allow the Holy Spirit to correct all your wrong thinking.

**Love, Sondra**

*October 9, 2020*

**❡ QUESTIONS ABOUT ATONEMENT**

❡ There were several questions about Atonement which I will attempt to answer. ACIM, Workbook, Lesson 139 is "I will accept Atonement for Myself."

❡ It is all about self-identity. Atonement can simply be remembered as AT-ONE-MENT. We are one with the father.

Our true identity is that we are as God created us: perfect, whole, complete, like the Father. If we doubt that, accepting the Atonement is the solution. This lesson more or less said that you will have to keep coming back until you get this! The Atonement is the restoration of the awareness of our Divine connection. The Atonement is also a correction of all our wrong thinking. What is asked of us is our acceptance of this. Every hour we are to say, "I will accept Atonement for myself, for I remain as God created me."

**Love, Sondra**

*October 10, 2020*

**❡ HEALING**

❡ I think the scary part of having a disease is the temptation to think *I will never get over this*. That fear and doubt has to be turned over to the Holy Spirit. Remember, anything you have created you can uncreate. It is actually less work to heal yourself than to make yourself sick. It takes a lot of effort and struggle to hang onto negative thinking to make yourself sick. Your natural state is health. You had to really work at going against your natural state to have created a condition.
❡ Also, remember that symptoms are the cure in process. In other words, anything on its way up is on its way out. At least it is no longer suppressed. You may need to get a Breathworker to find out the cause of your condition if you cannot figure it out yourself. That person can also help you breathe out the thoughts causing the condition.
❡ You have to be ready for healing. You have to get that you deserve it. Say, "I am going to have faith that I am healed of this _____" (symptom, disease, or pattern).

❡ The will to live is the most important factor in your healing. If your life urge is strong enough, you can definitely overcome. If you get stuck in fear or the thought *I might die* that will greatly inhibit the natural healing abilities of the body. Your body does have natural healing abilities. You know this because when you cut yourself, it starts healing by itself.

**Love, Sondra**

*October 11, 2020*

### ❡ A RELATIONSHIP CAN HEAL OR HURT YOU

❡ Whether a relationship heals or hurts you depends on how you play the game of relationships. You may want your mate to agree with you on everything and back you up no matter what. Or as a mate, you may think that is what you are required to do—agree with him or her and back them up no matter what. That might LOOK like a healed relationship, but what if it is just collusion and co-dependency that you are creating? If so, watch out later.

❡ What if your mate agrees with you just to make you happy and what if you are into your ego (your "case") at the time? He or she would then be supporting your ego, supporting that which will eventually make you sick. How is it then healing you? It is not. If you re-enforce your ego, you will just get more stuck. The same is true vice versa.

❡ This has been called "the tyranny of agreement." The ego cannot conceive that there is any love when two people disagree. If you support behavior that could be hurtful to your mate, this is the ultimate co-dependency. Peace does not come from the agreement of two egos. The truly healthy relationship has room for disagreement. You can even disagree without an upset! If you listen carefully to a mate who disagrees, you can learn what you need to change to stay healthy.

**Love, Sondra**

*October 12, 2020*

## ℐ THE GOAL IS THE IDEAL RELATIONSHIP

ℐ A relationship should strengthen you, not weaken you. You should be happier because of the relationship, not more miserable. You should expand because of the relationship, not contract. You should get financially more prosperous as a result, not less. You should get healthier, not sicker. This is the goal, the ideal.

ℐ To handle everything that comes up in a relationship and keep getting stronger, enlightenment is needed. Instead of saying it feels impossible, try reading A Couse in Miracles and see why this is happening to you. Read our books on loving relationships and spiritual intimacy.

ℐ I know many people who stay in dead or destructive relationships because they are too afraid to leave and be alone. Don't lie to yourself. Pray for the relationship to be healed or for something better for both of you.

**Love, Sondra**

*October 13, 2020*

## ℐ THE GOAL IS THE IDEAL RELATIONSHIP II

❡ Many people think or say, "I won't be happy until I am healthy." This is understandable, but the truth is that you will be healthy when you are happy. Unhappiness is due to loss of contact with the Source, which means that people forget that they are one with God.

❡ Maharishi, the founder of transcendental meditation, said that bliss is ultimately the most powerful agent of physiology. The idea is to be happy no matter what is going on around you. And your happiness should not depend on material things.

❡ Mother Teresa said that most people are spiritually deprived and that is the problem with the world.

**Love, Sondra**

*October 14, 2020*

**❡ LOVE AND FREEDOM**

❡ Amma says that love and freedom are interdependent. Many people think love makes you trapped, but when there is love, there is freedom from bondage of the ego.

❡ She says, "People are bound by the past and the future. That is why it is so difficult to find true love in the world. In order to be able to love, both the past and future must dissolve and disappear. You will then experience the present moment as it is. When you live in the moment you are completely here. You do not worry about anything; you have no fears or preconceived ideas. The past does not matter to you anymore, you forget it. Nothing can bind you...you are ever free. To truly be able to love, you need to be free of everything. But at the same time, if you are to be completely free, you must have love within. Only when we learn to love everyone and everything can we be completely free."

(From *Awaken Children Volume VIII* by Amma)

**Love, Sondra**

*October 15, 2020*

**♪ PAST-LIFE GUILT**

♪ I was having some of that, but then I read a passage from Amma that I found very helpful. A devotee came to her and said she was having a lot of guilt about having two abortions and she could not forgive herself. Amma consoled her and said, "Don't think of what you have done as a great sin. It was the karma of both you and the two children to go through that experience. The fetuses were destined to live only for that long.

♪ "Don't react to the past. There is a force and aggression implied in reaction. Reaction creates more turbulence in the mind and the very thought you are trying to forget will come up with more strength. To react is to fight. Fighting the wounds of the past will only deepen those wounds. Relaxation is the method that heals the wounds of the mind, not reaction. The mere realization of your wrongdoing has freed you from it. You have already been forgiven. Any sin will be washed away by the tears of repentance. From now on you should not carry this burden in your mind. Forget it and be at peace."

**Love, Sondra**

*October 18, 2020*

## ℘ RELATIONSHIPS ARE ASSIGNMENTS

℘ God brings together people who have the maximum opportunity for mutual growth. He appraises who can learn most from whom at any given time then he assigns them to each other. Those who are to meet will meet because together they have the potential for a holy relationship.

℘ There are casual encounters and in the second level, there are more sustained relationships. In the third level is a relationship once formed, lasts all our lives. If a couple separates it is not necessarily a failure. If both people learned what they were meant to learn, then the relationship was a success.

℘ People who have the most to teach us are often the ones who reflect to us the limits to our own capacity to love, those who consciously or unconsciously challenge our fearful positions. They show us their walls. Our walls are our wounds. We are in each other's lives to help us see where we most need healing.

(From Marianne Williamson)

**Love, Sondra**

*October 20, 2020*

## ℘ ACIM AND THE HOLY SPIRIT

℘ A Course in Miracles talks a lot about turning over everything to the Holy Spirit. So what is the Holy Spirit anyway? In church they talked about the Father, Son, and the Holy Spirit but I never knew for sure what that was then.

❡ The Holy Spirit is God's answer to the ego that we made up. He is God's eternal communication link with the separated Sons. The Holy Spirit is God's alternative to fear. Often the Holy Spirit is referred to as the "comforter." The Holy Spirit is a force of consciousness within us that "delivers us from hell" (or fear) whenever we consciously ask Him to. He transforms our thoughts from fear to love. In asking the Holy Spirit to help us, we are expressing our willingness to perceive a situation differently. We give up our interpretations and opinions and ask that they be replaced by His.

❡ What we give to God, He gives back to us renewed through the vision of the Holy Spirit. Say to the Holy Spirit, "Decide for me." For sure we need to turn over our intimate relationship to the Holy Spirit!

**Love, Sondra**

*October 21, 2020*

❡ **CREATING MIRACLES**

❡ Let's say you have a strong negative pattern or condition in the body that you want to get rid of. You cannot have a miracle if you are hanging out in two minds (the ego's and the Holy Spirit's). You cannot be thinking you are Divine today and then have doubt tomorrow. You must KNOW that you can overcome this because of God in you. You cannot be bound by any condition unless you accept it. Say, "I am one with my perfection."

❡ If you want a miracle, you must have passion, determination, and strong feeling. Only with this conviction can your miracles manifest. You must be in joy, courage, and total faith.

❡ You have to stop thinking of the problem and think of perfect manifestation; think of the wholeness of Your Divine Self. Once you learn the spiritual purpose of the condition it is no longer necessary. Expect to have miracles. Set your sight to the highest state of being you can conceive of. It may be hard at first to think of JOY but that is what will change things.
(Reverend Dr. Linda De Coff *Living the Life of Miracles*)

**Love, Sondra**

*October 22, 2020*

**❡ THE SUM OF ALL NEGATIVITY**

❡ "Guilt is really the sum of all negative feelings, beliefs, and experiences that we've ever had about ourselves. Guilt can be any form of self-hatred or self-rejection, feelings of incompetence, feelings of failure, feelings of emptiness, feelings that there are things in us that are lacking or are missing or are incomplete. Most of this is unconscious and that is why the image of the iceberg is helpful. The ultimate guilt is that we think we separated from God. Once we feel guilt it is impossible not to think we should be punished. You will then be afraid. We are then afraid of God. Everything is an opportunity being given by the Holy Spirit to see ourselves as guilty or guiltless.
❡ This is from a lecture given by my teacher Ken Wapnick. I think it is important because most people keep their guilt suppressed and then they get old and get all these sicknesses and die as a result. If you are willing to look at your guilt and have some Liberation Breathing, you can have another outcome.

**Love, Sondra**

*October 23, 2020*

### ℘ MANIFESTING THE MIRACLE YOU WANT

℘ This is my prayer inspired by Reverend Dr. Linda De Coff:

℘ "I have the passion, determination, and strong feeling and trust that my miracle _____will manifest by your grace. I am staying with the goal of _____. I affirm the truth of You God in this situation. I choose that miracle. I choose it and I believe in it. I let go of all doubt and fear. I choose not to hang out in any defeat. I am going to insist on this perfect manifestation by the power of God in me. This miracle is here now. I claim my good. Nothing that I say, think, or do can stop this miracle. I am working with the word of God. I have moved beyond my petty fears. I am grateful in advance. I am in conscious love and a high state of openness and receptivity. I accept my Real Self. I have all the help I need. I believe in this. You, Babaji, are my immediate solution. I give thanks now that I have this by your grace. Your infinite wisdom gives me the way. I now receive ultimate fulfillment. I bless this situation leading to my ultimate good. God, you are bringing it through for me. What I have claimed for myself is coming forth in perfect ways. I am now healed through the miraculous power of pure God consciousness. There is only the perfection of God here. The Perfect One is in me now. I give thanks."

**Love, Sondra**

*October 24, 2020*

### ℘ THE SPECIAL RELATIONSHIP

℘ ACIM says that the special relationship is the ego's chief weapon to keep you from God. That is quite a statement. It starts with us saying we have certain special needs that God can't meet (because we have made God an enemy). But when we find a special person with special attributes then that person will meet our needs. If they do, we will love them; if they don't, we will then hate them. This person begins to change and stops meeting our needs and then we make them feel guilty (which is a projection of our suppressed guilt because we threw away God). So much hate sets in the relationship that we leave the relationship and shift the dynamics from one person to another person. This is an unholy relationship and so one goes from one unholy relationship to another unholy relationship. Most people are stuck in unholy relationships.

♪ A holy relationship is where each person looks within and sees no lack. Accepting their completion, they join with another, also complete and come together to share the light. We wrote a whole book on this called *Spiritual Intimacy* which I recommend!

**Love, Sondra**


*October 26, 2020*

♪ **FORGIVING ABUSE**

♪ We have had quite a few clients who have been abused physically or emotionally. Sometimes it is tricky to get them to look at how they attracted that, especially if it happened when they were young. However, usually, even if it happened when they were young, they attracted it to them because of a past life karma or a negative thought they came in with, usually "I am bad" or "I am guilty."

♪ Perhaps one parent was abusive to them, and they feel a victim of that. However, they attracted abusive parents in this life because they came in with those thoughts. Those thoughts attract abuse as a punishment. If they do not change those thoughts, they will attract more abuse.

ℐ It is important for healing to understand that the abusers were actors in their own creation. They need to say this: "I have made a mistake in my thinking to allow you to seemingly hurt me. I recognize you were merely doing what I invited and that in reality neither you nor anyone can hurt me."

ℐ ACIM says, "I can be hurt by nothing but my thoughts." If they remain victims, they won't be healed from the abuse. Taking responsibility for attracting it makes it easy then to forgive.

**Love, Sondra**


**October 27, 2020**

**ℐ TWIN FLAMES AND SOUL MATES**

ℐ This is from the book *Finding a Higher Love* by Elizabeth Clare Prophet:

ℐ "You and your twin flame share the same blueprint of identity, like the design of a snowflake, unique in all of cosmos. The two twin flames are each stamped with the same divine blueprint. This is a frequency unique to those two and not duplicated elsewhere. When twin flames are present with one another, there is a mutual reverence and a deep inner spiritual interchange. No matter what the situation appears to be outwardly, twin flames are never separated at the level of God Presence. Twin flames share a tremendous love that is the creative energy of God. The twin flame love carries an intensity that can be translated into productive work of the hour and service to others. They ponder what magnificent creation they can bring forth so that the whole human race is elevated." An example she gives is Winston Churchill and his twin flame Clementine.

¶ The problem I had with what she wrote was that one's twin flame may or may not be in embodiment upon earth at the same time. I guess that means one has to go through more lifetimes to find it. I feel so fortunate to have found my twin flame, but who knows how many lifetimes we had to go through to find each other.

**Love, Sondra**

*October 28, 2020*

### ¶ SOUL MATES HAVE A SIMILAR SOUL DEVELOPMENT

¶ Many relationships are the loves of close, kindred souls, called soul mates. Soul mates have a similar soul development and paths of self-mastery. They come together because they are working on balancing the same type of karma and developing similar qualities and they tend to be complimentary. They are compatible because their soul development is at the same level. You could have several such associations throughout your lifetime. Even if you are with your twin flame, you could have others in your life who are soul mates.

¶ A girlfriend could be your soul mate or even coworkers or friends. The two of you work well together and are project orientated. Elizabeth Clare Prophet in her book *Finding a Higher Love* gives the example of President John Adams and his wife Abigail. She says that ultimately the relationship is more like brother and sister. It is not as profound as the twin flame relationship. The relationship is not automatically intended to be romantic. One may complete a project with a soul mate and be ready for the next step which could involve a new circle of people and perhaps another soul mate.

**Love, Sondra**

*October 31, 2020*

**॰ BLOCKING A NEW LOVE**

॰ We have had quite a few clients who are wanting a partner now. One of the reasons they cannot let one in is because they are stuck in the past. They are remembering a former relationship that did not work or they are still attached to a former relationship and not letting it go. There is no room for a new love to come in when either of these are going on.

॰ Some people are so scared of the void they would feel if they totally let go of the past that they are clinging to the memory. Some people are hanging on to a past phantom relationship because they don't want to feel the fear of there not being someone else who will love them. This is a trap. Your chances are zero if you don't clear the space.

॰ If your previous relationship was devastating (or an even earlier one) maybe you have not healed and so you are too scared to repeat that. If you face that devastation and breathe out the trauma, and understand your part in creating that, then you can start anew. If you have not healed, start journaling all your feelings and get some breathwork sessions so you can let it go. Then you can consciously prepare yourself to love again. It is important to realize you cannot have an open heart if you are still bitter.

॰ Maybe if a relationship ended in the past, that was not a failure. Maybe you just had some karma to clear. Don't let the past stand in the way.

**Love, Sondra**

*November 1, 2020*

## ℐ LETTING YOUR MATE IN

ℐ Your prayer can be as simple as this: "Please send me the love of my life" or affirm "The love I desire, the love that will bring me the greatest joy and fulfill my highest purpose is already on the way to me." What finally worked for me was, "My perfect mate is here now." I started then writing letters to him addressed "Dear Beloved" and I would write him as if he was already here.

ℐ When Markus came, I read him ten letters I had saved. It was fun! I also had purchased four presents for him and wrapped them: a men's white gold ring, a Brooks Brothers shirt, a wallet, and cologne. The ring fit him perfectly which is amazing as I did not know who I was buying it for. The shirt fit also. These purchases helped bring down the reality of his presence.

**Love, Sondra**

*November 2, 2020*

## ℐ WHOEVER YOU ARE CONNECTED TO

ℐ Joel Osteen says this: "You are going to become like whoever you are connected to. When you connect with someone who is blessed, someone who is favored, as they increase, you will increase. Who you are connected to is extremely important. If you are not seeing any fish, you need to evaluate who you are connected to.

ℐ "If you are sowing into horizontal relationships, into people who are at your level, then you are going to see horizontal favor. When you are secure enough in who you are to sow

385

into vertical relationships, into people who are ahead of you, you are going to reap some of this vertical favor.""
(From *The Power of Favor* by Joel Osteen)

**Love, Sondra**

*November 4, 2020*

## ♫ TENSION IN THE AIR

♫ There is no solution yet to the election stress and tension here in Washington. To calm down I started reading Gandhi. His words:

♫ "There is no one without faults, not even men of God. They are men of God, not because they are faultless but because they know their own faults. They strive against them, they do not hide them, and they are ever ready to correct themselves.

♫ "No matter how insignificant the thing you have to do, do it as well as you can, give it as much of your care and attention as you would give to the thing you regard as most important. For it will be by those small things that you will be judged."

**Love, Sondra**

*November 5, 2020*

## ♫ THE INTENSITY OF THE POLITICAL SITUATION

♫ The intensity of the political situation was driving me crazy and giving me a headache. So we did our devotions and read from ACIM and it said. "The Only Sanity is the Love of God." It also says that the only joy and peace that can be fully known is to fulfill the will of God perfectly. The gifts of the Kingdom are many:

- Start with perfect love
- There is only certainty
- All power is yours and you are the way, the truth, and the life
- You recognize other people as equals
- You are at peace
- You have everything and there is no competition
- Everything is unified and healed
- There is no lack
- There is only joy
- You have God's blessing forever and you share it
- You have abundance and you share it
- Self-fullness is the result
- Grace is the natural state
- There is no strain
- You are happy because you are with God, and this is where you belong.

**Love, Sondra**

*November 6, 2020*

### ꕯ PEACE THROUGH POLITICS AND PANDEMICS

ꕯ Now even my supermarket is boarded up. So far, we can still get in. I want to be at peace no matter what happens. Here is what ACIM says to do when we are feeling other than joy and peace. Say this:

🎵 "When I do not feel good and if I am not joyous, I realize I have chosen wrongly.

🎵 "I must have decided wrongly because I am not at peace.

🎵 "I made the decision myself, but I can also decide otherwise.

🎵 "I want to decide otherwise, because I want to be at peace.

🎵 "I do not feel guilty because the Holy Spirit will undo all the consequences of my wrong decision if I will allow it.

"I choose to allow it to decide for God for me."

**Love, Sondra**

*November 7, 2020*

## 🎵 MARKUS WRITES TO THE DIVINE MOTHER

🎵 Last night my husband wrote this to the Divine Mother:

> *Mother, Oh Mother*
> *In the depths of division*
> *A Plea is put to Your*
> *Supple care and clear vision:*
> *We cannot help by vilify*
> *We cannot insist to unify*
> *We will not desist from attack*
> *We only persist to react.*
> *The election is done but not done,*
> *A decision was made but not made.*
> *The Candidates completed their run*
> *But the public debate will not fade.*
> *What shall we do?*
> *A nation divided cannot stand.*
> *The world is watching for sure*
> *To see what decision will land.*

*Speak O Mother for us
to restore our sanity.*

*Child, will the birds still fly,
And the river down the street
Make its flow to the ocean
of Joy always around you?
The men who pretend to
have power have none,
and they will be swept
asunder unremembered.
The men who know All
Power is from God will
tap into a resource that
stays the course of ages.
I am in charge, so
do not worry, nor need you
to fear the passing of
seasons. You my son
are safe in my arms.*

**Love, Sondra**

*November 8, 2020*

### ℥ STAY IN PEACE NO MATTER WHAT

℥ I was happy to see so many people celebrating on the streets. But others are saying it is not over until it is over. We are trying to stay in peace no matter what happens. We are voting for Babaji every day.

℥ "To give a problem over to the Holy Spirit to solve for you means that you want it solved. To keep it for yourself to solve without His Help is to decide it should remain unsolved. The

Holy Spirit's problem-solving is the way in which the problem ends. It has been solved because it was met with justice."

**Love, Sondra**


*November 9, 2020*

**꒓ MOTIVATION FOR ALL OUR ENDEAVORS**

꒓ "Our motivation for all our endeavors in life should be happiness and peace. Real peace is an enlivened state of being, unclouded by fear or conflict. It is the most energetic and joyous state available to us. The best choices we make are those that create the least amount of pain and conflict. Conflict in any area simply reflects errors of choice.
꒓ "No one is in your life by accident. No one is in your life without a specific purpose and learning goal. Some people offer major lessons, others minor. They are all here to offer a lesson. The lesson is always the same: to remove the fears and judgments that are in the way of our loving each person unconditionally."
(Robert Roskind)

**Love, Sondra**


*November 10, 2020*

**꒓ THE GIFT OF FAILURE**

꒓ We tend to think of failure as something very negative and that it indicates a failure in us as a person. But in a benevolent universe, every situation in our lives is a gift. Failure can bring our fears into sharp focus so we can handle them. The failure could be due to lack of knowledge. Maybe it means you just lacked certain sufficient information. What is really going on is an opportunity to learn and grow and a chance to clear some fears.

ℊ If we honestly review the different failures, we will see that we made decisions that led to failure based on fears. For example, we may fear we do not have enough money, so we jump into a business without thoroughly investigating it.

ℊ In my history of relationships, I felt like failure when I got divorced long ago. But later I saw it was absolutely the best thing. After that I had several relationships that lasted only two years or so. I never saw the ending of those as a failure. I realized I was just clearing karma with those men and after I completed that, it was over. So I moved on. I learned so much that I felt each relationship was success in that way.

**Love, Sondra**

*November 11, 2020*

## ℊ PEACEFUL WAY OF EXISTING

ℊ Turning over our will to the guidance of our Higher Self and asking our Spirit to guide us is what works. However, this is perceived as frightening and dangerous to our ego. Or it may feel like self-sacrifice based on weakness. But we are not giving over to some being outside ourselves. We are asking that our true nature (which is love) manifest in our lives. We are not giving away control, but rather taking it back from our illusions.

ℊ Until our true Higher Self is given permission and encouragement to manifest its will through us, our lives will remain painful. Asking our Divine Self to dominate in our actions and decision making is the better way to fulfillment and peace.

**Love, Sondra**

*November 12, 2020*

❡ **ACIM, LESSON 340**

❡ "I can be free of suffering today."
❡ "Be glad today! Be glad! There is no room for anything but joy and thanks today. Our Father has redeemed us His Son this day. Not one of us but will be saved today. Not one who will remain in fear and none the Father will not gather to Himself, awake in Heaven in the Heart of Love."

**Love, Sondra**

*November 13, 2020*

❡ **HELP YOUR MATE SUCCEED**

❡ Here are three simple questions you can ask to help your mate succeed:

1. What can I do to help you?
2. How can I make your life easier?
3. How can I be a better mate, husband, or wife?

**Love, Sondra**

*November 15, 2020*

### ❡ BENEFITS OF COUPLE PRAYERS

❡ This is like a pill that will make you instantly 20 percent happier. (A study actually showed this.) Couple prayer has been found to be the most powerful correlate of marital happiness, or couple happiness.

❡ Try to choose a regular time of the day and a consistent place. For us, we get up, make the bed together, shower and then sit down every day to do this 5-point prayer. I may have said it before; but it is worth repeating.

1. Read a few paragraphs from the Text of ACIM.
2. 2 State forgiveness: who you want to be forgiven for, who you want to forgive, and especially what you want to forgive yourself for.
3. State what you are grateful for.
4. State your petition (ask and it is given).
5. Close by reading a lesson in ACIM.

❡ This is for people who have already read A Course in Miracles for years. In other words, you can open the book anywhere. But if you are new to the Course, start with Lesson 1 and go on.

❡ Couple prayer is a shared, intimate conversation with God that brings you closer to Him and to each other. It is good if you have a partner to talk out loud to. If you are alone, you can still talk out loud to God. I do it. It is ALWAYS good to say, "God, thank you for . . ." or "Please help me with . . ." You would be surprised how effective it is to thank a higher power (God or whatever you call it) for something. This draws you closer to the Source and then you are clearer, and your life clears up. TRY IT.

**Love, Sondra**

*November 17, 2020*

## ꧁ EXCEPTIONAL RELATIONSHIPS

꧁ Couples in exceptional relationships will not allow themselves to be walked over nor do they keep a running tally of offenses. They value each other as essential partners in helping them to live up to all their values and goals in life. Their primary goal in life is to become a loving, godly person who becomes more and more enlightened. They want that more than anything else.

꧁ You have to see your partner as instrumental in helping you achieve this goal. Your partner should be your best friend and there should be no secrets between you. You have to know how to create peace so, in other words you have to give up your addiction to anger and fighting. This is easier if your number one priority is God, and your partner is second to that. You both need a commitment to pursue the good in each other.

꧁ Exceptional couples are liberal with compliments and generous with affection. Love is generous.

**Love, Sondra**

*November 18, 2020*

## ꧁ WILLINGNESS TO BE A VICTIM

꧁ Are you in a verbally abusive or physically abusive relationship?

꧁ A woman went to see a therapist because she was in an abusive relationship. During the very first meeting, the therapist asked, "So you must like it when he abuses you?" The client became incensed and said, "Of course I don't like it! Why would you say that?" The therapist looked directly at her and replied, "Because you are still in that relationship." So then, the woman had to look at her willingness to be a victim.

**Love, Sondra**

*November 19, 2020*

**♪ LOVE IS GOOD FOR HEALTH**

♪ Research studies prove that love boosts our immune system. It is said if you stay alone your energy can get unbalanced. Yin and yang energy equals synergy which forms a powerful mix to improve your health. People in relationships are healthier. When we share and receive love many chemicals in the brain are activated allowing our overall energy to grow stronger. Just holding hands is good so if you are healing something, be sure to spend time holding hands with your partner. Research shows that people in good marriages have better mental and physical health.

♪ BUT staying in a relationship that is unhealthy has consequences. For people in conflicting relationships, that health benefit is lost. Bitching at your spouse is a recipe for bad health.

**Love, Sondra**

*November 20, 2020*

**♪ BREAK UP WITH THE INNER JUDGE**

ℊ You might be telling yourself that you failed such and such and that you are not good enough, etc. How do you berate yourself when things don't go well? Self-flagellation darkens your mood considerably. And how you speak to yourself affects your relationships with others. When you listen to your inner judge, you are more likely to judge others also. We can rarely live up to perfect expectations, so we end up rejecting ourselves. Then you end up in a vicious cycle leading to fear of being rejected by others.

ℊ Make a commitment to yourself to break up with the inner judge. When you make a mistake say this, "Even though I made a mistake, I still completely love and accept myself."

**Love, Sondra**


*November 21, 2020*

## ℊ GOING TO A HIGHER COURT

ℊ "The ego speaks in judgment and the Holy Spirit reverses the decision, much as a higher court has the power to reverse a lower court's decisions in the world. You need not fear the Higher Court will condemn you. It will merely dismiss the case against you. There can be no case against a child of God, and every witness to guilt in God's creations is bearing false witness to God Himself.

ℊ "Appeal everything you believe gladly to God's Own Higher Court, because it speaks for Him and therefore speaks truly. It will dismiss the case against you, however carefully you have built it up. The case may be fool proof, but it is not God-proof. The Holy Spirit will not hear it, because He can only witness truly. His verdict will always be "thine is the Kingdom" because He was given to you to remind you of what you are."

(From A Course in Miracles, Text, Chapter 5, Section VII)

**Love, Sondra**

*November 22, 2020*

**₰ ACIM, LESSON 139**

₰ "I will accept Atonement for myself."

₰ We have been reviewing this lesson, and I think it is the key one. It is deciding to accept ourselves as God created us. God did not create us with problems. So, this takes away problems. It says, "To be alive and not to know yourself is to believe that you are really dead." When we are sick, we are killing ourselves. God did not create us that way. When we accept the Atonement for ourselves, we can go our way rejoicing in the endless Love of God!

₰ I saw for myself that when I am creating problems, I am not accepting the Atonement. So then to get out of my problems I return to this statement: "I will accept the Atonement for myself for I remain as God created me."

₰ The lesson asks that you think this statement five minutes in the morning and at night.

**Love, Sondra**

*November 23, 2020*

**₰ AN OPPORTUNITY TO BLESS**

₰ When a brother acts insanely, he is offering you an opportunity to bless him. Every loving thought is true, everything else is an appeal for help. When a brother behaves insanely, you can heal him only by perceiving the sanity in him. (A Course in Miracles, Text, Chapter 7)

ℐ Once I was sitting on a park bench and a man sat down next to me and said, "I am a paranoid schizophrenic, you know." I said to him, "In my presence you are not." He shaped right up, and we had a normal conversation.

ℐ To perceive errors in anyone and to react to them as if they were real, is to make them real to you. You will not escape paying the price for this. Accept his errors as real and you have attacked yourself. The Holy Spirit will teach you to look on everything without condemnation. This is a lifelong training, I think, as it is so easy to form judgments.

**Love, Sondra**


*November 24, 2020*

**ℐ TOTAL GRATITUDE**

ℐ "When your forgiveness is complete, you will have total gratitude, for you will see that everything has earned the right to love by being loving, even as your Self. Today we learn to think of gratitude in place of anger, malice, and revenge." Our gratitude will pave the way to Him and shorten our learning time by more than you could ever dream of.

ℐ Gratitude goes hand in hand with love and where one is the other must be found. Your gratitude toward your brother is the only gift God wants. To know your brother is to know God. If you are grateful to your brother, you are grateful to God.

ℐ It is insane to fail in gratitude to one who offers you the certain means whereby all pain is healed and suffering is replaced with happiness. We thank our Father that we are separate from no living thing and are therefore one with Him. (From A Course in Miracles, Text, Lesson 195)

**Love, Sondra**

*November 26, 2020*

### ♫ HAPPY THANKSGIVING

♫ "What I've learned is there is a scientifically proven phenomenon that's attached to gratitude, and that if you consciously take note of what is good in your life, qualified benefits happen." (Deborah Norville, television journalist and anchor)

♫ So why not keep a gratitude journal? May McCarthy recommends you get a lovely book with blank pages. On the left you write "Dear CSO," (Chief Spiritual Officer) and then you write "I am so grateful for . . ." (things you have). On the right side you write "Dear CSO, I am so grateful for . . ." (things you want to manifest AS IF you already have them). So you have a list on the left and a list on the right. I have found this to be a wonderful thing to do. TRY IT.

**Love, Sondra**

*November 27, 2020*

### ♫ BE IMPECCABLE WITH YOUR WORD

♫ "Speak with integrity. Say only what you mean. Avoid using the Word to speak against yourself or to gossip about

others. Use the power of your Word in the direction of truth and love." (From *The Four Agreements* by Don Miguel Ruiz)
ℐ Affirm out loud: "The all-knowing power of the universe can turn this situation into something good."

**Love Sondra**

*November 28, 2020*

## ℐ THANK THE UNIVERSE

ℐ The Universe will never give you anything you cannot handle. If a big test comes your way, try saying this:
ℐ "Thank you, Universe, for presenting me with this Divine Assignment for spiritual growth and healing. I am ready and willing to show up for this assignment with love. I welcome your support. Show me where to go, what to do, and what to say. I trust I am being guided." (Gabrielle Bernstein)

**Love, Sondra**

*November 29, 2020*

## ℐ THE PATH OF DEVOTION:

ℐ The path of Devotion only gives:

- Gives much contentment
- Gives enthusiasm and vigor
- Gives a compassionate heart
- Gives a childlike innocence
- Gives a pleasing nature

- Gives calm in adversity
- Gives unshakable faith
- Gives relaxation and optimism
- Gives strength and courage
- Gives fearlessness
- Gives protection

❡ Everything that happens is a gift!

**Love Sondra**

*November 30, 2020*

❡ **FAITH STATEMENT**

❡ "I know that the Universe is an ever-present energy field of Love. I know that when I align with the energy of love with thoughts, actions, and beliefs, I am given Infinite support and guidance. I know that I can co-create my reality with this loving presence, and I can live in joy!" (Gabrielle Bernstein)
❡ Spend your day looking at what is right. Focus your attention on love that is around you and expect miracles. Put all situations in the hands of Infinite Love and Wisdom. Cast all burdens on the Christ within and let the light of Christ stream through you. Ask for a definite unmistakable lead as to what to do in any situation.

**Love, Sondra**

*December 1, 2020*

❡ **TEN COMMANDMENTS FOR CLEAN COMMUNICATION**

§ The book *Couple Skills* by Matthew McKay and Patrick Fanning presents ten commandments for clean communication:

1.  Avoid judgmental words and loaded terms.
2.  Avoid global labels. (generalized condemnations).
3.  Avoid "you" messages of blame and accusations.
4.  Avoid old history.
5.  Avoid negative comparisons.
6.  Avoid threats.
7.  Describe your feelings rather than attack with them.
8.  Keep body language open and receptive.
9.  Use whole messages (observations, feelings, needs).
10. Use clear messages (don't contaminate with judgements).

**Love, Sondra**

*December 2, 2020*

## § SOME BELIEVE THERE IS NO GOD

§ A devotee told Ammachi that some people believe there is no God, and her answer was this: "To say that there is no God is like saying with your own tongue, "I have no tongue." Likewise, when we say, "There is no God" at that very moment we have agreed that there IS a God. To say that a particular object is NOT, we must have previously had a general knowledge of the existence of that object."

§ Then she asked the devotee what he ate that morning. He said, "Chutney." She asked, "What is that made of?" He said, "Coconut." She asked where he got the coconut from. He said it came from a coconut tree. She asked, "Which came first, the coconut or the tree?" He could not answer. And then she replied, "Now, you should agree that there is a power beyond the coconut and the coconut tree. That power is the substratum of everything. That is God."

**Love, Sondra**

*December 3, 2020*

### ♫ GOD WANTS THE BEST FOR YOU

♫ "God does not want you in unhealthy, toxic relationships. You are not obligated to remain with someone while they continue to behave in a toxic manner. They need to be actively trying to correct it, and to be clear, active does not mean they continue the actions while claiming to be making the corrections. There has to be a visible change. Red flags cannot be ignored. It does not get better later in the relationship and it does not get better once you marry the person, nor does it magically stop. The more you continue to pacify the behavior and dismiss the problem the more you enable them. If you end the relationship, but take them back, you are then saying, "This is acceptable." It is not.

♫ Be sure you are not the one creating the problem and setting the stage for these toxic battles. How are you contributing to the situation?

♫ "The point is: God does not want you to be with someone who is consistently disrespectful to you or mistreats you." (From *The Man God Has for You* by Stephan Labossiere)

**Love, Sondra**

*December 4, 2020*

## ℘ YOU ARE NOT YOUR PARTNER'S CRUTCH

℘ Once one of my teachers told me not to go forward in a relationship I was starting because she said I would be the one who would have to do all the work. She knew I would work on myself, and she also knew that he would not work on himself. So I ended it. You want to avoid being someone who is constantly giving and not getting anything in return.

℘ You are not your partner's crutch. Support his effort in doing his part in the relationship. If this is not visible, you do not need to be there. If this partner is serious about being with you, he or she will have to step up their game. Do not settle! If you think there is nothing better out there, you might be "settling." When you are with someone you are not happy with, you will always feel a void. That is no way to live!

**Love, Sondra**

*December 5, 2020*

## ℘ HIGHLY EVOLVED BEINGS

℘ "Highly Evolved Beings are simply more aware of their eternal connection with Original Source, would never deny that they are expressions of it, experience that they are in constant communication with the Essential Essence that you call God, and find both joy and fulfillment in passing on what they have come to understand and experience as a result of their eternal connection and continual unity with God."
(From *Conversations with God, Book 4* by Neale Donald Walsch)

**Love, Sondra**

*December 6, 2020*

## ₰ WORSHIPPING DEATH AS SAVIOR

₰ "Death is a thought which takes on many forms, often unrecognized. It may appear as sadness, fear, anxiety, doubt, as anger, faithlessness, and lack of trust; concern for bodies, envy, and all forms in which the wish to be as you are not may come to tempt you. All such thoughts are but reflections of the worshipping of death as savior and giver of release. The frail, the helpless, and the sick bow down before its image, thinking it alone is real and inevitable."

₰ I think this ACIM, Lesson 163 is shocking in a way because one does not usually think of those things.

**Love, Sondra**

*December 7, 2020*

## ₰ WHATEVER TROUBLES YOU

₰ Whatever troubles you, be certain that the Holy Spirit has the answer and will gladly give it to you if you simply ask it of Him. He will not withhold answers that you need for anything that seems to trouble you. He knows the way to solve all problems, resolve all doubts. The Holy Spirit is the answer to all problems you have made.

**Love, Sondra**

*December 8, 2020*

## ₰ OUR WISH REPRESENTED

꽃 ACIM says that nothing occurs but represents our wish. That is often hard to accept in the case of pain and suffering. We don't want to see that we somehow wanted that.

꽃 "No one suffers pain except his choice elects this state for him. No one can grieve nor fear nor think him sick unless these are the outcomes that he wants. And no one dies without his own consent."

꽃 Why would we WANT suffering and sickness? The answer that comes to me is that we feel guilty about something, and we think we deserve punishment. So if you have pain, suffering, or sickness, look deeply within and see what you are guilty about.

**Love, Sondra**


*December 9, 2020*

### 꽃 GOD'S PRESENCE IN THE PRESENT

꽃 "God's presence can only be experienced in the present instant. The moment we dwell upon experiences from our past, or become preoccupied with the future, we let the ego block our ability to experience God's love in the present.

"To awaken to the possibility of the reality of love—in which worry and anxiety are totally absent—we must first be willing to let go of our attachment to the past and anticipation of the future. It is possible for all of us to focus on the peace of God as our only goal and forgiveness as our only function for just one instant. In that instant we can give up judging and evaluating and trust that the voice of love will direct us."
(Gerald Jampolsky, MD)

**Love, Sondra**

*December 10, 2020*

**❡ AMMACHI ON RELATIONSHIPS**

❡ "Always try to recognize and admire the good qualities in each other. Don't ever mention the weaknesses in front of others. You should work out your problems together with a positive attitude, without provoking or hurting each other with accusations. Never use your partner's faults as a weapon against him or her. See your weaknesses as obstructions and learn to remove them. Try to look at your own faults. By seeing your own weaknesses and bad habits you become aware of how ugly they are.

"A true relationship is possible only when one is able to let go of all one's preconceived ideas and prejudices, and when one stops being possessed by the past. Stop clinging to the past and you will be free and peaceful. To cling to the past is like living in the dark. You should be willing to forgive and forget each other's faults and weaknesses.

❡ "Men should try not to be aggressive, arrogant, or self-important in front of women and they should not try to dominate them. A woman should be respected, and her feelings should be given proper consideration. Men are mostly intellectually centered, while women tend to be more emotional. Their different natures should be understood and accepted."

(From *Awaken Children, Volume VIII* by Amma)

**Love, Sondra**

*December 11, 2020*

**❡ THE TONE OF WHAT YOU SAY**

407

꿈 The tone of what you are saying is everything in communication. Tone communicates care or lack of it. A frustrating, angry tone communicates rejection. We must vigilantly watch our tone to make sure we are communicating respect, care, and value.

꿈 A woman's great need that should be met by her man is security. Nothing makes a woman feel more secure than a selfless, sensitive man. If a man wants to successfully communicate with his woman, he must understand that every word he speaks must be encrypted with security. A man's deeper need is honor. He is very concerned with respect. A woman who wants to successfully communicate with her man must encrypt every word with the tone "You are a good man. You have what it takes. I believe in you." (Inspired by the book *The Four Laws of Love* by Jimmy Evans)

꿈 Early in our marriage we worked on tone. If the tone was off, I would say to Markus, "I cannot hear you well with that tone." He would then correct it. Since then, we try to communicate with each other as we would to an honored guest. THAT WORKS!

Love, Sondra


*December 12, 2020*


## 꿈 BEING TAKEN CARE OF

꿈 "A small child living in a normal healthy environment is free and relaxed because he or she assumes that an adult is handling his or her needs. That is meant to be a model for the development of our healthy relationship to the Divine. You are meant to trust the universe like a child trusts an adult.

❡ "If, however, you came to feel as a child that your adult authority figures could NOT be trusted, then you have had a harder time transitioning into a healthy dependence on the ultimate nature of reality. You think you are on your own and have to handle everything by yourself. That could make you feel heavy." That was from Marianne Williamson. I think it is valuable to consider those words.

❡ Think of yourself in the womb when all your needs are met. Can you then picture yourself in the womb of the Divine Mother? The Divine Mother wants you to have everything. The Mother is Supreme. She is supreme power, supreme peace, the supreme of the supreme. When you discover the Divine Mother inside of you, life will become much easier. Even Babaji worshipped the Divine Mother. For more info try reading my books *Rock Your World with The Divine Mother*.

**Love, Sondra**

*December 13, 2020*

❡ **THE TYRANNY OF AGREEMENT**

❡ "The ego's notion of love is based on agreement. It cannot conceive of love being present when two people disagree. Yet unless you are free to agree or disagree with your brother in any given situation, you cannot love him." (Paul Ferrini)

❡ Commitment to the truth is not so popular. Often it means saying yes when others would say no or saying no when others would say yes. Some people cannot imagine that saying no could be a loving act. You cannot support behavior that you know would be hurtful to another person.

A real friend is free to agree or disagree. A friend tells the truth and reminds you that you are free to make your own choice.

**Love, Sondra**

*December 15, 2020*

### ♫ OUR IMPECCABLE GUIDE

♫ ACIM describes this guide as the Holy Spirit. The Holy Spirit is the part of your mind that remains connected to the mind of God. It says the Holy Spirit is the one true friend we can trust who loves you more than the ego ever will. His voice will direct you specifically and you will be told all you need to know.

♫ A powerful prayer is this: "Please show me."

♫ You can discern between the advice of the Holy Spirit and that of the ego by noticing the feeling or energy the voice or advice generates. Spirit is founded in love. The ego operates from fear. Love feels good, light, and peaceful and brings relief. Fear feels bad, heavy, limiting; it deepens distress.

(From *A Course in Miracles Made Easy* by Alan Cohen)

**Love, Sondra**

*December 16, 2020*

### ♫ REMOVE ALL NEGATIVITY

♫ Couples who do this have a joyful relationship. This involves getting rid of blatant forms such as anger, shame, and criticism; but also eliminating more subtle forms as well, including such well known ploys as "helpful" criticism, inattention, condescension, "the silent treatment," and using a bored or weary tone of voice. Ideally this ban would extend all the way to eliminating even negative thoughts.

₰ This does not mean you repress your feelings. Bring them out and see them as some aspect of the relationship that needs work. The best way is to look at your own contribution. "What am I doing or not doing?" The rewards of this work are great!

(Inspired by *Getting the Love You Want* by Harville Hendrix)

**Love, Sondra**

*December 18, 2020*

### ₰ AVOIDING INTIMACY

₰ In *Getting the Love You Want*, Dr. Harville Hendrix talks about the things partners do to avoid intimacy. The couple lives in a state of invisible divorce. Why do partners avoid intimacy? The authors claim it is due to anger and fear. One partner is angry at the other for not meeting his or her needs. So they look elsewhere for gratification. They even state that when one thinks his or her needs are not met, they feel they might not make it. Or maybe the relationship is so filled with conflict that one feels his or her life is in danger.

₰ I would also say it could easily be due to the fact that their own personal issues are coming up from the subconscious. In our work we look at the results of a) the birth trauma b) specific negative thought structures c) the parental disapproval syndrome d) the unconscious death urge e) other lifetimes. In our work we call these the "5 Biggies." A person has these usually suppressed until they cannot keep them suppressed anymore. Let's say they are not doing any breathwork for themselves. So avoiding intimacy and seeking gratification in an addiction might be the result.

**Love, Sondra**

*December 19, 2020*

## ♫ A CLEARED CONSCIOUSNESS

♫ Leslie Thurston told me that a cleared consciousness is the most valuable asset to life. I totally agree. That happens to be one of the best contributions I originally made to the rebirthing movement. It is essential to know where you are stuck and to be able to do something about it by breathwork and changing your thoughts. A humble person is someone who recognizes his errors, admits them, and does something about them.

♫ When we process, we inquire deeply into the nature of our unbalanced ego patterning. We try to find the truth. We become more flexible and freer. We learn to function to the best of our ability. We let go of obsolete stuff from our childhood. We become free of the past. We let go of baggage. We can cope with life's challenges better. If you have a session with us, you will see how we do it. If you want to learn how to do it perfectly, we offer a 5-day intensive training.

**Love, Sondra**

*December 20, 2020*

## ♫ REAL SERVICE

§ "One must love and serve every creature of this world as one's own Self. Through our selfless service, we realize ourselves. It is we who gain .. . We shall be able to discover our happiness in the happiness of others. If one does not have love and compassion for others, years of spiritual practice and austerities are of no use . . . Real service is extending help without expecting anything: that is when we serve out of real love and compassion."
(Ammachi)

**Love, Sondra**


*December 21, 2020*

**§ THE POWER OF THE HUMAN MIND**

§ "The power of the human mind is immeasurable. This infinite power is in all human beings. Nothing is impossible for a human being. Nothing can enslave him, overpower him, or control him if he is courageous enough to dive deep into his own mind, his own consciousness. He can hit the very fundamental basis of the source of power. Amma can guarantee this, provided the efforts are sincere. There are many masters around the world who have attained that ultimate state. If they could do it, you too should be able to do it. Why have doubts? TRY. Doubting is learned: You learn to doubt. You never learn to believe, to have faith. Doubt is your number one enemy. Faith is your best friend. Have faith and put forth effort. You will see the outcome."
(Ammachi)

**Love, Sondra**

*December 22, 2020*

## ♫ KARMA AND ITS RESULTS

♫ "Many undesirable events happen in your life. You suffer without knowing why. A certain hereditary disease may afflict your family, newborn babies are born physically deformed. Are such events accidental? NO. Each thing that happens in life has a cause. Sometimes the cause is visible and other times it is not. Sometimes the cause is to be found in the immediate past, but in some cases, it is from the remote past. Nothing is accidental. The remote past is all the previous lifetimes.

♫ "We must be alert and careful about what we do today because we do not know what effect it will produce tomorrow. Karma and its results must inevitably be experienced by every living being until the mind is stilled and one is living moment by moment in God."

(Ammachi)

**Love, Sondra**

*December 23, 2020*

## ♫ AMMA SPEAKS ON GOD

♫ "God is love. God is not a person. He is Consciousness. God is compassion. He is waiting at the door of every heart. Whether you are a believer or non-believer. He is within you. Behind every form, behind everything. He is the hidden formula of life. But you won't feel Him unless you call Him. His glory and splendor are ever-present, but unrevealed because you have not invoked the power of His presence. Through your invitation, through your prayers and meditation, God will step into your heart and reveal His presence. Then you will know that He was always there waiting for you to call Him."

**Love, Sondra**

*December 24, 2020*

**♫ CHRISTMAS EVE DAY**

♫ "The sign of Christmas is a star, a light in darkness. See it not outside yourself but shining in the Heaven within and accept it as the sign the time of Christ has come. He comes demanding nothing. No sacrifice of any kind of anyone is asked by Him. In His Presence, the whole idea of sacrifice loses its meaning. For He is Host to God. And you need but invite Him in Who is there already by recognizing that His Host is One and no thought alien to His Oneness can abide with Him there. No fear can touch the host who cradles God in the time of Christ, for the Host is as holy as the Perfect Innocence Which He protects and Whose power protects Him.

♫ "This Christmas give the Holy Spirit everything that would hurt you. Let yourself be healed completely that you may join with Him in healing and let us celebrate our release together by releasing everyone with us."
(From A Course in Miracles)

**Love, Sondra**

*December 25, 2020*

## ♫ CHRISTMAS DAY

♫ "Let no despair darken the joy of Christmas, for the time of Christ is meaningless apart from joy. Let us join in celebrating peace by demanding no sacrifice of anyone, for so will you offer me the love I offer you. What can be more joyous than to perceive we are deprived of nothing? Such is the message of the time of Christ which I give you that you may give it and return to the Father, Who gave it to me. For in the time of Christ, communication is restored, and He joins us in the celebration of His Son's creation." (ACIM)

♫ We have been listening to the Messiah all day yesterday. For Christmas Eve dinner we set a place at the table for Babaji. I was once in Herakhan for Christmas and Babaji came out every hour by the cave to honor Jesus.

**Love, Sondra**

A place for Babaji – Christmas, 2020

*December 26, 2020*

## ℐ THE ALTAR

ℐ Hoping everyone had a wonderful holiday. We started a new practice this Christmas. We don't just look at our altar, we sit in front of it every morning now and do our devotions out loud. It is so beautiful.

ℐ The Divine Mother painting was done by Babaji's temple painter. I came home from a tour and my decorator had had a dream where to hang it after he picked it up. I walked in at midnight and when I turned on the light and saw it a miracle happened. The scent of roses came out of it for ten minutes! I threw myself on the floor and prostrated myself before it. It has not happened since, but we love it.

ℐ On the altar cloth is the Virgin on the left, Ammachi on the right, and the Quan Yin in the middle.

ℐ On the lower shelf are our male gurus: Muniraj, Shastriji, Babaji's feet, and Jesus. The Divine Mother is Supreme.

**Love, Sondra**

Our Divine Mother altar, the "command central" of our spiritual life

*December 27, 2020*

## ❡ RELATIONSHIPS

❡ We always say in the Loving Relationships Training (LRT) that people tend to pick partners with whom they can re-create whatever was relationally dysfunctional in their formative years. That always sounds like a bad recipe. Why would we do it? Because there is a deep-seated impulse to heal it. So then we choose a partner who has a character similar enough to one or both of the parents so with that person one can recreate most unresolved childhood dramas.

❡ The problem becomes that one tries to get from the partner what he or she should have gotten (but did not get) from their parents. This is a losing strategy and leads to failure. It really helps to know all this, otherwise there is a lot of fighting.

❡ The way out is to totally forgive your parents and the situations in your childhood. WHAT YOU DON'T FORGIVE YOU ATTRACT. You also have to be enlightened enough to be an adult in the relationship and change your thoughts.

**Love, Sondra**

*December 28, 2020*

## ❡ OUR UNFINISHED BUSINESS

❡ So then, we all marry our unfinished business, at least the first time around. In the book *The New Rules of Marriage* by Terrence Real, it says: "A GOOD RELATIONSHIP IS NOT ONE IN WHICH THE RAW PARTS OF OURSELVES ARE AVOIDED. A GOOD RELATIONSHIP IS ONE IN WHICH

THEY ARE HANDLED. AND A GREAT RELATIONSHIP IS ONE IN WHICH THEY ARE HEALED."

ᛦ I certainly agree with that. And that is why I wrote The Loving Relationships Training which is all about healing those patterns. Unfortunately, many people project the anger they have at their parents (unfinished business) onto their mates, and this creates a hell.

**Love, Sondra**

*December 29, 2020*

**ᛦ JOY**

ᛦ "There is one thought in particular that should be remembered throughout the day. It is a thought of Pure Joy; a thought of peace, a thought of limitless release, limitless because all things are freed within it. LIVING IS JOY, but death can only weep. You see in death escape from what you made, and it is but illusion of an end. Death cannot be escape, because it is not life in which the problem lies. Life has no opposite, for it is God.
You must learn to think with God. To think with Him is to think like Him. This engenders JOY."
(From A Course in Miracles)

**Love, Sondra**

*December 30, 2020*

**ᛦ GET MORE JOY**

¶ Liberation Breathing is a celebration of Pure Joy. It is a breathing process which fills the body with oxygen and aliveness, life energy, spirit, prana, chi, and a sense of God. Often one's separation from joy can start at birth. The effects of our first experience of life outside the womb have been well documented. Most people are stuck in their birth trauma and don't even realize how it is running them. Liberation Breathing helps to dissolve the sense of separation at birth and puts one back in touch with the original source of joy.

¶ As a physical experience, it cleanses away physical tension and pain. The result is greater peace and aliveness physically. Life energy seems to neutralize anything which is contrary to it. This practice is like letting God in to clean house, sweeping away the tensions and stuckness.

¶ My whole life changed when I started doing breathwork. I got over a condition I had had for 13 years in just two sessions! So you can see why I became one of the first Breathworkers in 1974.

¶ Personal growth comes through conscious awareness of one's issues and taking practical action to choose out of one's negative habits. This work has helped me to invoke spiritual energy and joy. I want that for all of you.

**Love, Sondra**

***December 31, 2020***

**¶ PRACTICING SPIRITUAL PURIFICATION**

¶ Some people say they don't have time to do spiritual purification techniques, and yet you can get a lot more done in a shorter period when you are clear. It used to take me a year to write a book. The time began to shrink to a period of months (especially after I shaved my head the first time!).

Now I can write one in a matter of weeks. I have literally saved years by practicing spiritual purification. The best investment you can make is in yourself. When you remove the blocks to receiving, you only gain.

§ If you love life, it will always work for you.

**Love, Sondra**

When we first came to Washington, D.C. Maureen Hessel took us to the Peruvian embassy for an art exhibit

# About the Authors

**SONDRA RAY**, author of 30 books on the subjects of relationships, healing, and spiritual matters, was launched into international acclaim in the 1970s as one of the pioneers, along with Leonard Orr, of the Rebirthing Experience. She has trained thousands of people all over the world in this conscious connected breathing process, and is considered one of the foremost experts on how the birth trauma affects one's body, relationships, career and life. As she puts it, "This dynamic breathing process produces extraordinary healing results in all of your relationships—with your mate, with yourself and with Life—very fast. By taking in more Life Force through the breath, limiting thoughts and memories, which are the cause of all problems and disease, come to the surface of the mind so they can be 'breathed out', forgiven and released."

Applying over 50 years of metaphysical study, she has helped thousands of people heal their negative thought structures, birth trauma, habitual family patterns and unconscious death urge have affected their life. She encourages people to make lasting positive changes through Liberation Breathing® to be more free, happy and productive. No matter what Sondra Ray is doing, she is always trying to bring about a higher consciousness. Recently she has written new books on the subject of **Revolutionary Spiritual Healing** and **Outside the Box with Babaji**. Her book on **Physical Immortality** is provocative, in which she envisions a shift in the current paradigm in relationships around the world to a new level of consciousness—free from anger, conflict and even death.

**MARKUS RAY**, artist, poet, and twin flame of Sondra Ray, received his training in the arts, holding degrees from the Cleveland Institute of Art and Tyler School of Art of Temple University in Philadelphia. He is the author of a major work, *Odes to the Divine Mother*, which contains 365 prose poems in praise of the Divine Feminine Energy. Along with the Odes are his paintings and images of the Divine Mother created around the world in his mission with Sondra Ray.

Markus is a presenter of the profound modern psychological/spiritual scripture, *A Course in Miracles*. He studied with his master, Tara Singh, for 17 years in order to experience its truth directly. His spiritual quest has taken him to India many times with Tara Singh and Sondra Ray, where Muniraj, Babaji's foremost disciple, gave him the name Man Mohan, "The Poet who steals the hearts of the people". In all his paintings, writings and lectures, Markus creates a quiet atmosphere of peace and clarity that is an invitation to go deeper into the realms of inner stillness, silence and beauty. He teaches, writes and paints along-side Sondra Ray, and many have been touched by their demonstration of a holy relationship in action. His iconic paintings of the Masters can be viewed on markusray.com which he often creates while Sondra Ray is lecturing in seminars.

*SONDRA RAY'S Author's Portal :*

*Bit.ly/SondraRay*

*MARKUS RAY'S Author's Portal :*

*Bit.ly/MarkusRay*

# Other Resources

**Sondra Ray** / – author, teacher, Rebirther, creator of the Loving Relationships Training®, Co-founder of Liberation Breathing® and Quests to Sacred Sites around the world.
Facebook: www.facebook.com/sondra.ray.90
Facebook Fan Page:
www.facebook.com/LiberationBreathing
Twitter: www.twitter.com/SondraRay1008
YouTube: www.youtube.com/SondraRay
Website: www.sondraray.com


**Markus Ray** / – poet, author, artist, Rebirther, presenter of *A Course in Miracles*, co-founder of Liberation Breathing®,
Facebook: www.facebook.com/markus.ray.169
Facebook Fan Page:
www.facebook.com/LiberationBreathing
Twitter: www.twitter.com/MarkusRay1008
Website: www.markusray.com/

Receive Markus's articles on ART here:

*"Art Look" – an art lovers companion –*
**www.markusray.com**

301 Tingey Street, SE, #302, Washington, D.C. 20003

E-mail: contact@sondraray.com
E-mail: contact@markusray.com

**Babaji and The Divine Mother Resources:**

**Babaji's Ashram in Haidakhan (India)**
E-mail: info@haidakhanbabaji.com

**Haidakhandi Samaj (India)**
E-mail: Info@HaidakhandiSamaj.org

*See Sondra Ray & Markus Ray on these Websites:*

www.sondraray.com   www.markusray.com

www.facebook.com/LiberationBreathing

We encourage you, our reader, to attend *The Loving Relationships Training* (LRT) which is produced by Immortal Ray Productions all over the world. You can see Sondra Ray & Markus Ray's worldwide teaching schedule on:

*www.sondraray.com/programs-seminars/*

Also, we encourage you to attend The INDIA QUEST, The BALI QUEST, or other Spiritual Quests that teach and disseminate Liberation Breathing practices, and principles of *A Course in Miracles*, as well as enhance your Divine Connection to various Spiritual Masters. These are also available on: *www.sondraray.com*

Artwork and paintings of the Spiritual Masters by Markus Ray are available on: *www.markusray.com*

*Liberation Breathing® Sessions*

*with SONDRA RAY & MARKUS RAY*

*Book a Session at*  bit.ly/LBSession

CHANGING LIVES AROUND THE WORLD

430

# Notes

# Notes

# Notes

www.ingramcontent.com/pod-product-compliance
Lightning Source LLC
Chambersburg PA
CBHW050448270326
41927CB00009B/1654